**Engineering Applications
Software Development
Using FORTRAN 77**

Engineering Applications Software Development Using FORTRAN 77

GREGORY A. MOSES
University of Wisconsin—Madison

WILEY

A Wiley-Interscience Publication
JOHN WILEY & SONS
New York • Chichester • Brisbane • Toronto • Singapore

Library of Congress Cataloging in Publication Data:

Moses, Gregory A.
   Engineering applications software development : using Fortran 77 /
Gregory A. Moses.
      p.   cm.
   "A Wiley-Interscience publication."
   Bibliography: p.
   Includes index.
   ISBN 0-471-63851-X
   1. FORTRAN (Computer program language)   2. Computer software-
-Development.   3. Engineering—Data processing.   I. Title.
QA76.73.F25M67   1988
620'.0028'551—dc19   88-20887
                                                                CIP

Printed in the United States of America

10 9 8 7 6 5 4 3 2 1

To Sharon and Laurel

■ CONTENTS

■ PREFACE

Today all engineering students graduate with some understanding of computer programming. Although a single undergraduate course in FORTRAN or Pascal introduces the basic concepts of programming, it is not intended to turn engineers into software developers. Yet many engineers, as graduate students or employees, face the prospect of writing or modifying computer programs that are larger and more complex than any they have experienced in their undergraduate career. Left with only their own untested intuition to guide them, they use trial-and-error methods to complete this part of their thesis or work project. This unguided approach to software development is wasteful of both time and money.

To remedy this situation, this text serves as a follow-up to the first course in FORTRAN programming for engineers with a need to advance their software development skills. Our goal is to train engineers to efficiently write and debug large-scale software written in the FORTRAN 77 language. FORTRAN 77 language features that are crucial to large-scale program development, such as subroutine arguments and dummy arguments, global and local variables, and formatted and unformatted input and output, are covered with an emphasis on the conceptual picture of computer hardware and FORTRAN compiler combining to accomplish the intended result. These topics are treated unusually lightly in the first programming course due to time constraints. The binary number system, fixed and floating point data representation on IBM, DEC VAX, and Cray computers, and ASCII and EBCDIC character codes are reviewed along with the concept of machine code. This conceptual picture of machine code operating on various forms of binary data helps the engineer to understand "what the computer is doing" during the debugging stage of program development. The topics of programming style, portability, and debugging and their relation to efficient software development are discussed. The use of symbolic debuggers and other software development tools is emphasized. Finally, the advanced topics of structured analysis and structured design are introduced to guide the engineer in the specification of an engineering problem in a form that is suitable for a large-scale software solution. These methods, borrowed from the business systems software community, have proven over the years to yield high-quality software products. The team approach to software development and the idea of quality assurance through a formal software inspection process are introduced. The material chosen for inclusion is intended to turn the reader into a knowledgeable, albeit novice, engineering applications software developer.

The text was motivated by my frustration over training each of my graduate students in the vagaries of large-scale engineering software. This was becoming increasingly inefficient as the number of students grew, until I finally offered a special course in the subject. The text has its roots in the lecture notes of this course, taught several times over the past four years in the College of Engineering at the University of Wisconsin–Madison.

I wish to thank Max Carbon, my department chairman, for allowing me the time to teach this course. I gratefully acknowledge the many helpful suggestions and criticisms offered by the students who served as guinea pigs in this endeavor. I also thank Bob Peterson, who has worked with me on numerous large-scale FORTRAN programs over the past eight years.

On a historical note, I acknowledge Glenn Knoll for introducing me to computer programming a long time ago and Jim Blinn, Glenn Kern, Steve Mooney, and Sid Karin for our hours of discussion about computers and programming. I thank Jim Duderstadt for introducing me to the rewards of authorship.

GREGORY A. MOSES

Madison, Wisconsin
October 1988

**Engineering Applications
Software Development
Using FORTRAN 77**

━ 1

Introduction

The role of engineering in today's society is the same as it has been since antiquity: to use our basic understanding of the physical world to create products, structures, and processes to improve the living of humanity. This rather general definition of engineering encompasses practically every man-made thing that we find in the world around us. It includes the design and manufacture of automobiles and space shuttles, the building of bridges and dams, the refinement of oil, and the pasturization of milk. It includes the design and manufacturing of computers. On the road to reaching an engineer's creative goal it is necessary to solve problems. In fact, most of the time spent in this creative enterprise is spent solving problems. Thus, engineers are often described as problem solvers and much of their education is devoted to learning the solutions and solution methods for many different types of problems. The solution of complex engineering problems necessitates a basic understanding of physics, chemistry, and mathematics along with the utilization of specialized tools. In the past, these tools were the drafting board, the slide rule, the engineering handbook, and, perhaps most importantly, physical intuition. In today's world of engineering the most important tool after intuition is the digital computer. The role of the digital computer in engineering problem solving will continue to expand at an increasing rate in the years to come. Therefore, it is incumbent on the modern engineer to have a complete functional understanding of digital computers to most effectively utilize them in such problem-solving activities. For this reason, computer science must be added to physics, chemistry, and mathematics as a fourth building block of engineering science.

Except for the electrical engineers who design computers, the typical engineer interacts with computers solely through creating and executing computer programs. Executing computer programs requires skill in the use of the computer operating system, an understanding of the computational method implemented in the computer program, and knowledge of the problem to be solved. Mastery of these skills to the degree necessary to intelligently run computer programs and use them as tools for the solution of a problem is what we define as *computer literacy*. All engineers should have these skills.

For all of the computer-literate engineers using computer programs as tools to solve their problems, there must be other engineers who view their task as creating the programs for their literate colleagues to use. Notice that we have been careful to use the words "create a computer program" rather than "write a computer program." This is because good computer programs are in fact "created" through careful design. The skills required to create good computer programs transcend those of basic computer literacy. One requires fluency in the computer language used to write the program and a working knowledge of the methods used to solve the problem. Furthermore, one must have an understanding of software design, for the program itself is likely to be a large and complex problem in its own right. The creation of such programs as engineering tools we call *engineering applications software development*. This is the subject of this book.

The demands of society are making engineering problems more complex. Conservation of materials and energy requires a more fully optimized design than in the past when these resources were in abundant supply. No longer can the engineer simply substitute overdesign in the form of more material for uncertainty in the design limits of the system. Greater concern exists over the safety of engineered systems such as space craft, nuclear power plants, chemical-processing plants, and automobiles. Answering these safety questions requires more effort at the design stage to reduce the uncertainty in the calculations and allow for enough overdesign to ensure that the system functions adequately to protect the public under accident situations.

These constraints require the engineer to perform additional and more sophisticated computational analysis than in the past. There is therefore greater demand for more sophisticated analysis tools. These tools themselves represent complex systems that challenge the current methods of software development. Along with greater modelling sophistication in the tools there is also demand for tools that are easier to use, so that the engineer can direct more attention to the problem at hand rather than to preparing the input and deciphering the output of the program. This ease in use is called *user friendliness*.

The major limiting factor in the use of computers for engineering design and analysis is the development of this sophisticated and user-friendly applications software. Why is this the case? The answer is simple: software is very expensive to develop and maintain and there are not enough qualified engineers to keep up with the demand. Software is expensive for two reasons: (1) it is specialized and (2) it is labor-intensive. Once a computer has been designed, it is manufactured on an assembly line at the rate of dozens or perhaps even thousands per day. The computer hardware is used for almost limitless applications. Software, on the other hand, is specialized. An accounting program only keeps the books and a finite element program only computes stresses and strains. Thus each application necessitates a customized program. Estimates show that 50–90% of computing costs are in the software.

Let us take a look at just how expensive software is to develop. A typical engineer earning $35,000 per year working for AT&T, AMOCO, Rockwell, Exxon, or any other large company probably costs the company $100,000 per year when overhead charges and fringe benefits are included. Monitoring of programming productivity shows that debugged, documented computer software is generated at the rate of 10 lines per day by an experienced programmer. If our engineer works 48 weeks per year, 5 days per week, then a total of 2400 lines of debugged program per year will result. This is at a cost to the employer of $40 per line of program. A typical 20,000-line applications program to model fluid flow, electrical circuits, chemical process control, or whatever will cost $800,000 to create! In contrast to this, a scientific workstation computer to execute the program over many years costs only about $40,000. Hence, if this paltry 10 lines of program per day could be improved to 12.5 lines per day, the company could save $200,000, enough to buy five more computers. Looking at this another way, if the engineer spends 25% more time in developing a program that runs 10% faster than without this extra time investment, is this really cost-effective? If the program is used a lot, then it certainly is. On the other hand, if the program is used only for a short time or is used infrequently, then the extra time investment is definitely not worth the cost.

Research by computer scientists in *software engineering* offers the possibility of programming productivity improvement through creation of better programming tools. Software engineering has many facets. It involves coupling the text editors used for source program editing and compilers that convert the source program into machine instructions so that once a syntax error is discovered by the compiler, it automatically transfers back to the text editor to allow the programmer to correct the error. It then continues with the compilation. It involves a coupling between the compiler, linker, and file management system so that all files modified since the last link step are recompiled before relinking. It involves symbolic debugging aids that allow the programmer to interactively step through the program, statement by statement, and examine the contents of variables during execution to track down bugs in the program. All of these features can be implemented in a "window" interface with the user, so that the programmer can view several different steps simultaneously. This is an active area of computer science research. Obviously, improvements in the programmer's tools have a tremendous payoff if they improve productivity.

A related approach, and the subject of this book, is to better prepare engineers to meet their tasks. To be most productive in applications software development the engineer should be familiar with all of the features of the programming language and tools that are available. Here we do not invent new tools or methods, but try to make the best use of the ones that are already available to us. And maybe along the way we will also contribute to the development of better methods of software development.

A final question that should have been asked at the start of this discussion is: why should engineers be concerned with software development? Don't engineers do "engineering" and computer scientists or programmers write computer programs? No. In most industrial and research laboratory situations where computers are not the revenue center (i.e., the company uses computers and does not design or sell them), the applications programming is done by engineers and scientists with backgrounds in the area that is the revenue center of the company. Chemical engineers at AMOCO and Dow write computer programs to model chemical processes in their plants. Nuclear engineers at Westinghouse and General Electric write computer programs to model nuclear fuel burnup in their reactors. Mechanical engineers at Combustion Engineering write computer programs to model steam conditions in the boilers and feedwater heaters of a power plant. In addition to these examples, there are many companies that specialize in the development of applications software. These companies employ engineers to work on these programs.

We hope that with this brief introduction we have made the point that there is a need for engineers with strong backgrounds in applications software development. In the remainder of this chapter we present an overview of the important elements of the software development process. We assess the current status of computing in the engineering world before proceeding to the specifics of software development.

1.1. BASIC CONCEPTS

1.1.1. Large-scale Software

Engineering applications software spans a spectrum of program size and complexity. At one extreme are the so-called canned production programs that have taken many years to develop and are used regularly by engineers for design purposes. Such programs are typically 20,000–100,000 lines in length. Many man-years are required to create and maintain them and they cost as much as $1 million or more. We will consider programs in excess of 20,000 lines to be large scale. These programs generally require more than one person to develop and maintain them. As such, they exhibit management and structural problems that are not found in smaller programs. At the other extreme are the little programs that the engineer is required to write in a hurry to help solve some immediate problem. These programs are 100–1000 lines in length and are written in less than a week or so. This program size is typical of those written as part of either beginning programming or engineering courses.

A small, few-hundred-line program developed by an engineer for immediate use and limited in its scope of application can be easily debugged and quickly implemented with only modest attention paid to the structure of the program. In this case the best choices might be a simple language such as BASIC to write the program and a versatile, user-friendly microcomputer to execute it. The level of sophistication of the programmer need not be very high. A working knowledge of the microcomputer operating system and an understanding of BASIC are the requirements to make the engineer a productive problem solver.

Most large-scale applications software products are developed by teams of engineers and programmers. At a productivity of 10 lines of debugged and documented program per man-day, a 100,000-line program would require 10,000 days (or 40 years of workdays) to develop if only one person were to work on it. This is clearly unacceptable. The team approach cuts the time to completion significantly, provided that all of the team members are as productive as though they were working alone on a single small program.

A large, many-thousand-line program developed by a team of engineers and programmers must be carefully planned and managed to avoid serious debugging problems associated with the interaction of the different parts or modules of the program. The so-called structure chart for such a large program is shown in Figure 1.1. Each module of this program, denoted by a box in the structure chart, contains roughly 100–200 lines of program (i.e., it is the same size as the small-scale program mentioned above). Years of experience have provided documented proof that a well-organized program, adhering to a simple set of structured design guidelines, is more likely to be developed and implemented on schedule than a program that receives little structured design attention. Such large programs are designed by defining the function of each module and its relation to other modules in a systematic way that closely parallels the structure of the problem to be solved. Much like the organization chart

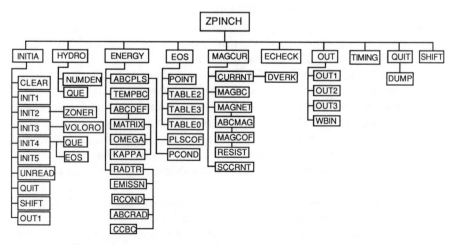

Figure 1.1 Structure chart for large-scale FORTRAN program.

of a corporation, the modules near the top of a structure chart are devoted to decision making, while the modules near the bottom of the chart make few decisions and mostly perform computations. The data passed between modules, like the information passed between people in a corporation, is limited to only those modules that need access to the data. We can see that this complication only exists for large programs since small programs consist of only one module. It is this large-scale software and its associated design problems that are the subject of this book. However, the design guidelines that are presented for large-scale software development can be effectively used for smaller scale programs as well.

1.1.2. FORTRAN 77

The programming languages most frequently used for engineering applications software are FORTRAN, BASIC, C, and Pascal. The languages used on most microcomputers are BASIC, C, and Pascal, although most microcomputers have FORTRAN compilers. This is in contrast to large mainframe computer systems where FORTRAN has historically been the language of choice for scientific applications. The optimum choice of language for a particular applications software project depends on the type of problem being solved and on the type of computer system being used to solve it.

The FORTRAN 77 language produces fast-running, executable machine code. It allows the compilation of separate modules with an intermediate linking step between the compilation and execution of the program as shown schematically in Figure 1.2. This feature is essential for the development of programs with hundreds of different modules.

The BASIC language, on the other hand, is not compiled into machine code at all. The source program is interpreted by a BASIC language interpreter program that "executes" the program line by line as it interprets it, as shown in Figure 1.3. Therefore interpreted BASIC programs execute more slowly but are very convenient because only one step is involved in the software development process. In addition to the BASIC interpreters there are also BASIC compilers that actually produce executable machine code.

The Pascal language is compiled into executable code by the Pascal compiler; however, the language is not designed to support the creation of separately compiled modules (Figure 1.4). It requires that all modules be in the same compilation step. This is really no limitation for programs of modest length but becomes a problem for the large-scale programs like the one shown in Figure 1.1. Many implementations of the Pascal compiler have "extended" features to allow the separate compilation of modules, thus removing this limitation.

The C language allows the separate compilation of modules and produces fast-running code. It has low-level language features as well as high-level ones like the others discussed here. For this reason it is used as a replacement for assembly language for many applications. Its structure is similar to that of

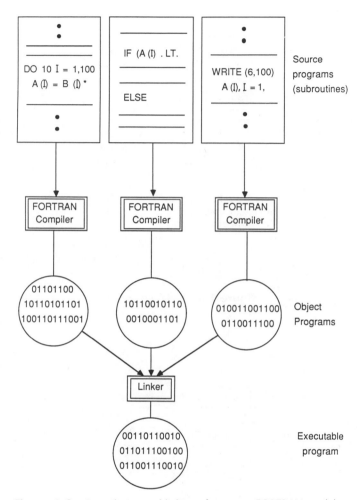

Figure 1.2 Compilation and linking of separate FORTRAN modules.

Pascal and follows the state-of-the-art concepts in structured language design. It has no elaborate input and output capabilities, but instead depends on extensive libraries of modules to perform these functions. It was developed for minicomputer applications but is available on many microcomputers as they become more powerful. It is closely associated with the UNIX operating system, which is largely written in C.

The last 10 years have seen extensive debate over the relative merits of the FORTRAN language in comparison to more modern languages such as Pascal and C. The Pascal language is predicated on the principles of modern computer language theory and therefore allows a much better implementation of the structured design principles that form the basis of modern software development. On the other hand, FORTRAN 77 remains the standard language

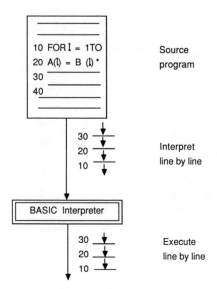

Figure 1.3 BASIC interpreter.

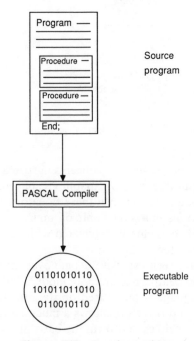

Figure 1.4 Pascal compilation.

used for most large scientific applications. Since this book is meant to serve as a practical guide to large-scale engineering applications software development, we acknowledge these distinctions between FORTRAN 77 and other languages such as Pascal, but adopt the FORTRAN 77 language as our reference.

FORTRAN is a procedure-oriented language, that is, it is defined in a way that closely resembles the problem being solved rather than the computer on which it is executing. Examples of other procedure-oriented languages are COBOL, Pascal, C, PL/1, and BASIC. FORTRAN is designed to solve mathematically oriented problems and is an acronym for "formula translation." A powerful feature of the FORTRAN 77 language is its adherence to a set of standards that define it in an unambiguous way. This allows FORTRAN 77 programs to be moved from one computer type to another and to be recompiled and executed on the new machine without modification. We honor these standards in all programming examples used in the text.

1.1.3. Scientific Computers

The current status of computer hardware for scientific applications shows a hierarchy of machines, each of which is specially adapted to a specific purpose. Computers are classified according to the hierarchy shown in Figure 1.5. At the top are supercomputers that execute at state-of-the-art speeds, about 100 million floating point operations per second (Mflops). These machines cost in excess of $10 million. A Cray XMP-48 supercomputer is shown in Figure 1.6. Below these are the classic mainframe computers that execute at about 10 Mflops and cost in excess of $1 million. The IBM 30xx series of computers is a good example of this machine. An IBM 3094 is shown in Figure 1.7. Below these are the popular superminicomputers that usually run a convenient timesharing system and are used by researchers for program development and to interface to supercomputers. This class of computer has execution speeds of 1 Mflops and costs in excess of $100,000. The DEC VAX 8600 is such a machine and is shown in Figure 1.8. Next there is the high-performance scien-

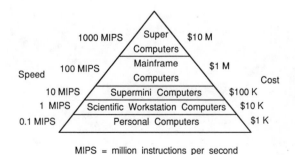

MIPS = million instructions per second

Figure 1.5 Computer hardware hierarchy of speed and cost.

Figure 1.6 Cray XMP/48 supercomputer. (Courtesy of Cray Research Incorporated.)

Figure 1.7 IBM 3090 series 400 mainframe computer. (Courtesy of International Business Machines, Inc.)

Figure 1.8 VAX 8600 supermini computer. (Courtesy of Digital Equipment Corporation.)

tific workstation that sits on the engineer's desk. This machine costs in excess of $10,000 and is capable of quite sophisticated computations and, most importantly, high-resolution graphics. Its execution speed is about 0.1 Mflops. The Apollo Domain Series 4000 is shown in Figure 1.9. Finally, there is the personal computer that costs in excess of $1000 and executes at a rate of 0.01 Mflops. This machine is useful as a smart terminal and can serve as a low-cost alternative to the scientific workstation. The Apple MacIntosh computer is shown in Figure 1.10.

Figure 1.9 Apollo Domain Series 4000 scientific workstation computer. (Courtesy of Apollo Computer.)

Figure 1.10 Apple MacIntosh personal computer. (Courtesy of Apple Computer, Inc.)

No single computer is the total solution to an engineer's computing needs. This hierarchy of hardware is most effective when networked together as shown in Figure 1.11. With such networking of computers, engineers can move up or down in the hierarchy to the machine that best matches their computational needs.

In the future we expect that each of these layers in the hierarchy will be redefined by hardware with a performance equal to those of a higher class, but at the same cost as the earlier slower machines. This trend will place ever greater amounts of computer power in the hands of engineers. The limiting factor in the utilization of this computing power will be the engineer's ability to efficiently program the computers.

Considering the state of the art in computer hardware, the large-scale engineering applications programs discussed in this book could be developed and executed on any of the machines in the hierarchy, from microcomputers to supercomputers. The optimum situation would probably be to develop the program on a microcomputer or workstation in the engineer's office, and then ultimately execute it on a supercomputer.

1.2. SCOPE OF THE TEXT

Beginning courses in FORTRAN or Pascal programming do not qualify an engineer to design and write large-scale engineering applications software. A popular beginning FORTRAN 77 programming text[1] specifies as its objective:

1. Achieving a *modest* level of programming and problem-solving skills
2. Acquiring a basic knowledge of computer concepts, uses, and limitations

Advancing from computer-programming novice with modest levels of programming skill to large-scale applications software developer requires knowledge beyond the beginning programming level. Binary representation of numerical and character data and the concept of machine code executed by the computer are important to the understanding and debugging of the executing program. Features of the FORTRAN 77 language, lightly treated in elementary FORTRAN programming courses but crucial to large-scale software development, must be learned. Programming style and its relation to readable and error-free programs, symbolic debugging, program portability, and optimization are important to the creation of high-quality FORTRAN programs. Principles of structured analysis and structured design, suitably modified and augmented to be most applicable to problems of a numerical nature, are another essential ingredient in successful applications software design.

This book is designed to serve as a text for an advanced course in engineering applications software development. We assume that the student has had prior experience in FORTRAN 77 or some other suitable procedure-oriented language such as Pascal. The examples used in the text are taken from the

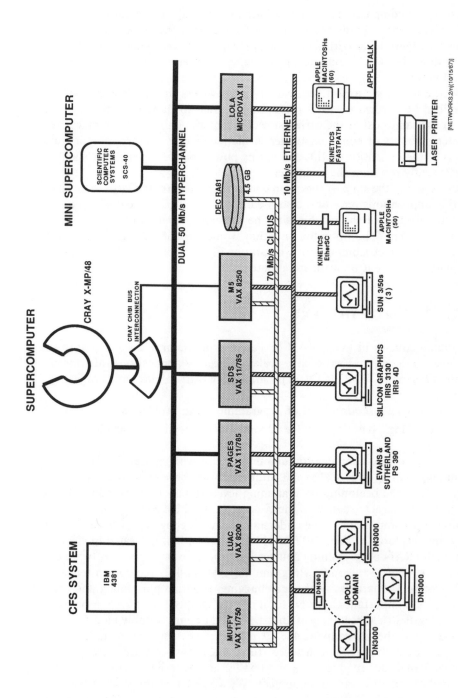

Figure 1.11 Computer network connecting many different types of computers. (Courtesy of San Diego Supercomputer Center.)

engineering world, and therefore some background in a field of engineering or physical science is required. In addition, an undergraduate level background in numerical analysis would be helpful but is not mandatory. An important aspect of a course based on this text is of course the homework. To allow the student to practice the principles discussed in the text, the final three or four homework exercises must be additive so that the final product of these is a computer program in excess of 1000 lines. Team projects are desirable. In this case a larger program is developed, with each student responsible for about 1000 lines. Because the text has not been keyed to a particular field of engineering, we must leave to the instructor the definition of the large-scale software application used as the basis for the last homework exercises.

Another use of the text is as a companion text to the one used in an engineering course that requires students to develop a large-scale computer program. In this case the emphasis would be on the engineering discipline itself (perhaps in the form of modeling particular physical systems) rather than on the software development aspect. In this circumstance, the student could use the text as a reference.

Along these same lines, the text ideally serves as a reference to the practicing engineer or scientist in either a production or research environment.

The book has been organized into 11 chapters. The introductory chapter is followed by a chapter devoted to a discussion of computer hardware and arithmetic. Topics include the binary number system, fixed and floating point representation of data, and the problems of finite precision arithmetic or round-off error. Chapter 3 introduces the FORTRAN language. It is expected that the material in this chapter is a review for students. The next two chapters cover advanced features of the FORTRAN 77 language. The topics covered here are generally only briefly covered in a beginning programming course. These include a discussion of subroutines and of input and output. These chapters cover such topics as subroutine linkage, global and local variables, pseudodynamic vector dimensioning through argument lists, internal files using CHARACTER variables, and direct access input/output. The next three chapters are devoted to programming style and optimization, debugging, and portability. These are all related to FORTRAN 77 with specific examples used to clarify the discussion. The final three chapters cover large-scale applications software development utilizing the methods of structured analysis and structured design. This includes definitions of module coupling and cohesion, program morphology, interface definitions, and software development design strategies using the graphical tools of structured design. A detailed example is given in Chapter 11.

REFERENCES

1. R. Ageloff and R. Mojena, *Applied FORTRAN 77, Featuring Structured Programming,* Wadsworth, Belmont, CA, 1981.

EXERCISES

1. Name an applications program in your engineering discipline and write a report on it, including the machines on which it executes, the number of lines of program, the function of the program, its age, who wrote it, and so on.

2. Read the *Wall Street Journal* for a week and write a report on all stories and advertisements related to computers, computer technology, and computer applications. Report on the relative health of the computer-related stocks such as IBM, CDC, Cray, DEC, and Apple.

3. Acquire the operating system manual, FORTRAN compiler manual, linker manual, debugger manual, and file editor manual for the computer system you will use for this course. List the commands required to execute each of these program development processors. Familiarize yourself with the terminal or workstation that you will use.

4. For all of the computers to which you have access, list the following items:
   (a) Purchase price
   (b) Execution speed in million instructions per second (MIPS) and million floating point instructions per second (Mflops).

5. For all of the terminals or workstations that you have access to, list the following items:
   (a) Resolution of the CRT screen in pixels,
   (b) Graphics and text or only text on the screen,
   (c) Windowed environment or not,
   (d) Keyboard and mouse or only keyboard.

6. Estimate the time required to write your last computer program and the number of lines per day that this represents. Why do you suppose it is so different from the 10 lines per day often quoted as typical productivity?

▬2

Computer Fundamentals

A FORTRAN programmer need not understand every detail of a computer's hardware. After all, FORTRAN was originally created to remove the requirement that all applications programmers also be computer hardware experts. Given a program that is operating correctly, simply executing it to obtain a result does not require an in-depth understanding of the computer hardware. However, a general understanding of digital computer fundamentals will help the applications software developer to diagnose error messages during execution and to ask the correct questions of the computer systems expert when a particularly difficult problem arises. A conceptual understanding of computer hardware speeds up the debugging process by giving the applications software designer greater insight into what the computer is doing when an error occurs. In this chapter we review the binary number system and the computer hardware components that use binary numbers to execute programs and store data.

2.1. BINARY NUMBER SYSTEM

Digital computers today, from the fastest supercomputers to inexpensive micros, use the *binary number system* as the basis for computations, data representation, and communications with peripheral devices. Although high-level languages like FORTRAN shield the user from these considerations by compiling mathematical statements into machine code and by formatting input and output in the more familiar form of decimal numbers, it is important for the software developer to be acquainted with the actual representation of the FORTRAN data forms and the methods whereby computations are done. This is most important in the debugging stage of software development where subtle

17

errors may only be uncovered by understanding and viewing the internal binary coding of the data.

The binary number system is most easily understood by comparison with the more familiar decimal number system. The decimal number system consists of the symbols

$$0 \ 1 \ 2 \ 3 \ 4 \ 5 \ 6 \ 7 \ 8 \ 9$$

and a positional arrangement that multiplies each of the symbols by powers of 10 (the so-called base or radix of the decimal number system). For instance, the number

$$937.42$$

represents

$$9 \times 10^2 + 3 \times 10^1 + 7 \times 10^0 + 4 \times 10^{-1} + 2 \times 10^{-2}$$

The binary number system has only two symbols:

$$0 \ 1$$

The positional arrangement is analogous to that of the decimal system, only now each position corresponds to a power of 2. The binary number

$$1011.1101$$

represents (in decimal notation)

$$1 \times 2^3 + 0 \times 2^2 + 1 \times 2^1 + 1 \times 2^0 + 1 \times 2^{-1} + 1 \times 2^{-2} \\ + 0 \times 2^{-3} + 1 \times 2^{-4}$$

Of course the decimal number 2 is represented by "10" in the binary number system. Thus a totally binary representation of this is

$$10^{11} + 10^1 + 10^0 + 10^{-1} + 10^{-10} + 10^{-100}$$

The *radix point* (called the decimal point in the decimal number system) is shifted by multiplying a number by the base of the number system to an appropriate power. The decimal number

$$937.42$$

can be rewritten as

$$0.93742 \times 10^3$$

Any decimal number can be written in this so-called scientific notation with a fractional part times a power of 10. Similarly, in the binary system, the number

$$1011.1101$$

can be rewritten as

$$0.10111101 \times 10^{100}$$

where this is totally in binary notation (i.e., "10" represents 2).

A drawback of the binary system is that powers of 2 are so small that many binary digits or *bits* are required to represent numbers of large magnitude. For instance, the decimal number 1003 is represented in the binary number system as

$$1111101011$$

or

$$2^9 + 2^8 + 2^7 + 2^6 + 2^5 + 2^3 + 2^1 + 2^0$$

Binary numbers are represented in a shorthand notation using either the *octal* or *hexadecimal* number system. These are number systems based on a base of 8 or 16. The octal number system consists of the symbols

$$0\ 1\ 2\ 3\ 4\ 5\ 6\ 7$$

and follows the same positional rules as the decimal and binary systems only using eight as the base. Binary numbers are represented as equivalent octal numbers by grouping the binary digits into groups of three starting from the radix point and working to the left or the right, since $8 = 2^3$. Thus, the binary number

$$1111101011.010110$$

is written as

$$001\ 111\ 101\ 011\ .\ 010\ 110$$

and in octal has the value

$$1753.26$$

The hexadecimal system uses the symbols

$$0\ 1\ 2\ 3\ 4\ 5\ 6\ 7\ 8\ 9\ A\ B\ C\ D\ E\ F$$

In this case the base of 16 is greater than our familiar value of decimal 10. Thus we must invent unique symbols to represent the decimal numbers

10 11 12 13 14 15

These are chosen to be

A B C D E F

Binary numbers are conveniently represented as hexadecimal numbers by grouping the binary digits into groups of four. The same binary number is now represented "in hex" as

0011 1110 1011 . 0101 1000

3EB.58

The correspondence between decimal, binary, octal, and hexadecimal whole numbers is summarized as follows:

Decimal	Binary	Octal	Hexadecimal
0	0	0	0
1	1	1	1
2	10	2	2
3	11	3	3
4	100	4	4
5	101	5	5
6	110	6	6
7	111	7	7
8	1000	10	8
9	1001	11	9
10	1010	12	A
11	1011	13	B
12	1100	14	C
13	1101	15	D
14	1110	16	E
15	1111	17	F
16	10000	20	10
17	10001	21	11
18	10010	22	12
19	10011	23	13
20	10100	24	14

While the whole numbers are exactly represented in any number system, fractions are not. Consider the decimal number

$$0.4$$

This is represented exactly as

$$4 \times 10^{-1}$$

in the decimal number system. However, the binary representation of the decimal number

$$0.4$$

is

$$0.011001100110011001 \ldots 1001 \ldots$$

Thus there is no finite length binary fraction to exactly represent decimal 0.4. This creates subtle errors when finite precision arithmetic is performed on a digital computer.

Most computer hardware performs two kinds of arithmetic: *fixed point* and *floating point*. Corresponding to these, there are binary data formats for fixed point and floating point numbers. In fixed point arithmetic only integer numbers are used, while in floating point, fractional numbers are allowed. The binary data formats are considerably different for these two types of numbers. Each data format is discussed with reference to its FORTRAN designation.

2.1.1. Binary Representation of Fixed Point Numbers

The INTEGER data type in FORTRAN is associated with numbers that are in the fixed point data format. These numbers are often used as counters in loops or other repetitive calculations. This INTEGER data type (fixed point) is implemented in actual hardware using either *one's complement* or *two's complement* format.

2.1.1.1. *One's Complement Fixed Point Data Format.* Fixed point numbers must be represented on actual hardware as a finite number of binary digits (bits). The number of bits that are used usually corresponds to the number of bits in a *word* on the particular computer. See Section 2.2.1 for a discussion of words. Most modern computer designs use 32-bit word lengths. For the purposes of our discussion we will use eight bits as the word length to avoid long strings of binary digits.

The one's complement notation for positive fixed point numbers is identical to the earlier discussion of binary numbers. The question is how to represent negative fixed point numbers. Obviously, we want to ensure that sums of positive and positive, positive and negative, and negative and negative numbers are correct. This is accomplished in one's complement notation by reversing the values of all digits from 0 to 1 or 1 to 0 to form the negative value of a number. For example, the decimal numbers 50 and 40 are represented in eight-bit binary notation as

$$00110010 \text{ and } 00101000$$

and the one's complement value of -50 is

$$11001101$$

Thus, if we add -50 and 40 using our eight-bit computer, we get

$$\begin{array}{r} 11001101 \\ +\,00101000 \\ \hline 11110101 \end{array}$$

We expect the answer to be decimal -10, so hopefully the binary result is the one's complement for -10. We check this by reversing the 0's and 1's in the answer to get

$$00001010$$

and in fact this is the binary value for the decimal 10. We now try this again, but instead we add 50 and -40. The one's complement value of -40 is

$$11010111$$

Thus, if we add 50 and -40 using our eight-bit computer we get

$$\begin{array}{r} 00110010 \\ +\ 11010111 \\ \hline 1 \leftarrow 00001001 \end{array}$$

In this case the sum of the leftmost digits in each number results in a carry digit, but the finite word length of the eight-bit computer leaves no place for this bit to go. This is a so-called *overflow*. Looking now at the result, we find the decimal value of 9. This is incorrect, since we know that the result is 10. To correct this, we must always add the overflow carry bit to the result when using one's complement notation.

$$
\begin{array}{r}
00110010 \\
+\ 11010111 \\
\hline
1 \leftarrow 00001001 \\
\rightarrow +\qquad 1 \\
\hline
00001010
\end{array}
$$

Now the result is correct.

Suppose that we add 40 and -40

$$
\begin{array}{r}
00101000 \\
+\ 11010111 \\
\hline
11111111
\end{array}
$$

What number does all 1's represent? The negative of this number in one's complement form is

$$
00000000
$$

Hence, we see a peculiarity of the one's complement notation. There are two values for zero, so-called *positive and negative zero*. This ambiguity about zero is eliminated by using two's complement notation.

2.1.1.2. Two's Complement Notation for Fixed Point Data.

In two's complement notation, the negative of a number is taken by reversing all of the 1's and 0's and then adding 1 to the result. In this way, the carry bit need not be added to the result during the addition operation. Thus the number -40 is given by

$$
00101000 \rightarrow
\begin{array}{r}
11010111 \\
+\qquad 1 \\
\hline
11011000
\end{array}
$$

and the sum of 50 and -40 is

$$
\begin{array}{r}
00110010 \\
+\ 11011000 \\
\hline
1 \leftarrow 00001010
\end{array}
$$

We see that the result is now the decimal value 10 and is correct. Furthermore the two's complement notation eliminates the ambiguity about positive and negative values of zero because if we add 40 and -40:

$$
\begin{array}{r}
00101000 \\
+\ 11011000 \\
\hline
1 \leftarrow 00000000
\end{array}
$$

we get zeroes.

The maximum positive and minimum negative INTEGER numbers represented on a computer with an n-bit word length using two's complement notation are

$$2^{n-1}-1 \quad \text{and} \quad -2^{n-1}$$

Table 2.1 gives the maximum positive and negative values allowed in fixed point notation for several different computers.

2.1.2. Fixed Point Arithmetic

Addition and subtraction of fixed point numbers is straightforward, with the exception of the overflow problem. Consider the addition of the decimal numbers 70 and 80 on our eight-bit computer.

TABLE 2.1 Binary Number Characteristics for Different Computers

Computer Type	IBM 30xx, 43xx	DEC VAX	Cray XMP
Addressing	Byte	Byte	Word
Byte (bits)	8	8	—
Word (bits)	32	32	64
Fixed point notation	Two's comp.	Two's comp.	Two's comp.
Maximum positive number	2,147,483,647	2,147,483,647	9,223,372,036, 854,775,807
Minimum negative number	−2,147,483,648	−2,147,483,648	−9,223,372, 036,854,775,808
Floating point notation	Biased exp.	Biased exp.	Biased exp.
Sign (bits)	1	1	1
Characteristic (bits)	7	8	15
Bias	64	128	16384
Mantissa (bits)	24	23[a]	48
Decimal digits	~7	~7	~15
Maximum number	7.2×10^{75}	1.7×10^{38}	10^{2466}
Minimum number	5.4×10^{-79}	0.29×10^{-38}	10^{-2466}
Double-precision	Biased exponent	Biased exponent	Biased exponent
Sign (bits)	1	1	1
Characteristic (bits)	7	8 or 11[b]	—
Mantissa (bits)	56	55 or 52[a,b]	—
Decimal digits	17	17 or 16[b]	—
Maximum number	7.2×10^{75}	1.7×10^{38} or 0.9×10^{308}	—
Minimum number	5.4×10^{-79}	0.29×10^{-38} or 0.56×10^{-308}	

[a]Plus one phantom bit.
[b]D_floating or G_floating options.

$$01000110 \quad (70)$$
$$+\,01010000 \quad (80)$$
$$\overline{10010110} \quad (-106) \; ???$$

Each operand is represented with no problem, but the sum exceeds decimal 127, the largest positive number that can be represented in eight bits using two's complement notation. This is a *fixed point overflow error*. Such finite magnitude arithmetic errors are detected by the hardware on most scientific computers. Following the error, the operating system *traps* to an error routine and a message is returned to the user.

Multiplication of fixed point numbers is again straightforward, with the exception of the overflow problem. Division of fixed point numbers creates the problem of fractional quotients resulting from integer operands. There is of course no provision for fractions in fixed point arithmetic and fixed point notation. Therefore, fractional results are simply discarded or the result is said to be truncated (as opposed to rounded). Consider the fixed point division

$$29 \; / \; 10 \; = \; 2$$

The only error that can occur in fixed point division is division by zero. This error is trapped by the computer and an error message is returned to the user.

2.1.3. Binary Representation of Floating Point Numbers

Numbers with whole and fractional parts are represented in floating point notation on actual computer hardware and are referred to as REAL numbers in FORTRAN. Floating point is very different from fixed point notation. Floating point numbers are expressed in a form similar to that for scientific notation. The floating point number consists of three parts: (1) the sign of the number, (2) the biased exponent to which the radix is raised, and (3) the fractional part, normalized so that the first nonzero digit is immediately to the right of the radix point. A floating point number generally is stored in a single word. This is usually 32 bits. Again, for the purposes of demonstration, we use an eight-bit word length. We allow one bit to represent the sign of the number, three bits to represent the exponent, and four bits to represent the fraction.

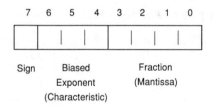

Consider the decimal number 2.75. In the binary number system this is written as

$$10.11$$

or in normalized scientific notation (binary) it is written as

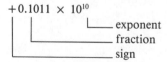

In floating point notation the fraction is called the *mantissa* and is the same as the normalized fraction in the binary notation or

$$\text{Mantissa} = 1011$$

The sign is denoted by a single bit where 0 represents positive and 1 represents negative. In our case

$$\text{Sign} = 0$$

The exponent, called the *characteristic* in floating point notation, is *biased* such that zero is represented by a number halfway between zero and the maximum number that can be expressed in the number of bits available for the exponent. In the case of the three bits in our example, this bias is decimal 4, or 100 in binary. The actual exponent is found by subtracting 100 from the value given in the floating point number. In our example,

$$\text{Characteristic} = 110$$

Thus the floating point representation of 2.75 is

```
0  110  1011
|   |    |__ mantissa or fraction
|   |_____ characteristic or biased exponent
|_____ sign
```

Examples of floating point numbers are given in Table 2.2.

2.1.4. Floating Point Arithmetic

The computer hardware performs floating point arithmetic in the same way that one does when using scientific notation. For instance, in decimal scientific notation, to multiply

$$0.125 \times 10^{-2} \quad \text{and} \quad 0.264 \times 10^{4}$$

TABLE 2.2 Representative Floating Point Numbers

IBM 30xx, 43xx (Lowest to Highest Byte Address)

1.0	41100000[a]
0.1	4019999A
0.125	40200000
6.023×10^{23}	547F8AC0
1.67×10^{-24}	2D204D71

DEC VAX (Lowest to Highest Byte Address)

1.0	00008040
0.1	CDCCCC3E
0.125	0000003F
6.023×10^{23}	7F15FF67
1.67×10^{-24}	C2350119

Cray XMP

1.0	4001800000000000
0.1	3FFDCCCCCCCCCCCD
0.125	3FFE800000000000
6.023×10^{23}	404FFF157F317BAB
1.67×10^{-24}	3FB28135C2027034

IEEE Standard, IBM PC (Lowest to Highest Byte Address)

1.0	0000803F
0.1	CDCCCC3D
0.125	0000003E
6.023×10^{23}	7F15FF66
1.67×10^{-24}	C2350118

[a]Hexadecimal representation of binary format.

we would multiply the fractional parts and add the exponents to get

$$0.033 \times 10^2$$

This number is now *unnormalized* because the leftmost digit of the fraction is zero. We *normalize* it by writing

$$0.33 \times 10^1$$

Suppose that we want to multiply 0.25 and 2. The floating point numbers are

$$0\ 011\ 1000 \quad \text{and} \quad 0\ 110\ 1000$$

We multiply the mantissas and add the characteristics (after adjusting for the bias) to get

$$0\ 100\ 1000$$

While multiplication and division are straightforward when using scientific notation, addition requires more steps. Two normalized numbers with unequal characteristics cannot be added. One of the numbers must be unnormalized until its characteristic is equal to the other number and then the mantissas can be added. Suppose we wish to add 0.25 and 2. We follow these steps.

Step 1: Shift the mantissa of the number with the smaller characteristic and increment the characteristic until it equals that of the other number.

0 011 1000   →   0 100 0100   →   0 101 0010   →   0 110 0001

Step 2: Add the mantissas.

$$\begin{array}{r} 0\ 110\ 1000 \\ +\ 0\ 110\ 0001 \\ \hline 0\ 110\ 1001 \end{array}$$

Step 3: Normalize the result if it is unnormalized. Shift the resultant mantissa until the leftmost digit is one and increment or decrement the characteristic by as many as the number of rightward or leftward shifts. In this example the result is normalized.

Table 2.1 gives information on the floating point representation on several computers. Each different computer vendor has a unique method for representing floating point numbers. We survey four different representations that are often encountered.

2.1.5. Floating Point Representation on IBM Mainframe Computers

The floating point representation on IBM mainframe computers (distinguished from microcomputers) uses the hexadecimal rather than binary number system. The 32-bit word is divided into sign, characteristic, and mantissa using the format.[1]

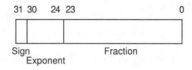

The seven-bit characteristic is biased using decimal 64 or hexadecimal 40. Using the hexadecimal characteristic has the advantage of representing numbers with magnitudes that range from 16^{-64} to 16^{63}. In other words, the characteristic raises the base of sixteen to a power rather than the base of two. Using seven bits in the characteristic and a base of two would only allow magnitudes of decimal 2^{-64} to 2^{63}. A disadvantage of using hexadecimal is that the normalized mantissa does not necessarily have a one as its leftmost digit. Consider the decimal number 0.375. In binary notation this is

$$0.011$$

In IBM floating point notation this would be

$$0 \ 1000000 \ 01100000000000000000000$$

or 40600000 hexadecimal.

Another disadvantage of the hexadecimal representation is that the precision of the mantissa is actually less than in the binary format. This is because the mantissa of a smaller number is shifted in hexadecimal digits to align the characteristics for addition and subtraction operations. Consequently, more bits are shifted out of the calculation than would be if binary representation were used. Furthermore, the leftmost bit in the mantissa is equally likely to be 0 or 1 since the normalization requires that the leftmost hexadecimal digit be non-zero. On IBM computers the precision is an average of 22.5 bits rather than the 24 bits that one would expect.

Double-precision representation on IBM computers simply adds 32 additional bits to the mantissa. The characteristic remains unchanged.

2.1.6. Floating Point Representation on DEC VAX Computers

Floating point representation on the DEC VAX computer, called F_floating, closely follows our discussion in Section 2.1.3.[2] Conceptually, the format is

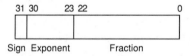

The exponent is biased by 128 and the floating point numbers are always normalized so that the leftmost bit in the mantissa is 1. However, this digit is not actually stored in the word but is "understood" to be there by the hardware. In this way, 24 bits of precision are achieved with only 23 bits in the actual mantissa. An added complication is that the sign, characteristic, and mantissa bits are not arranged in the 32-bit word in the order shown above. In fact, the bytes from lowest to highest addresses are

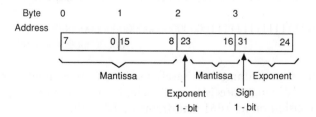

To rearrange the bits into the standard format, the first and second 16-bit words are reversed and then the two bytes within each 16-bit word are reversed. This arrangement allows the 32-bit VAX to be compatible with its predecessor, the 16-bit PDP-11. Hence, on the DEC VAX computer the decimal number 0.375 is represented conceptually by

$$0 \quad 01111111 \quad 10000000000000000000000$$

but in the computer memory, from lowest to highest byte address it is

$$00000000 \quad 00000000 \quad 00111111 \quad 11000000$$

There are two forms of double-precision floating point, so-called D_floating and G_floating. In the more common D_floating format the 64-bit number is divided into a sign bit, an eight-bit characteristic that is biased by decimal 128, and a 55-bit mantissa with the leftmost bit a phantom giving 56 bits of precision. The D_floating double-precision number has the same sign and characteristic as the F_floating, with the additional 32 bits devoted to the mantissa. This is similar in principal to the IBM double-precision format. The G_floating double-precision representation has a sign bit, 11 bits of characteristic, and 52 bits of mantissa. Again the most significant bit in the mantissa is a phantom. Thus, 53 bits of precision are achieved. The advantage of the G_floating format is of course the much larger range of magnitudes provided by the 11-bit characteristic.

2.1.7. Floating Point Representation on Cray Computers

Floating point representation on Cray computers[3] again follows our discussion in Section 2.1.3. The Cray computer has 64-bit words and floating point numbers are thus represented by 64 bits. There is one sign bit, 15 bits in the characteristic, and 48 bits in the mantissa. The 15-bit characteristic is biased by decimal 16,384 or octal 40000.

The decimal number 0.375 is represented on a Cray computer as

$$0 \quad 0111111111111111110000000000000000000000000000000 \ldots$$
$$\ldots 00000000000000000$$

Double-precision arithmetic is rarely used on Cray computers because of the lengthy word. Single-precision arithmetic on a Cray is roughly equivalent to double-precision on an IBM mainframe or DEC VAX.

2.1.8. IEEE Standard Floating Point Representation

Some microcomputers do not have hardware to perform floating point arithmetic. Floating point calculations are performed by calling subroutines that use the integer arithmetic instructions and algorithms to simulate floating point operations. To achieve uniformity between different computers the IEEE has proposed a standard for floating point representation and arithmetic called "A Proposed Standard for Binary Floating-Point Arithmetic," also known as IEEE Task P754. This is the standard used in IBM personal computers,[4] for instance, and is therefore useful to include along with the different vendor floating point formats.

The IEEE standard is similar to the DEC VAX format both in principle and in its implementation. It has one sign bit, eight bits of exponent biased by 127, and 23 bits of mantissa with the most significant bit a phantom that is not stored. On the IBM PC these 32 bits are stored in four successive bytes in a manner similar to the VAX.

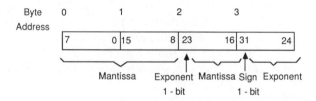

Thus, the number 0.375 appears conceptually as

$$0\ \ 01111101\ \ 10000000000000000000000$$

but is stored in the computer memory from lowest to highest byte address as

$$00000000\ \ 00000000\ \ 11000000\ \ 00111110$$

The double-precision format is one sign bit, 11-bit biased exponent, and 52-bit mantissa with the most significant bit a phantom. In this way a 53-bit mantissa is used.

2.1.9. Binary Representation of Characters

Thus far, we have discussed the binary notation of fixed and floating point numbers used for arithmetic operations. From a scientific point of view, it is natural to first think of computers as calculators of numbers. However, computers are used to store and operate on other kinds of data as well. Foremost among these is *character* or *textual data*. In fact, the vast majority of computer applications in the business world involve the storage and manipulation of textual data for employee records, payrolls, inventories, and so on. The word processor used to prepare this text deals exclusively with textual data. In the realm of scientific programming, the source programs that are entered into disk files and edited are character data. The compiler reads this character data and converts it to machine code. The input and output files used to transfer information to FORTRAN programs are often in the form of character data. The FORTRAN formatted READ and WRITE statements convert the input from characters to the fixed or floating point binary format suitable for arithmetic operations and back again to characters for output. The FORTRAN 77 language has operations and variables specifically for character data. These are discussed further in Chapter 5.

Fortunately, character data is standardized so that textual information is transferrable from one computer to another with little difficulty using magnetic tapes or directly over an electronic network. Each character is represented by a unique pattern of bits. Generally these unique bit patterns are stored in eight bits or a *byte* of computer memory. See Section 2.2.1 for a discussion of bytes. The standard set of bit patterns used to represent characters on many computers is called ASCII (American Standard Code for Information Interchange) and is given in Table 2.3. The ASCII character codes range from decimal 0 to 127. Mainframe computers manufactured by IBM use their own character set called (EBCDIC) the Extended Binary Coded Decimal Information Code also shown in Table 2.3. The EBCDIC character codes range from 0 to 255. Most computer systems have programs to translate from one character set standard to the other.

Thus the FORTRAN source program statement

$$\texttt{DO 10 I = 1,35}$$

is represented in the computer by the following sequence of ASCII bit patterns (where each eight bits is written as two hexadecimal digits for convenience):

$$\texttt{202020202020444F2031302049202A20312C3335}$$

All characters, even blanks, have an ASCII code. The code for the blank is obviously hexadecimal 20. All of the ''control characters'' on the keyboard of a CRT terminal have their own unique bit pattern, even though they don't appear on the screen when typed. The computer recognizes these bit patterns as special instructions and takes appropriate action when it receives one of them. The ''escape key,'' for instance, has the ASCII code 1B.

Peripheral devices such as terminals and printers have circuitry that translate these ASCII bit patterns into characters to display on the CRT screen or print on the paper. The ASCII codes for the carriage return and line feed are 0D and 0A. These must be added to the end of each line of text sent from the computer to the peripheral device to advance the cursor to the beginning of the next line or to advance the paper to the next line.

TABLE 2.3 ASCII and EBCDIC Character Codes

Dec	Hex	Octal	ASCII	EBCDIC
0	00	000	NUL	NUL
1	01	001	SOH	SOH
2	02	002	STX	STX
3	03	003	ETX	ETX
4	04	004	EOT	PF
5	05	005	ENQ	HT
6	06	006	ACK	LC
7	07	007	BEL	DEL
8	08	010	BS	
9	09	011	HT	
10	0A	012	LF	SMM
11	0B	013	VT	VT
12	0C	014	FF	FF
13	0D	015	CR	CR
14	0E	016	SO	SO
15	0F	017	SI	SI
16	10	020	DLE	DLE
17	11	021	DC1	DC1
18	12	022	DC2	DC2
19	13	023	DC3	TM
20	14	024	DC4	RES
21	15	025	NAK	NL
22	16	026	SYN	BS
23	17	027	ETB	IL
24	18	030	CAN	CAN
25	19	031	EM	EM
26	1A	032	SUB	CC
27	1B	033	ESC	CU1
28	1C	034	FS	IFS
29	1D	035	GS	IGS
30	1E	036	RS	IRS
31	1F	037	US	IUS
32	20	040	SPACE	DS
33	21	041	!	SOS
34	22	042	"	FS
35	23	043	#	
36	24	044	$	BYP
37	25	045	%	LF
38	26	046	&	ETB
39	27	047	'	ESC
40	28	050	(	
41	29	051	)	
42	2A	052	*	SM
43	2B	053	+	CU2
44	2C	054	,	

(continued)

TABLE 2.3 (*Continued*)

Dec	Hex	Octal	ASCII	EBCDIC
45	2D	055	—	ENQ
46	2E	056	.	ACK
47	2F	057	/	BEL
48	30	060	0	
49	31	061	1	
50	32	062	2	SYN
51	33	063	3	
52	34	064	4	PN
53	35	065	5	RS
54	36	066	6	UC
55	37	067	7	EOT
56	38	070	8	
57	39	071	9	
58	3A	072	:	
59	3B	073	;	CU3
60	3C	074	<	DC4
61	3D	075	=	NAK
62	3E	076	>	
63	3F	077	?	SUB
64	40	100	@	SPACE
65	41	101	A	
66	42	102	B	
67	43	103	C	
68	44	104	D	
69	45	105	E	
70	46	106	F	
71	47	107	G	
72	48	110	H	
73	49	111	I	
74	4A	112	J	¢
75	4B	113	K	.
76	4C	114	L	<
77	4D	115	M	(
78	4E	116	N	+
79	4F	117	O	
80	50	120	P	&
81	51	121	Q	
82	52	122	R	
83	53	123	S	
84	54	124	T	
85	55	125	U	
86	56	126	V	
87	57	127	W	
88	58	130	X	
89	59	131	Y	
90	5A	132	Z	!

TABLE 2.3 (*Continued*)

Dec	Hex	Octal	ASCII	EBCDIC
91	5B	133	[	$
92	5C	134	\	*
93	5D	135	]	)
94	5E	136	^	;
95	5F	137	–	
96	60	140	`	—
97	61	141	a	/
98	62	142	b	
99	63	143	c	
100	64	144	d	
101	65	145	e	
102	66	146	f	
103	67	147	g	
104	68	150	h	
105	69	151	i	
106	6A	152	j		
107	6B	153	k	,
108	6C	154	l	%
109	6D	155	m	–
110	6E	156	n	>
111	6F	157	o	?
112	70	160	p	
113	71	161	q	
114	72	162	r	
115	73	163	s	
116	74	164	t	
117	75	165	u	
118	76	166	v	
119	77	167	w	
120	78	170	x	
121	79	171	y	`
122	7A	172	z	:
123	7B	173	{	#
124	7C	174	|	@
125	7D	175	}	'
126	7E	176	~	=
127	7F	177	DEL	"
128	80	200		
129	81	201		a
130	82	202		b
131	83	203		c
132	84	204		d
133	85	205		e
134	86	206		f
135	87	207		g

(*continued*)

TABLE 2.3 (*Continued*)

Dec	Hex	Octal	ASCII	EBCDIC
136	88	210		h
137	89	211		i
138	8A	212		
139	8B	213		
140	8C	214		
141	8D	215		
142	8E	216		
143	8F	217		
144	90	220		
145	91	221		j
146	92	222		k
147	93	223		l
148	94	224		m
149	95	225		n
150	96	226		o
151	97	227		p
152	98	230		q
153	99	231		r
154	9A	232		
155	9B	233		
156	9C	234		
157	9D	235		
158	9E	236		
159	9F	237		
160	A0	240		
161	A1	241		~
162	A2	242		s
163	A3	243		t
164	A4	244		u
165	A5	245		v
166	A6	246		w
167	A7	247		x
168	A8	250		y
169	A9	251		z
170	AA	252		
171	AB	253		
172	AC	254		
173	AD	255		
174	AE	256		
175	AF	257		
176	B0	260		
177	B1	261		
178	B2	262		
179	B3	263		
180	B4	264		
181	B5	265		

TABLE 2.3 (*Continued*)

Dec	Hex	Octal	ASCII	EBCDIC
182	B6	266		
183	B7	267		
184	B8	270		
185	B9	271		
186	BA	272		
187	BB	273		
188	BC	274		
189	BD	275		
190	BE	276		
191	BF	277		
192	C0	300		{
193	C1	301		A
194	C2	302		B
195	C3	303		C
196	C4	304		D
197	C5	305		E
198	C6	306		F
199	C7	307		G
200	C8	310		H
201	C9	311		I
202	CA	312		
203	CB	313		
204	CC	314		
205	CD	315		
206	CE	316		
207	CF	317		
208	D0	320		}
209	D1	321		J
210	D2	322		K
211	D3	323		L
212	D4	324		M
213	D5	325		N
214	D6	326		O
215	D7	327		P
216	D8	330		Q
217	D9	331		R
218	DA	332		
219	DB	333		
220	DC	334		
221	DD	335		
222	DE	336		
223	DF	337		
224	E0	340		\
225	E1	341		
226	E2	342		S

(*continued*)

TABLE 2.3 (*Continued*)

Dec	Hex	Octal	ASCII	EBCDIC
227	E3	343		T
228	E4	344		U
229	E5	345		V
230	E6	346		W
231	E7	347		X
232	E8	350		Y
233	E9	351		Z
234	EA	352		
235	EB	353		
236	EC	354		
237	ED	355		
238	EE	356		
239	EF	357		
240	F0	360		0
241	F1	361		1
242	F2	362		2
243	F3	363		3
244	F4	364		4
245	F5	365		5
246	F6	366		6
247	F7	367		7
248	F8	370		8
249	F9	371		9
250	FA	372		|
251	FB	373		
252	FC	374		
253	FD	375		
254	FE	376		
255	FF	377		

2.2. COMPUTER HARDWARE COMPONENTS

Most computers are conceptually quite similar in their general features. On the other hand, the details vary greatly in implementation and complexity from microcomputers to mainframes. In this discussion we are interested in developing a conceptual picture of the computer's hardware components. For our purposes we assume that the computer consists of three different parts:

1. Random access memory—RAM
2. Central processing unit—CPU
3. Input/output processing unit—IOPU

The computer is connected to external devices or peripherals:

1. Magnetic disk storage
2. Magnetic tape storage
3. Timesharing terminals
4. Printers
5. Communications network

This is shown schematically in Figure 2.1. This whole system stores data and communicates among its components using *digital circuitry*. The electrical signals are either (on or off) or (1 or 0). Everything else builds on this basic feature in the form of binary logic and arithmetic. The more one understands about this computer hardware, the easier it is to debug programs and thus develop applications software. This discussion of hardware represents the minimum knowledge required for applications software development.

2.2.1. Random Access Memory (RAM)

The memory of the computer stores information as binary digits or bits. The memory is designed such that all of this information is equally accessible and thus it is called random access memory. The bit is such a small unit of information (1 or 0) that it is not convenient to allow random access to each individual bit in the memory. Instead, bits are grouped together into larger units of information. One common unit of information in the memory is the *word*. A word of memory usually consists of 16–64 bits, depending on the type of computer. A word usually holds the information associated with a fixed or floating point number. Each word of memory has a unique *address* that is used to reference

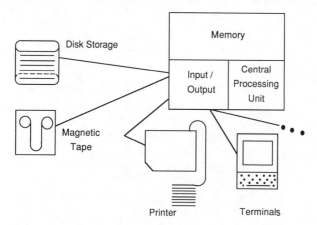

Figure 2.1 Schematic of computer hardware.

the information contained in that word. Hence we can think of memory as a large array of postal boxes, all able to hold the same amount of information, and each with an address as shown in Figure 2.2.

Another useful unit of information in the memory is called the *byte*. A byte is smaller than a word. A byte is the amount of memory that is required to store the information associated with one character to be printed on the terminal or line printer, using the ASCII or EBCDIC character codes. It usually consists of eight bits. In some computers (e.g., Cray) each word has an address and the bytes within the word are accessed with special instructions. On other computers (e.g., VAX and IBM) each byte has a unique address and the address of each succeeding word is incremented by the number of bytes per word. This is demonstrated in Figure 2.3.

The memory is used to store three different types of information:

1. Numerical data (floating or fixed point)
2. Character data
3. Machine instructions

Each type of information is simply in the form of 1's and 0's. Just looking at the 1's and 0's, one could not tell what kind of information is stored in each word. The information only makes sense when it is interpreted by the CPU or IOPU to be one of these three types of information. This is analogous to written languages. Newspapers written in English, German, French, and Spanish all use the same alphabet. However, the English newspaper only makes sense to the English, and the French newspaper only makes sense to the French. In the same way, the 1's and 0's in the computer memory only make sense to the CPU if they are arranged as legitimate machine operations and they only make sense to the IOPU if they are arranged to make strings of legitimate characters to be printed on the terminal or whatever device is being used.

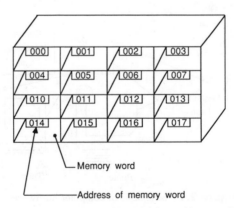

Figure 2.2   Computer memory words are like postal boxes.

BYTE ADDRESSABLE (IBM, DEC)

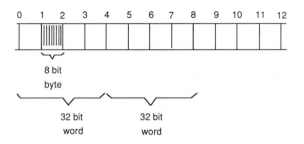

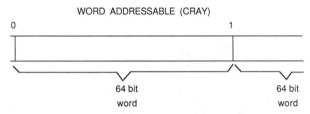

Figure 2.3 Byte and word addressable memory.

As we have already seen, most computers use the same bit arrangements to represent fixed point data using two's complement notation and they use standard character set representations such as ASCII for communications with peripheral equipment. Each computer uses its own form of floating point number notation although they are all based on the same principles.

In contrast to data representation, each type of computer has its own unique set of patterns of 1's and 0's to represent machine instructions. Machine instructions are a sequence of coded information that tell the CPU what functions to perform on the data. This is discussed in more detail in the next section. However, it should be emphasized that the machine instructions are stored in the same random access memory that holds the data to be operated upon.

2.2.2. Central Processing Unit (CPU)

The central processing unit is the "active" part of the computer. The memory simply passively stores the information it is given and returns it back when requested. The CPU asks for information from the memory and sends information back to the memory. It operates on the information within the CPU. A diagram of a generic CPU is shown in Figure 2.4.

The computer's CPU and memory operate according to a digital *clock*. Each operation on the computer takes a fixed number of clock periods (CP). Some instructions require more clock periods than others. Retrieving a word

Functional Units

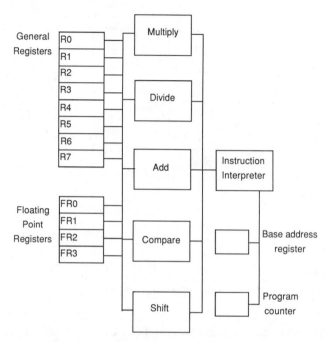

Figure 2.4 Schematic of central processing unit.

from memory requires a number of clock periods. For instance, on the Cray XMP, four CPs are required to move a word from memory to the CPU.

Within the CPU, information is stored in *registers* that usually hold the same number of bits as a memory word. There are often different types of registers, such as

1. Address registers
2. Fixed point registers
3. Floating point registers

Each of these different kind of registers holds different types of information. Machine instructions that operate on floating point numbers do so using the floating point registers. Addresses are manipulated in address registers. The CPU contains *functional units* that add, multiply, test, compare, or perform other functions on the data in the registers. Data in the memory is accessed using the address of the memory word that contains the data. The CPU gets its instructions from memory, where a program in the form of machine instructions is stored. The CPU always executes the instruction contained in the memory word whose address is in the *base address* and *program counter* registers in the CPU. The CPU fetches the contents of this word from memory and interprets it as a *machine instruction*. A generic machine instruction appears as follows:

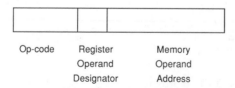

Op-code   Register   Memory
               Operand   Operand
               Designator   Address

The first seven or eight bits of the machine instruction are the *operation code*. This "op-code" tells the CPU which operation (e.g., LOAD, STORE, ADD, MULTIPLY, . . .) is to be performed. The operation is usually performed on data that is contained in the registers of the CPU and a word in memory, much in the same way that a hand-held calculator multiplies a number in a register with the one just entered on the keypad. The register operand is designated by the next bits in the machine instruction. The address of the memory words operand is the last 12–22 bits of the machine instruction. Once this instruction is performed, the program counter is incremented to the address of the next instruction and this instruction is fetched by the CPU to interpret and the process is repeated. In this way the CPU steps through memory *executing* a program stored in the memory.

A single FORTRAN statement may be translated into several machine instructions by the compiler. For instance, the FORTRAN statement A = B * C would be translated by the FORTRAN compiler into the following machine instructions (written here in a nmeumonic form called *assembly language* to represent the machine instructions):

```
LOAD  FPR1,  B
MULT  FPR1,  C
STOR  FPR1,  A
```

The first instruction loads floating point register 1 with the contents of the memory word that has been designated by the compiler to hold the value of the variable B. The second instruction multiplies the contents of FPR 1 with the contents of the memory word that has been designated to hold the value of the variable C and puts the result of the multiplication back into FPR 1. The third instruction stores the contents of FPR 1 into the memory word designated to hold the contents of the variable A.

In the text we will represent programs and program units called subprograms in the schematic form shown in Figure 2.5. Each subprogram will reside in contiguous words of memory. This memory will contain machine code for

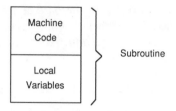

Figure 2.5 Schematic of machine code and variables in a subroutine.

that subprogram and the words required to hold the local variables on which the machine code operates. It will not be necessary to represent the actual details of the machine code.

2.2.3. Input/Output Processing Unit

On most larger computers there is an IOPU (called many different names by different manufacturers). The IOPU communicates with all of the I/O devices connected to the computer. It is actually like a CPU itself, with its own set of instructions that it can execute. However, it is a slave to the CPU which tells it what to do. The IOPU accepts input signals from the various input devices and puts this data into the memory, at a position designated by the CPU under control of the operating system. It also reads data from memory and sends it out to output devices. This can occur simultaneously with the execution of a program by the CPU.

If the IOPU takes character data from the memory and sends this out to a terminal, then the terminal receives this information and its circuitry translates each byte of data into a character to be displayed on a screen or printed on a page. Each character has a unique set of bits to identify it as shown in Table 2.3.

2.2.4. Virtual Memory

Many of today's supermini- and mainframe computers have *virtual memory* (VM). The virtual memory is "virtual" because the addresses in the *virtual address space* which a program references are only loosely related to addresses in the *real memory* of the computer. Virtual memory is a powerful feature for timesharing environments because it lets the operating system better manage the swapping of programs into and out of the real memory where they are executed. To understand VM we must review how timesharing operating systems manage real memory.

A schematic picture of real memory, disk storage, and user programs is shown in Figure 2.6. In this timesharing environment there are five users with five programs that in combination exceed the size of the real memory. Thus, one of the programs has been *swapped* out of memory to the disk. Timeshar-

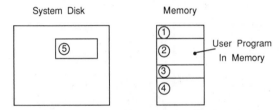

Figure 2.6   Real memory environment for multiple users.

ing operating systems give the illusion that each user has full control of the computer by rapidly rotating use of the CPU to each user for usually less than a second apiece. This is called a *time slice*. In the situation in Figure 2.6, when it is time for program 5 to execute, it must be swapped back into the memory. Since there is no more memory available to hold it, another program must be swapped out to leave space. This is shown schematically in Figure 2.7. Each program must be swapped into and out of memory as a complete unit.

In a virtual memory environment the picture changes to that shown in Figure 2.8. The addresses referenced in the users program are in a virtual address space. This virtual address space is considerably larger than the amount of real memory in the computer and each user program has its own virtual address space. The virtual address space or virtual memory is divided into units called *pages*. These pages are usually 1024 or 4096 words. The real memory is also divided into pages of the same size. When a user program executes, each page of its virtual address space is located either in real memory or on the disk. In this way, parts of all programs can be in real memory at one time. So long as the virtual memory references within the executing program correspond to addresses in pages that are located within real memory, the program can execute. These address references include both the fetching of machine instructions by the CPU and the access to the memory words devoted to variable storage. When the executing program references a virtual memory address that is not in real memory but is on the disk, a *page fault* interrupts the execution and returns control to the operating system. The timesharing operating system notes the page that is needed and begins the process of swapping that page back into the real memory so the program can continue execution. If the

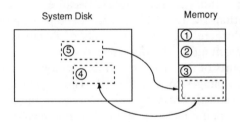

Figure 2.7   Program swapping between real memory and disk.

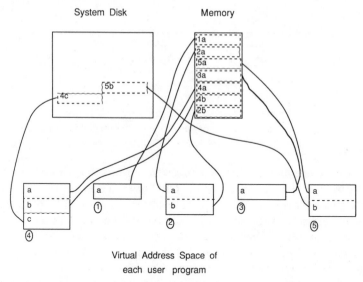

Virtual Address Space of
each user program

Figure 2.8   Virtual memory environment for multiple users.

real memory is full, then this page will replace the page that was referenced least recently. Thus the most frequently referenced pages in all of the users programs tend to remain in the real memory. In the interim, control of the CPU is given to another user program. If managed properly, this virtual memory scheme improves the efficiency of the timesharing environment and gives each user a "better response" from the computer. Obviously, more hardware components are needed to translate the virtual memory addresses referenced by the programs into the corresponding real memory addresses where the information actually resides. When executing on a VM computer the user never "sees" the real addresses where the program is executing.

Virtual memory has many advantages. Suppose that all five programs in our example use large amounts of memory but that 50% of the memory in each is referenced infrequently. In a VM environment, the 50% of virtual memory that is frequently referenced tends to remain in the real memory and little swapping to the disk occurs. Suppose that a single program is so large that it does not fit within the real memory. Because the virtual address space is so much larger than the real address space, the programmer can write the program as though there were large amounts of memory. This considerably simplifies the programming. The operating system manages the swapping of pages so that the parts of the program that are referenced are in real memory.

There are disadvantages to VM as well. The paging system can become overloaded. This is called *thrashing*. In this situation the computer spends all of its CPU time swapping pages in and out of real memory and has no time left to execute user programs. This can occur because too many users are logged onto the computer at the same time or because the user programs are poorly written.

2.2.5. Vector Computers

The most recent generation of supercomputers are called vector computers. These high-speed computers make use of *parallel* and *pipeline* processing to increase the rate at which arithmetic operations are performed by the CPU.

The idea of parallel processing within a CPU is to keep all hardware as busy as possible. Different functional units perform operations simultaneously on different operands so long as the result of one calculation does not impact the other. It is the task of the optimizing compiler to evaluate the FORTRAN program and generate machine code that makes best use of the hardware.

The pipeline aspect involves the design of each functional unit. The functional unit is treated as an assembly line where two operands enter and move along to a different station on each clock period until the result emerges at the other end after the required clock periods. This is shown schematically in Figure 2.9. On a vector computer the functional units are designed so that new

Unsegmented Functional Unit

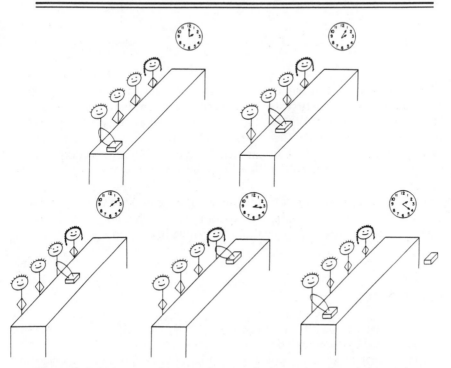

Figure 2.9 Schematic of functional unit producing results in four clock periods.

Segmented Functional Unit

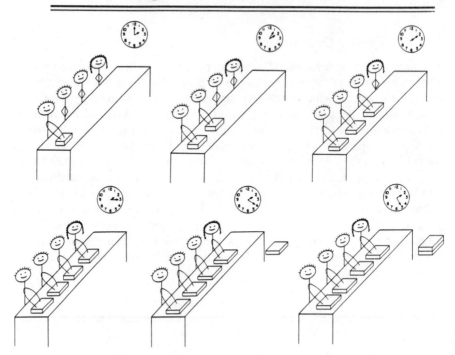

Figure 2.10 Filled pipeline producing a result on every clock period.

operands are started through the assembly line after the first two operands have completed just the first step of the total operation. In this way the assembly line or pipeline is "filled up" and a result emerges every clock period as shown in Figure 2.10. On a Cray XMP the clock period is 9.5 nanoseconds and two operations can be done in parallel. Thus a single CPU produces results at the peak rate of 200 million floating point operations per second, or 200 Mflops.

Both the virtual memory of superminicomputers and the vector processing of supercomputers requires special attention to programming. A brief introduction to these programming rules is presented in Section 6.9.

REFERENCES

1. VS FORTRAN Application Programming: Language Reference, Release 3.0, March 1983, IBM Corporation.
2. VAX-11 FORTRAN Language Reference Manual, Order No. AA-DO34C-TE, April 1982, Digital Equipment Corporation.

3. CFT Reference Manual, Cray Research Inc. Publication Number SR-0009, 1986, Cray Research, Inc.

4. IBM Personal Computer Professional FORTRAN Manual, November 1984, IBM Corporation.

Other Useful References

Operating system command language manual for the computer system used by the reader.

File editor manual for the computer system used by the reader.

FORTRAN implementation and language manual for the computer system used by the reader.

Linker manual for the computer system used by the reader.

EXERCISES

1. Write the first 20 numbers in a base four number system along with the corresponding numbers in decimal and binary systems.

2. Using our hypothetical eight-bit computer, write the one's and two's complement binary representation for the following decimal integer numbers.
   (a) 32
   (b) −21
   (c) −75
   (d) 12

3. Using our hypothetical eight-bit computer, write the binary representation for the following real numbers.
   (a) 2.0
   (b) 0.125
   (c) 0.1
   (d) −1.25

4. Using our hypothetical eight-bit computer, write the integer, real, and ASCII and EBCDIC character data that the following bit patterns represent.
   (a) 10010101
   (b) 01001110
   (c) 01101011
   (d) 01111111

5. Perform the indicated integer arithmetic operations using our eight-bit computer and convert the result to decimal. (a) and (b) are binary and (c) and (d) are hexadecimal representations of the eight bits.

(a)   00001010
       + 00011011

(b)   00001010
       − 00011011

(c)   3E
       + 4F

(d)   3E
       − 4F

6. Give the binary representation of the following data on your computer. [Hint: Write a program to assign each of these constants to a variable and write the output using a "Z" (hexadecimal) format specifier for variables assigned these values.]

   (a) 2.0
   (b) 3.14159
   (c) 0.3
   (d) −10.1

7. Give the characters corresponding to the bit patterns that represent the values in problem 6 for your computer. Some eight bit bytes may have bit patterns that correspond to no character.

8. Write a report on the hardware features of the computer you are using. Include the registers in the CPU (integer, address, and floating point) and the number of bits per register, the type of memory addressing (word or byte addressable) and the number of bits per word, the maximum number of memory words (both virtual and real), and the output devices attached to the computer such as disks, tape drives, and the like.

9. What is the smallest difference between two numbers that will yield a non-zero result when the numbers are subtracted on your computer? This is called the "machine epsilon" and is important for determining the maximum precision of calculations on your computer.

■ 3

The FORTRAN Language

Most large-scale scientific computer programs are written using the FORTRAN language. FORTRAN is a procedure-oriented language. That is, its syntax more closely resembles the problem being solved than the computer on which it is executing, in contrast to assembly language, which has a one-for-one correspondence between language statement types and machine instructions. FORTRAN is designed to solve mathematically oriented problems and is an acronym for *for*mula *tran*slation.

FORTRAN was originally developed by IBM and released for customer use in 1957. The language was a great success and quickly became the major scientific programming language. As the language has evolved over the 30 years of its life, new features have been added and a few features eliminated. In 1966 the American Standards Association published American Standard FORTRAN, which became known as FORTRAN 66, sometimes called FORTRAN IV ("FORTRAN four"). In the ensuing years new features were added to the language on an ad hoc basis to implement many of the ideas that computer scientists were developing and implementing in more modern languages such as Pascal. In 1978, the American National Standards Institute produced the first revision of the standard, known as *FORTRAN 77*. Throughout this text we base our discussion on FORTRAN 77, the current standard. The FORTRAN 77 language is defined in the document: American National Standard Programming Language FORTRAN, ANSI Document X3.9—1978, published by the American National Standards Institute, Inc., 1430 Broadway, New York, New York 10018.

In past years the beginning programming courses taken by engineering students were usually based on the FORTRAN language. In recent times, many computer science departments have switched to Pascal in their introductory

51

courses because Pascal is more suitable for teaching structured programming and has much "richer" data structures than FORTRAN. In any event, it is important for engineers and scientists involved in software development to understand the FORTRAN language because they are more likely to encounter it than any other language.

The FORTRAN 77 language consists of 51 statement types, given in Figure 3.1. Although FORTRAN 77 is categorized as a mathematical language suitable for solving scientific problems, in fact only one of the 51 statements in the language (the arithmetic assignment statement) actually resembles a mathematical formula! The other 50 statements control input and output, make decisions, transfer control, or give additional information about the program so that it can be translated into machine code. Statements are divided into executable and nonexecutable categories designated by (E) or (NE) in Figure 3.1. Executable statements result in the generation of machine code in the final executable version of the FORTRAN program. Nonexecutable statements are not translated into machine code but instead instruct the compiler in some way. The true essence of the program is embodied in the executable statements. The features invoked by the nonexecutable statements are the ones that distinguish advanced FORTRAN programs from the simple programs written in beginning courses.

The 51 statements are divided into eight general categories in Figure 3.1. The assignment category includes the arithmetic assignment statement that assigns the value of an expression (e) to a variable (v). Execution control includes the looping and decision-making constructs that make up structured programming. The input and output category includes not only read and write statements, but also statements that control the disk files from which FORTRAN programs normally read and write data on today's computers. Variable type definitions include six different variable types. Subprogram definition, invocation, and exit are included in one category. Variable initialization and the definition of constants, memory definition, and miscellaneous variable attribute definitions round out the categories. Comment statements are not included in any category because they have no effect on the program in any way.

In the next section, 11 statements normally covered in elementary courses are selected for review. These are denoted by a 3 in the last column in Figure 3.1. Chapters 4 and 5 are devoted to advanced FORTRAN-programming topics. The statements described in these chapters are denoted by a 4 or a 5. Some of the remaining statements are also covered in beginning programming courses and others are not really necessary because they duplicate the function of other statements.

3.1. MASTERY OF ELEVEN SIMPLE STATEMENTS

While this text is not meant to serve as a beginners guide to FORTRAN programming, it is instructive to develop the language features of importance to

Category	Statements	Executable/ Non-executable	In text
Assignment	v = e (arithmetic)	E	3
	v = e (logical)	E	
	v = e (character)	E	5
Execution control	ASSIGN s TO i	E	
	CONTINUE	NE	3
	DO	E	3
	ELSE	E	3
	ELSE IF THEN	E	
	END	E	3
	ENDIF	E	3
	GOTO	E	3
	GOTO (...)	E	
	IF(e) st	E	
	IF(e) st1,st2,st3	E	
	IF(e) THEN	E	3
	PAUSE	E	
	STOP	E	
Input and output	FORMAT	NE	5
	PRINT	E	
	READ	E	3,5
	WRITE	E	3,5
	BACKSPACE	E	5
	CLOSE	E	5
	ENDFILE	E	5
	INQUIRE	E	
	OPEN	E	5
	REWIND	E	5
Variable type definition	CHARACTER	NE	5
	COMPLEX	NE	
	DOUBLE PRECISION	NE	6
	IMPLICIT	NE	6
	INTEGER	NE	6
	LOGICAL	NE	
	REAL	NE	6
	DIMENSION	NE	3
Subprogram definition and access	CALL sub	E	4
	ENTRY	E	4
	function invocation	E	4
	FUNCTION	E	4
	INTRINSIC func	NE	4
	PROGRAM	E	4
	RETURN	E	4
	SUBROUTINE sub	E	4
Initialization	BLOCK DATA	E	4
	DATA	NE	
	PARAMETER	NE	
Memory definition	COMMON	NE	4
	EQUIVALENCE	NE	
Miscellaneous variable attributes	EXTERNAL	NE	4
	SAVE	NE	4
Other	comment	NE	3

Figure 3.1 List of FORTRAN 77 statements.

the advanced programmer by starting from the simplest approach to FORTRAN programming. The references include several excellent texts on FORTRAN programming.[1-3]

FORTRAN programs are an ordered sequence of commands (statements) that either operate on the data (variables and constants) or test them and transfer control to other parts of the program. The 51 statement types that represent the entire language definition can be reduced to a subset of 11 statements which are:

1. Arithmetic assignment
2. CONTINUE
3. DIMENSION
4. DO
5. END
6. GOTO
7. IF-THEN-ELSE
8. READ
9. WRITE
10. Intrinsic functions (EXP, COS, ABS, . . .)
11. Comment

This subset of the FORTRAN language allows the engineer to write short yet powerful programs such as the one given in Figure 3.2. This program calculates the mean value and the root mean square deviation from the mean of the data inputted to it. Only four statements in this simple but realistic program can be directly related to the mathematical formulas that define the problem. The rest of the statements are extraneous to the understanding of the formulas.

```
1              DIMENSION DATA(1000)
2           5 READ(*,*)  NMAX
3              IF( NMAX .GT. 1000 ) GOTO 990
4              READ(*,*) (DATA(I), I=1,NMAX)
5              XBAR = 0.
6              DO 10 I = 1,NMAX
7              XBAR = XBAR + DATA(I)
8          10 CONTINUE
9              XBAR = XBAR / NMAX
10             XDIF = 0.
11             DO 20 I = 1,NMAX
12             XDIF = XDIF + (DATA(I) - XBAR) ** 2
13         20 CONTINUE
14             RMS = SQRT( XDIF / NMAX )
15             WRITE(*,*) 'THE NUMBER OF DATA VALUES IS', NMAX
16             WRITE(*,*) 'THE VALUES OF THE DATA ARE'
17             WRITE(*,*) (DATA(I), I=1,NMAX)
18             WRITE(*,*) 'THE VALUE OF THE MEAN IS', XBAR
19             WRITE(*,*) 'THE ROOT MEAN SQUARE VALUE IS', RMS
20             GO TO 5
21        990 WRITE(*,*) 'TOO MANY DATA VALUES - NMAX=', NMAX
22             END
```

Figure 3.2 Simple FORTRAN program.

However, they are vital to the program that must be written to solve the problem.

Mastery of these 11 statements gives engineers the capability to solve most simple problems. However, the limited features of these 11 statements are a great handicap when trying to write large applications programs. A reasonable rule of thumb is that these 11 statements are adequate for problems that require less than 300 FORTRAN program statements to solve. For problems that are larger than this, one requires an expanded set of FORTRAN statements. Following a first course in programming, the student should be quite familiar with these 11 statements and the associated variable and constant types.

It should also be noted here that for simple programs where these 11 statements are adequate to solve the problem in question there may be better alternatives to the FORTRAN language. The BASIC language is designed to have little more than these few statements and is well supported on personal computers where the engineer is likely to be solving simple problems.

3.1.1. FORTRAN Statement Format

All FORTRAN statements have a fixed format consisting of four fields shown in Figure 3.3.

Statement label. This field is an optional one- to five-digit number that can appear anywhere within columns 1–5. It is nice to right-justify these like the program in Figure 3.2. In any case it is best to keep numbers out of column 1 because this is used for "carriage control" on most systems, and a number here can fool some processors and cause bothersome spurious page ejects from the line printer.

Continuation. A digit or letter in column 6 signals that this is a continuation of the previous line. One can use up to 19 of these for a single statement. This is most convenient on FORMAT statements as we shall see later. Most FORTRAN compilers actually allow many more than 19 continuation lines, but 19 is the FORTRAN 77 standard. One cannot use a 0 (zero) as a continuation character.

FORTRAN Statement. This can appear anywhere within columns 7–72. Imbedded blanks may appear anywhere in the FORTRAN statement. In FORTRAN even variable names can have imbedded blanks.

Sequence Numbers. On a finished program, sequence numbers are often put in columns 73–80. Later when the program is modified (possibly by someone else), they can distinguish the original lines from later addi-

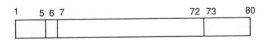

Figure 3.3 FORTRAN statement format.

tions. Also, when cards were used, this helped to resort them if the box was dropped.

3.1.2. Legitimate Symbols

The following symbols are part of the FORTRAN 77 standard. A letter is one of the upper case alphabet:

```
A B C D E F G H I J K L M N O P Q R S T U V W X Y Z
```

A digit is

```
0 1 2 3 4 5 6 7 8 9
```

Letters and digits together are called *alphanumeric symbols*. The following special characters are included:

```
(no symbol)  Blank
     =       Equals
     +       Plus
     -       Minus
     *       Asterisk
     /       Slash
     (       Left parenthesis
     )       Right parenthesis
     ,       Comma
     .       Decimal point
     $       Currency symbol
     '       Apostrophe
     :       Colon
```

No other symbols are included as part of the FORTRAN 77 standard. Yet most compilers accept many other symbols, with the most common ones being lower case letters.

3.1.3. Variable and Constant Types

Floating point variables start with letters A–H and O–Z and are called REAL variables. Six upper case letters or numbers are allowed in the variable name. Floating point constants are specified with an exponent and mantissa (or fractional part):

```
1.257E-6
10.674
6.023E22
```

Fixed point variables start with letters I–N and are called INTEGER variables. Again, six upper case letters and numbers are allowed in the variable name. Integer constants take the familiar form:

```
1, 102, 5563, etc.
```

There are also LOGICAL and CHARACTER variables and constants and COMPLEX variables and constants.

3.1.4. Assignment Statement—Executable

The assignment statement has the form:

```
Variable = Expression
```

where expression consists of variables, functions, constants, and arithmetic operators. This should be the easiest statement to understand because it is closest in form to the mathematical formulas that the program is meant to solve.

Arithmetic operations have an implicit precedence ordering as given below:

Highest	**	exponentiation
	+,−	plus, negation
	*,/	multiplication, division
Lowest	+,−	addition, subtraction

As an example the following expression is evaluated as shown.

```
B = 2.
C = 3.
D = 2.
E = 6.
F = 2.
G = 3.
A = B + C ** D - E / F * G
    2 + 3 ** 2 - 6 / 2 * 3
    2 +   9   -   3   * 3
       11      -       9
               2
```

The order of evaluation is altered using parentheses.

```
A = (B + C) ** D - E / (F * G)
     2 + 3  ** 2 - 6 / (2 * 3)
        5   ** 2 - 6 /    6
           25    - 1
                 24
```

It is important to note that "$=$" symbolizes "assignment" and not "equals." Thus the expression

```
A = 2.
A = A + 5. ⟶ A = 7.
```

is read as "add 5 to the value of A and replace the value of A with this new result".

3.1.5. DIMENSION Statement—Nonexecutable

The DIMENSION statement is used to declare *subscripted variables* and to define the minimum and maximum indices. It instructs the compiler to set aside this much memory to hold the values of the variables. Variables, either real or integer, can come in two varieties: scalars and subscripted. Subscripted variables with one subscript are called *vectors* and those with two subscripts are called *matrices*.

3.1.5.1. Scalars. We have only used scalars thus far. Here the variable holds a single number. A scalar variable is usually stored in a single word of computer memory.

```
VAR = 5.
ITEM = 9
```

3.1.5.2. Vectors. Here the variable holds a singly subscripted set of numbers and must be declared with a DIMENSION statement that specifies the minimum and maximum indices in the vector variable. When only a single index is specified, it is the maximum index and the minimum index is assumed to be 1. Thus

```
DIMENSION VEC(10)
```

is the same as

```
DIMENSION VEC (1:10)
```

Each element of a vector variable can be referenced.

```
    VEC(1) = 5.
    VEC(9) = 264.37
                or
    DO 10 I = 1,10
       VEC(I) = 5. + I
10 CONTINUE
```

Vector variables are stored in sequential words of memory with the address of each element of the vector being the address of the next word in memory as shown in Figure 3.4.

3.1.5.3. Matrices. Here the variable holds a doubly subscripted set of numbers and must be declared with a DIMENSION statement. Again, a single number designates the maximum index for that subscript.

```
    DIMENSION MAT(5,5)
    DO 10 I = 1,5
    DO 10 J = 1,5
    MAT(I,J) = I * J
10 CONTINUE
```

The ordering of the elements of matrices in memory is not obvious because memory addresses are sequentially ordered single numbers while the elements of the matrix are doubly subscripted. Hence, some scheme must be used to translate the two indices into a single index that is associated with memory addresses. In FORTRAN, the elements of multisubscripted variables are always ordered with the leftmost index varying fastest (just the opposite of the odometer on your car). This is also shown in Figure 3.4. The translation formula from a doubly subscripted to singly subscripted indexing scheme where 1 is the minumum index for both subscripts is

$$(i,j) \longrightarrow k \qquad K = I + (J-1) * IMAX$$

where IMAX is the maximum dimension of the I index. Subscripted variables can be defined with up to seven subscripts. This is useful for data that must be sequentially or randomly accessed.

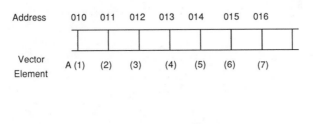

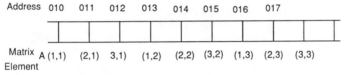

DIMENSION A (3,3)

Figure 3.4 Singly subscripted (vector) and doubly subscripted (matrix) variables and addresses.

3.1.6. CONTINUE Statement—Nonexecutable

The CONTINUE statement is normally used to end "DO loops." It does nothing itself, but has a statement label to hold a position.

```
    DO 10 I = 1,5          DO 10 I = 1,5
    A(I) = B(I) * D      10 A(I) = B(I) * D
 10 CONTINUE
```

These two sequences of program are equivalent, but if we want to add additional lines to the program the left one is easiest to modify.

```
    DO 10 I = 1,5
    A(I) = B(I) * D
    C(I) = A(I) * E
 10 CONTINUE
```

A good recommendation is to end all DO loops with CONTINUE statements rather than place the statement label on the last executable statement in the loop.

3.1.7. DO Statement—Executable

The DO statement allows looping or indexing through a vector. Sum the elements of the vector VECTOR.

```
    SUM = 0.
    DO 10 I = 1,100
    SUM = SUM + VECTOR(I)
 10 CONTINUE
```

Sum every other element of the vector VECTOR.

```
    SUMODD = 0.
    SUMEVN = 0.
    DO 10 I = 2,100,2
    SUMODD = SUMODD + VECTOR(I-1)
    SUMEVN = SUMEVN + VECTOR(I)
 10 CONTINUE
```

The DO statement specifies a beginning integer index, an ending index, and an optional increment if the increment is not 1. The statements included in the DO loop are identified by the statement label referenced in the DO statement. Negative as well as positive increments are allowed.

3.1.8. IF-THEN-ELSE Statement—Executable

The IF statement tests the relation between variables and/or constants to form a logical value and transfers control according to the outcome of the test.

```
IF( A .LT. 3. ) A = 3. (true test)
    (false test)
```

Set all elements of vector A with negative values to their absolute value.

```
   DO 10 I = 1,100
   IF( A(I) .LT. 0. ) A(I) = -A(I)
10 CONTINUE
```

The relational operators used in IF statements are

```
.LT. less than
.LE. less than or equal to
.GT. greater than
.GE. greater than or equal to
.NE. not equal to
.EQ. equal to
```

A variation on the IF statement is the IF-THEN-ELSE construct of statements. Using this combination of statements, sequences of FORTRAN statements can be conditionally executed depending on the outcome of the test in the IF statement.

```
IF( A .LT. 12. ) THEN
    Y = A * B
    Z = Y / X
ELSE
    Y = 0.
    Z = 0.
ENDIF
```

The IF-THEN-ELSE construct is one of the features of the FORTRAN 77 language that allows structured programming. It was the most important addition to the language in the revision from FORTRAN 66.

3.1.9. GOTO Statement—Executable

The GOTO statement transfers control in the program to a specified statement label. Count the number of nonzero elements in the vector A.

```
      NONZER = 0
      DO 10 I = 1,100
      IF( A(I) .EQ. 0.) GOTO 10
      NONZER = NONZER + 1
10 CONTINUE
```

Very often the GOTO statement is used with the IF statement to transfer control on one of the conditional branches. The argument about GOTO-less programming has raged since the original paper by Dijkstra.[4] The theory says that a language with sequential statements, IF-THEN-ELSE statements, and loops can be used with no GOTO's in the program. Although this is true in principle, in practice there are circumstances when a GOTO statement is more natural than the other options. Excessive use of GOTO statements certainly does turn a program into "spaghetti" and should be avoided.

3.1.10. END Statement—Executable

The END statement marks the end of the program. If control reaches this statement in the program, then the program terminates. All FORTRAN programs must have an END statement.

3.1.11. READ Statement—Executable

The READ statement reads data into specified variables. Data comes from a terminal, file, magnetic tape, and so on.

```
READ(*,*) NMAX
READ(*,*) (DATA(J), J=1,NMAX)
```

The second "*" in each statement indicates that the data can be any format. It is best to separate the data items with blanks. The first "*" in the above READ statements designates the default input device, usually the terminal. Data from a file can be read by assigning the file to an input/output *unit specifier* using either an operating system command or the OPEN statement and then using a READ statement of the form:

```
READ(u,*) NMAX
```

where u is an integer constant or variable designating the unit specifier.

3.1.12. WRITE Statement—Executable

The WRITE statement prints the contents of specified variables onto the default output device or into a designated file assigned to a unit specifier.

```
WRITE(*,*) 'NMAX EQUALS', NMAX
WRITE(*,*) 'THE DATA IS AS FOLLOWS'
WRITE(*,*) (DATA(I), I=1,NMAX)
```

Descriptive messages are included with the values of the variables by putting the message within apostrophes as shown above. Unit specifiers are treated the same as the READ statement:

```
WRITE(u,*) (DATA(I), I=1,NMAX)
```

where u is an integer constant or variable associated with a file through a system command or OPEN statement.

3.1.13. Intrinsic Functions—Executable

The FORTRAN language has a rich number of so-called intrinsic functions that perform common mathematical functions such as square root, cosine, sine, exponentiation, logarithm, and the like. These are given in Figure 3.5. Functions can be used in expressions in the same way that variables can be used.

```
Y = LOG(B) + COS(X) / SQRT(X + EXP(A))
```

3.1.14. Comment Statement—Nonexecutable

The comment statement is one of the most important statements in large-scale program development. It allows textual information to be included in the source program to describe what is going on. It is denoted by a "C" or "*" in column 1 of the statement line. The statistical analysis program in Figure 3.2 with comment statements included is given in Figure 3.6. Quite clearly, it is more understandable with the comments than without.

With these 11 statements and associated concepts one can write FORTRAN programs to solve many simple engineering problems. However, more complex problems, requiring greater computing resources, will require a more advanced knowledge of the FORTRAN language to most conveniently implement the solution. Advanced features of FORTRAN 77 are covered in Chapters 4 and 5.

3.2. MECHANICS OF "WRITING" A FORTRAN PROGRAM

The process of writing and executing a FORTRAN program actually involves four steps and three different "versions" of the program. These are shown schematically in Figure 3.7. Each of these steps is described in the following sections.

Function name	Definition	Function name	Definition
INT	Conversion to integer	REAL	Conversion to real
DBLE	Conversion to double precision	CMPLX	Conversion to complex
ICHAR	Conversion from character to integer	CHAR	Conversion from integer to char.
AINT	Truncation	ANINT	Nearest whole number
NINT	Nearest integer	ABS	Absolute value
MOD	Remaindering	SIGN	Transfer of sign
DIM	Positive difference	MAX	Choosing largest value
MIN	Choosing smallest value	LEN	Length of char. entity
INDEX	Index of a char. substring	LGE	Lexically greater than or equal to
LGT	Lexically greater than	LLE	Lexically less than or equal to
LLT	Lexically less than	AIMAG	Imaginary part of complex arg.
CONJG	Comjugate of complex arg.	SQRT	Square root
EXP	exponential	LOG	Natural logarithm
LOG10	Common logarithm	SIN	Sine
COS	Cosine	TAN	Tangent
ASIN	Arcsine	ACOS	Arccosine
ATAN	Arctangent	SINH	Hyperbolic sine
COSH	Hyperbolic cosine	TANH	Hyperbolic tang.

Figure 3.5 List of FORTRAN intrinsic functions.

3.2.1. Writing the Source Program

The program that you write is called the *source program.* This consists of the FORTRAN statements that are typed into a disk file using a text editor. This disk file actually contains the ASCII characters that correspond to the letters that are typed on the terminal. An example of this is shown in Figure 3.8 where

```
C  THIS IS A PROGRAM TO COMPUTE THE MEAN AND ROOT MEAN SQUARE
C  DEVIATION OF INPUTTED DATA
       DIMENSION DATA(1000)
C
C  READ IN THE NUMBER OF DATA ITEMS IN A SET OF DATA
     5 READ(*,*) NMAX
C
C  IF THERE ARE MORE THAN 1000 DATA ITEMS THEN WE HAVE AN ERROR
C  CONDITION
       IF( NMAX .GT. 1000 ) GOTO 990
C  ELSE EVERYTHING IS OKAY, PROCESS THE DATA
C
C  READ IN A DATA SET
       READ(*,*) (DATA(I), I=1,NMAX)
C
C  COMPUTE THE MEAN VALUE OF THE DATA
       XBAR = 0.
       DO 10 I = 1,NMAX
       XBAR = XBAR + DATA(I)
    10 CONTINUE
       XBAR = XBAR / NMAX
C
C  COMPUTE THE ROOT MEAN SQUARE
       XDIF = 0.
       DO 20 I = 1,NMAX
       XDIF = XDIF + (DATA(I) - XBAR) ** 2
    20 CONTINUE
       RMS = SQRT(XDIF / NMAX)
C
C  NOW PRINT OUT A SUMMARY OF THE RESULTS
       WRITE(*,*) 'THE NUMBER OF DATA VALUES IS", NMAX
       WRITE(*,*) 'THE VALUES OF DATA ARE"
       WRITE(*,*) (DATA(I), I=1,NMAX)
       WRITE(*,*) 'THE VALUE OF THE MEAN IS", XBAR
       WRITE(*,*) 'THE ROOT MEAN SQUARE VALUE IS", RMS
C
C  RETURN TO THE BEGINNING TO READ ANOTHER DATA SET
       GOTO 5
C
C  ERROR CONDITION - TOO MANY DATA ITEMS IN ONE SET
   990 WRITE(*,*) 'TOO MANY DATA VALUES - NMAX=", NMAX
       END
```

Figure 3.6 Simple FORTRAN program with comment statements.

a FORTRAN statement is given along with the hexadecimal representation of the bits that make up the characters that are typed to create this statement. The FORTRAN program is updated by modifying the source file.

Because the ASCII code that represents the letters and numerals in the source program is a standard in the computer industry, the source program is transferrable from one type of computer to another with no compatibility problem.

3.2.2. Compiling the Source Program to Create an Object Program

The *FORTRAN compiler* translates or *compiles* the source program, in the form of character strings, into an *object program,* in the form of machine code. The compiler produces an object file that contains more information than just the machine code that corresponds to the source statements. The

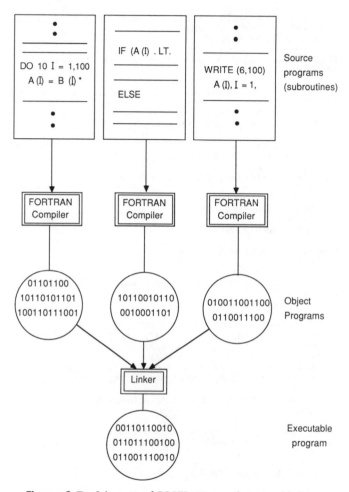

Figure 3.7 Schematic of FORTRAN compilation and linking.

compiler must supply other information because the machine code for a single isolated subroutine is not yet ready to be executed.

Recall that FORTRAN is a modular language. It allows parts of the program called subroutines to be written independently. Each subroutine is compiled separately. In a sense, each subroutine is like a separate program. To

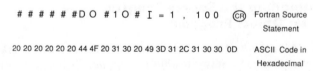

Figure 3.8 Schematic of ASCII characters in a disk file.

execute the combination of subroutines (i.e., the entire program), the linkages between the separately compiled subroutines must be established.

When the compiler writes the object code for a subroutine that calls other subroutines, it does not know at what address in memory the other subroutines will be located. Therefore it establishes an *external reference table* that records the addresses of instructions in the object code where memory addresses for other subroutines must be supplied. This is shown conceptually in Figure 3.9. This external reference table and the object code are used by the linker to complete the job of combining the subroutines into one program.

The object files of a FORTRAN program cannot be transferred between computers of different manufacturers because each computer has its own machine instruction coding. Many computer systems are compatible across a number of compilers, so that object files generated by different compilers such as FORTRAN, C, and the Assembler can be linked together into a single executable program. Many manufacturers also have a product line that allows machine code compatibility between different models of their computers.

OBJECT FILE FOR MAIN PROGRAM

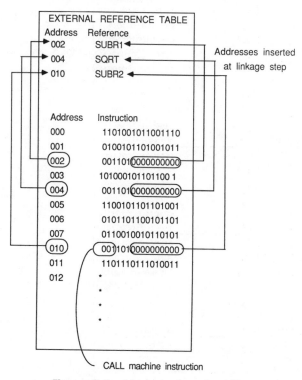

Figure 3.9 Schematic of an object file.

3.2.3. Linking the Object Codes into an Executable Code

The final step in preparing a program for execution is the *linking process*. The linker is a program that combines the object codes of all the subroutines into one *executable machine code*. This executable program is outputted by the linker to an *executable file*. This is shown schematically in Figure 3.10. The linker usually puts the main program first in the file, starting with address 000 and running up to some final address. A subroutine follows at the next address. If this subroutine is referenced by the main program, then the entry address of the subroutine must be put into the appropriate machine instruction in the main program. Another subroutine follows the first one and the process of address computation and insertion continues until all of the subroutines have been included. Only now is the program ready to be executed.

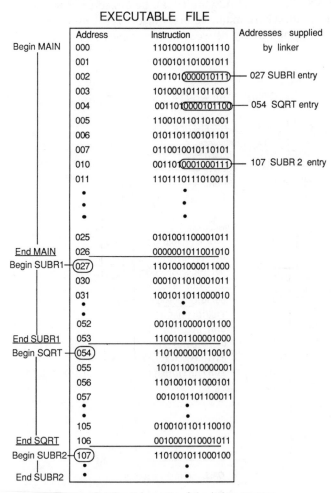

Figure 3.10 Schematic of the linking process.

3.2.4. Execution of the Executable Code

Once the object codes of the individual subroutines have been linked together, the executable form of the program is ready to be executed. At this point the operating system can load the executable code into memory and jump to the entry point of the main program. The executable code starts with address 000, yet the operating system can put the program anywhere in the memory of the computer. This is because the actual program addresses used by the computer hardware are equal to the address in your machine code plus the address stored in the base address register in the CPU (see Section 2.2.2). Hence there is one final address offset done by the hardware itself. As a user of the computer, you never see the actual addresses where your program is executing. You are always given the addresses used within the executable code produced by the linker.

3.2.5. The FORTRAN Compiler

The FORTRAN compiler is a computer program itself. Its input is the FORTRAN source program. Its task is to translate or compile the source program into the machine code that will perform the computations described by the source program. Its output is the object code as well as diagnostic information to aid the programmer. The object code is put into a file for the linking step. The diagnostic output is either put into a file or printed. The programmer can select a number of different options offered by the compiler to guide the compilation process. Each different vendor has its own unique FORTRAN compiler with its own options. The common features are that they all compile FORTRAN source programs written according to the FORTRAN 77 standard and should all produce the same results when executed on the different hardware of each computer maker.

It is instructive to study the options available on a FORTRAN compiler and we will use the DEC VAX FORTRAN Compiler as our example.[5] Most other compilers have similar options. The different options are listed in Figure 3.11. The CHECK or NOCHECK option controls the checking of vector and matrix references to ensure that the indexes are within the bounds of the subscripted variable dimensions. This is usually not checked and checking it requires additional machine code. This slows the execution of the program considerably and is only used during debugging. The option also controls the trapping of overflow and underflow conditions on integer and real arithmetic.

The CONTINUATIONS = n option determines the number of continuation lines allowed. The standard number is 19, but the compiler will allow up to 99 if set by this option.

The CROSS_REFERENCE or NOCROSS_REFERENCE option controls whether the compiler generates a cross-reference listing as part of the symbol table map.

The DEBUG or NODEBUG option controls whether the compiler generates

CHECK or NOCHECK	I4 or NOI4
CROSS_REFERENCE or NOCROSS_REFERENCE	LIST or NOLIST
CONTINUATIONS=n	MACHINE_CODE or NOMACHINE_CODE
DEBUG or NODEBUG	OBJECT or NOOBJECT
D_LINES or NOD_LINES	OPTIMIZE or NOOPTIMIZE
DML	SHOW or NOSHOW
F77 or NOF77	STANDARD or NOSTANDARD
G_FLOATING or NOG_FLOATING	WARNINGS or NOWARNINGS

Figure 3.11 Digital Equipment Corporation VAX FORTRAN compiler options.

information for the debugger (see Chapter 7). When this option is invoked, the compiler writes additional information into the object file so that the debugger can reference variables symbolically and can reference lines within the program by the line numbers generated by the compiler.

The D_LINES or NOD_LINES option indicates whether the compiler will treat source program lines with a "D" in column 1 as a comment or as true program statements. Using this option, statements can be conditionally compiled.

The DML option specifies that the FORTRAN Data Manipulation Language be used to preprocess the source program before compilation.

The F77 or NOF77 option controls whether the FORTRAN 77 standard or the FORTRAN 66 standards are used to interpret the statements where there is a difference.

The G_FLOATING or NOG_FLOATING option controls whether the G_FLOATING or D_FLOATING format is used for double-precision numbers.

The I4 or NOI4 option controls whether integer variables are stored in four or two bytes.

The LIST or NOLIST option controls whether a source listing is produced by the compiler. The MACHINE_CODE or NOMACHINE_CODE option determines whether the machine language generated by the compiler is included in the listing in the form of assembly language statements. The SHOW or NOSHOW option controls whether optionally listed source statements appear in the listing.

The OBJECT or NOOBJECT option controls whether the compiler generates an object file.

The OPTIMIZE or NOOPTIMIZE option controls whether the compiler optimizes the compiled program. The NOOPTIMIZE option is usually used with the DEBUG option to ensure that the machine code generated is in one-to-one correspondence with the FORTRAN statements. The optimizer reorders the machine code to produce faster execution, making debugging more difficult.

The STANDARD or NOSTANDARD option controls whether the compiler produces diagnostics for statements that do not follow the FORTRAN 77 standard. This is an important option because the compiler will allow many extensions of the FORTRAN 77 language if the STANDARD option is not used.

The WARNINGS or NOWARNINGS option controls whether the compiler generates messages for warning conditions.

Utilization of compiler options is an essential feature of software development. The options that control the debugging, diagnostics, and FORTRAN language standard should always be used. Becoming familiar with the options available on the FORTRAN compiler is a necessary prerequisite for successful software development.

REFERENCES

1. R. Ageloff and R. Mojena, *Applied FORTRAN 77, Featuring Structured Programming,* Wadsworth, Belmont, CA, 1981.
2. H. Katzan, Jr., *FORTRAN 77,* Van Nostrand Reinhold New York, 1978.
3. C. Hughes, C. Pfleeger, and L. Rose, *Advanced Programming Techniques, A Second Course in Programming Using FORTRAN,* Wiley, New York, 1978.
4. E. W. Dijkstra, "Go To Statement Considered Harmful," *Comm. ACM 11,* 147 (1968).
5. VAX-11 FORTRAN Language Reference Manual, Order No. AA-D034C-TE, April 1982, Digital Equipment Corporation.

EXERCISES

1. List and explain all of the compiler options available with the compiler you will use.

2. Which of the following are legal FORTRAN 77 statements?

   ```
   (a)  IF-THEN-ELSE     (e)  REAL*4
   (b)  DIMENSION        (f)  PARAMETER
   (c)  DO               (g)  EDIT
   (d)  DO WHILE         (h)  EXTERNAL
   ```

3. Using the file editor, type the program given in Figure 3.2 into a disk file. Compile and link the program and then execute it. Supply your own data sets to be analyzed.

4. Modify the program in problem 3 to read the data from a disk file rather than from the terminal. Prepare a data file and reexecute the program.

5. The Jacobi method is an iterative method for solving systems of linear alge-

braic equations, a problem that is common to many engineering problems. Given the N equations in N unknowns $\{X_i, i = 1 \ldots N\}$,

$$a_{11}X_1 + a_{12}X_2 + a_{13}X_3 + \ldots a_{1N}X_N = b_1$$
$$a_{21}X_1 + a_{22}X_2 + a_{23}X_3 + \ldots a_{2N}X_N = b_2$$

.
.
.

$$a_{N1}X_1 + a_{N2}X_2 + a_{N3}X_3 + \ldots + a_{NN}X_N = b_N$$

The values of X_i are determined by

$$X_i^{(m+1)} = (a_{ii})^{-1} [b_i - \sum_{\substack{j=1 \\ j \neq i}}^{N} a_{ij}X_j^{(m)}], \quad i = 1 \ldots N$$

where m is the iteration counter. Iteration continues until all values of X_i change by no more than a specified amount between two successive iterations. The iteration converges fastest if the initial guess of the solution $X_i^{(0)}$ is close to the final result. The Jacobi method may not converge at all if the matrix of coefficients a_{ij} is ill conditioned. For this exercise, we will avoid this problem by our choice of coefficients.

Write a FORTRAN program using only the 11 statements discussed in Chapter 3 to solve systems of linear algebraic equations with values of N up to 10. The program should input the coefficients from a file, print the coefficients in a format that appears like the matrix, solve the equations using the Jacobi method, and print the solution at the end of each iteration.

Use this program to solve the following problem.

$$6X_1 + X_2 + X_3 + X_4 = 15$$
$$X_1 + 9X_2 + 3X_3 + 2X_4 = 36$$
$$2X_1 + 2X_2 + 6X_3 + X_4 = 28$$
$$2X_1 + X_2 + 3X_3 + 8X_4 = 45$$

with a convergence parameter of 10^{-4} and an initial guess of

$$X_1 = 1 \quad X_2 = 1 \quad X_3 = 1 \quad X_4 = 1$$

4

FORTRAN Subprograms

The FORTRAN language supports the compilation of *modules* or *subprograms* in separate and independent steps. These compiled subprograms are then combined into an executable program in a linking step. This feature of FORTRAN makes it suitable for the development of large-scale applications software, where different independent parts of the solution are identified with corresponding subprograms. Once the software design is complete these subprograms can be written and debugged by different people and then assembled for debugging of the integrated program. The FORTRAN language includes three types of subprograms:

1. Subroutines
2. Functions, and
3. Intrinsic functions

Subroutines and functions are created by the programmer. Intrinsic functions are supplied as part of the FORTRAN language and include common functions such as cosine, logarithm, etc. Subroutines and functions have many common features. Their major distinguishing feature is the ability of subroutines to return an arbitrary number of results to the caller while functions only return a single scalar result. The common features of subroutines and functions are discussed together in the following sections.

Subroutines are considered to consist of two parts: (1) the interface and (2) the body. The body of the subroutine is the part that does the computation and is identical to a simple, single-module FORTRAN program with both nonexecutable declaration statements and executable statements that operate on the variables. The body of the subroutine is not emphasized in this chapter. The interface consists of the dummy arguments, dummy argument declarations, and COMMON blocks (global variables). The subroutine interface is the major focus of this chapter.

4.1. ARGUMENTS AND DUMMY ARGUMENTS

A subroutine is invoked from a main program or another subprogram through a CALL statement. When a CALL statement is executed, the flow of execution jumps to the first statement in the subroutine. The calling program communicates with the subroutine through the *argument list* associated with the call.

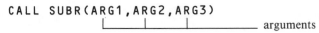

A subroutine is defined with a SUBROUTINE statement. The SUBROUTINE statement must have a *dummy argument list* that corresponds in number and type to the variables in the argument list in the calling program.

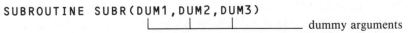

The arguments in the CALL statement are local variables to the calling routine, global variables that are accessible by the calling routine, or dummy variables from the dummy argument list of the calling routine (if it is a subroutine itself). These different variable categories are discussed later. The arguments in the SUBROUTINE statement are "dummy variables." These are names used in the subroutine to refer to the actual data coming from the calling routine. Because these names are just aliases for the actual data, they need not be the same names given to the variables in the calling program. This is best discussed with reference to an actual program and subroutine. These are given in Figure 4.1. For any real vector, VECTOR, of length, LENGTH, the subroutine BUBBLE sorts its elements into ascending numerical order using a bubble sort algorithm. The main program can be compiled separately from the subroutine. They could even be written by different people so long as they communicated properly through their argument and dummy argument lists. The communications is shown conceptually in Figure 4.2.

Multimodule programs have *local variables* that only play a role within a single subprogram. The main program has two local variables, VECT and I. The VECT variable is a REAL vector with 25 elements and the I variable is an INTEGER scalar. They are called local variables because the memory words used to store the contents of these variables are associated with the main program module. The subroutine BUBBLE has three local variables, TEMP, DONE, and I. The TEMP variable is a REAL scalar, DONE is a LOGICAL

```
C   A PROGRAM TO SORT DATA INTO ASCENDING ORDER

        PARAMETER (NIN=5, NOUT=6)
        DIMENSION VECT(25)
        READ(NIN,*)     (VECT(I), I=1,25)
        WRITE(NOUT,100) (VECT(I), I=1,25)
    100 FORMAT('1 THE RAW DATA IS THE FOLLOWING'/(5E12.4))

C   SORT THE DATA INTO ASCENDING ORDER USING THE SUBROUTINE BUBBLE

        CALL  BUBBLE ( VECT,25 )
        WRITE(NOUT,101) (VECT(I), I=1,25)
    101 FORMAT('0 THE SORTED DATA IS THE FOLLOWING'/(5E12.4))
        STOP
        END

        SUBROUTINE BUBBLE( VECTOR,LENGTH )

C   THIS SUBROUTINE PERFORMS A BUBBLE SORT OF DATA INTO ASCENDING
C   ORDER
C   INPUT   — VECTOR - RAW DATA (REAL VECTOR)
C           — LENGTH - NUMBER OF ELEMENTS IN THE VECTOR OF RAW
C                        DATA
C   OUTPUT  — VECTOR - SORTED DATA
C
        DIMENSION VECTOR(LENGTH)
        LOGICAL DONE

C   SET THE DONE SWITCH TO .TRUE. TO START
        DONE = .TRUE.

C   MAKE A PASS THROUGH THE DATA AND INTERCHANGE ELEMENTS THAT
C   ARE OUT OF ORDER
      5 DO 10 I = 1,LENGTH-1
          IF( VECTOR(I) .GT. VECTOR(I+1) ) THEN
            TEMP = VECTOR(I)
            VECTOR(I) = VECTOR(I+1)
            VECTOR(I+1) = TEMP
            DONE = .FALSE.
          END IF
     10 CONTINUE

C   CHECK TO SEE IF ANY CHANGES WERE MADE ON THIS PASS, IF NO
C   CHANGES WERE MADE THEN THE DATA IS SORTED
        IF( DONE ) RETURN

C   CHANGES WERE MADE, RESET THE SWITCH AND TRY AGAIN
        DONE = .TRUE.
        GOTO 5
        END
```

Figure 4.1 Main program and subroutine for a bubble sort.

scalar, and I is an INTEGER scalar. These local variables reside in memory words associated with the subroutine BUBBLE. This is shown schematically in Figure 4.2. Notice that each module has a local variable with the same name, I. This is no problem because the FORTRAN compiler treats each subroutine as a separately compiled unit. All local variable names are independent of other modules and there is no ambiguity so long as the association between local variables and local memory storage in each subprogram is made.

The argument list in the main program consists of the local variable VECT and the constant 25. The corresponding dummy argument list in subroutine

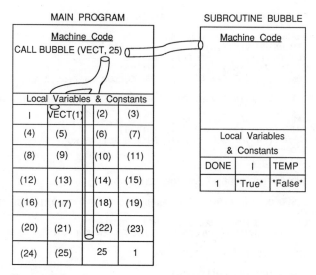

Figure 4.2 Conceptual picture of subroutine call to BUBBLE.

BUBBLE has VECTOR and LENGTH. These are *not* local variables to the subroutine. They are dummy arguments or aliases for the actual data stored in the elements of the argument list back in the calling routine. This distinction between dummy argument variables and local variables is important to make and is crucial to understanding the mechanics of subroutine linkage in FORTRAN.

Another distinction must be made here between the DIMENSION statement in the main program and the DIMENSION statement in the subroutine. This distinction helps to clarify the differences between the arguments and dummy arguments in the CALL and SUBROUTINE statements, respectively. The DIMENSION statements in the main program and the subroutine BUBBLE perform different functions. The DIMENSION statement in the main program *defines* the vector VECT. It instructs the compiler to define storage space in memory to put the values of the variable VECT. The memory for the vector VECT is associated with the main program. The variable VECT is a local variable to the main program. The DIMENSION statement in the subroutine BUBBLE does *not* define storage space for the dummy variable VECTOR. The dummy variable VECTOR is just a name used in subroutine BUBBLE to access the actual variable passed between the calling program and subroutine BUBBLE through its argument list. This dual use of the DIMENSION statement is very confusing. It would be best if the FORTRAN language had two different statements, one to serve each of these purposes, such as

```
DIMENSION VECT(25)
        .
        .
```

```
CALL BUBBLE(VECT,25)
        .
        .
        .
SUBROUTINE BUBBLE(VECTOR,LENGTH)
DIMENSION DUMMY VECTOR(LENGTH)
        .
        .
```

The subroutine allows the vector to have any length since LENGTH is given to the subroutine from the calling program. However, the creation of the vector VECT in the calling program requires a fixed, constant value for the length since this is where the memory space is defined for it and the memory space for local variables in a subroutine must be fixed at compile time. Unfortunately, FORTRAN does not have separate statements to help make this distinction.

However, the FORTRAN language does include two equivalent statements to define the dimension of subscripted variables, and these can be used by the programmer to accomplish the same distinction discussed above so long as a convention is established.

In the calling program where the vector variable is defined and memory space is reserved for it, one can use

```
DIMENSION VECT(25)
```

In the subroutine where the vector variable is a dummy variable and the dimension statement simply defines the variable type, one can use

```
REAL VECTOR(LENGTH)
```

By using DIMENSION statements *only* where subscripted variables are truly being defined and memory is reserved for them, the programmer helps to alleviate this confusion. This is further demonstrated by the following program segment:

```
DIMENSION VECT1(25), VECT2(200)
        .
        .
        .
CALL BUBBLE(VECT1,25)
        .
        .
CALL BUBBLE(VECT2,200)
        .
        .
END
SUBROUTINE BUBBLE(VECTOR,LENGTH)
        .
        .
```

```
REAL VECTOR(LENGTH)
      .
      .
```

In this example the calling program calls BUBBLE twice with vectors of different lengths. Each of these vectors is local to the main program. The subroutine does not care about the vector length because it is not storing the vectors. It only cares that the variable type is singly subscripted rather than scalar or multiply subscripted. In fact one can take this one step further and use the fact that the subroutine does not care about the length to write it in the following way:

```
SUBROUTINE BUBBLE(VECTOR,LENGTH)
      .
      .
REAL VECTOR (*)
      .
      .
```

In this case VECTOR is dimensioned with an unspecified length by using the "*". But remember that this is not an actual variable but is only a dummy variable, so that the subroutine does not care about its length, only the fact that it is singly dimensioned. If this is the case, why not use

```
SUBROUTINE BUBBLE(VECTOR,LENGTH)
      .
      .
      .
DO 10 I = 1,LENGTH-1
   IF( VECTOR(I) .GT. VECTOR(I+1) ) THEN
      TEMP = VECTOR(I)
      .
      .
```

Here we have not dimensioned the dummy variable VECTOR at all. This does not work. The FORTRAN compiler gives error comments because it thinks that VECTOR is a scalar variable and should not be used with subscripts "(I)" and "(I+1)". Hence the dummy variable VECTOR must be designated as singly subscripted so that the compiler will allow it to be used as such in the subroutine.

Now let's look at another potential trouble spot in calling subroutines. Suppose we modify the main program and add another subroutine as shown in Figure 4.3. The subroutine REVERS simply reverses the order of the numbers in a vector VECTOR and puts the result into a vector RVEC. But remember, VECTOR and RVEC are just dummy arguments in the subroutine REVERS. They are really aliases for the actual vectors supplied by the calling program in its argument list.

```
C   A PROGRAM TO SORT DATA INTO DESCENDING ORDER

      PARAMETER (NIN=5, NOUT=6)
      DIMENSION VECT(25), TCEV(25)
      READ(NIN,*)     (VECT(I), I=1,25)
      WRITE(NOUT,100) (VECT(I), I=1,25)
  100 FORMAT('1 THE RAW DATA IS THE FOLLOWING'/(5E12.4))

C   SORT THE DATA INTO ASCENDING ORDER USING THE SUBROUTINE BUBBLE
      CALL  BUBBLE( VECT,25 )

C   REVERSE THE DATA AND PUT IT INTO THE VECTOR - TCEV
      CALL REVERS( VECT,25,TCEV )

C   PERFORM THE SAME OPERATION ONLY PUT THE RESULT BACK INTO VECT
      CALL REVERS( VECT,25,VECT )

C   COMPARE THE RESULTS
      WRITE(NOUT,101) (VECT(I), I=1,25)
  101 FORMAT('0 THE SORTED DATA IS THE FOLLOWING-VECT'/(5E12.4))
      WRITE(NOUT,102) (TCEV(I), I=1,25)
  102 FORMAT('0 THE SORTED DATA IS THE FOLLOWING-TCEV'/(5E12.4))
      STOP
      END

      SUBROUTINE REVERS(VECTOR,LENGTH,RVEC)

C   THIS SUBROUTINE REVERSES THE ORDER OF THE ELEMENTS IN VECTOR
C   AND PLACES THE RESULT IN RVEC.
C   INPUT       VECTOR - DATA TO BE REVERSED
C               LENGTH - DIMENSION OF VECTOR
C   OUTPUT      RVEC   - REVERSED DATA

      REAL  VECTOR(LENGTH), RVEC(LENGTH)

C   PERFORM THE REVERSAL
      DO 10 I = 1,LENGTH
         RVEC(I) = VECTOR(LENGTH+1-I)
   10 CONTINUE
      RETURN
      END
```

Figure 4.3 Subroutine call with two dummy arguments assigned to the same variable in the calling routine.

What error was committed here? The first call to REVERS is okay. However, the second call does not accomplish the desired result because both the "input" dummy variable in REVERS (i.e., VECTOR) and the "output" dummy variable (i.e., RVEC) correspond to the same actual variable (i.e., VECT) in the calling program. Hence the "DO loop" in REVERS destroys elements in VECT that are needed at a later pass through the loop since VECTOR and RVEC are actually the same variable in this case.

When information is shared between subroutines in this way the variables are said to be *referenced by location* or, equivalently, *referenced by address,* that is, the memory addresses of the variables in the argument list are passed to the called subroutine. The called subroutine references its dummy arguments using these addresses. The called subroutine does not contain any memory words to hold the contents of the dummy variable. This is the way that subscripted variables are passed between subroutines on all computers. However, it is not always the way that scalar variables are treated. On IBM computers, for instance, scalar dummy variables are *referenced by value* as the default option. This means that the called subroutine has memory words to store the contents of all of the scalar dummy variables in its dummy argument list. The data is actually transferred from the calling program at the start of the subroutine execution and it is retransferred back to the calling program when the subroutine RETURNs. This difference in compilers leads to very baffling errors in programs that are moved from one computer to another if the FORTRAN program is improperly written. Consider the program in Figure 4.4. What do we expect to happen in the calling program?

```
C   THIS PROGRAM DEMONSTRATES PROBLEMS WITH ASSOCIATING TWO DUMMY
C   ARGUMENTS WITH THE SAME VARIABLE IN THE ARGUMENT LIST

        PARAMETER (NIN=5, NOUT=6)
        DIMENSION DATA(25)

        READ(NIN,*) MAX
        READ(NIN,*) (DATA(I), I=1,MAX)
        READ(NIN,*) COMPAR

C   RETURN NUMBER OF VALUES IN DATA GREATER THAN COMPAR IN COMPAR
        CALL COMDAT(VECTOR,MAX,COMPAR,COMPAR)

C   RETURN NUMBER OF VALUES IN DATA GREATER THAN ZERO IN COUNT
        CALL COMDAT(VEC2,MAX,-5.,COUNT)

C   USE THE SAME CONSTANT IN AN EXPRESSION
        X = 0.
        X = -5. + X

C   LOOK AT THE RESULTS
        WRITE(NOUT,100) COMPAR, COUNT, X
100 FORMAT('0 COMPAR = ', E12.4/
   1        '  COUNT  = ', E12.4/
   2        '  X      = ', E12.4)

        STOP
        END

        SUBROUTINE COMDAT(DATA,MAX,TEST,COUNT)
C
C   THIS SUBROUTINE COMPARES THE VALUE OF TEST WITH EACH ELEMENT
C   OF THE VECTOR DATA AND RETURNS THE NUMBERS OF ELEMENTS OF
C   DATA THAT ARE GREATER THAN TEST IN THE VARIABLE COUNT
C   IF TEST IS LESS THAN 0., THEN THE SUBROUTINE RETURNS THE
C   NUMBER OF ELEMENTS OF DATA THAT ARE GREATER THAN 0.
C   INPUT      DATA   - VECTOR OF VALUES
C              MAX    - DIMENSION OF DATA
C              TEST   - VALUE TO TEST DATA AGAINST
C   OUTPUT     COUNT  - NUMBER OF SUCCESSFUL TESTS

        REAL DATA(MAX)

        IF( TEST .LT. 0. ) TEST = 0.
        COUNT = 0.
        DO 10 I = 1,1000
          IF( DATA(I) .GT. TEST ) COUNT = COUNT + 1.
 10 CONTINUE
        RETURN
        END
```

Figure 4.4   Troubles with argument passing.

On the first call to COMDAT the testing works improperly if the arguments are "referenced by location" but works properly if the arguments are "referenced by value." In the latter case there are memory locations set aside in COMDAT for the dummy variables TEST and COUNT, even though they correspond to the same variable back in the calling program. Hence COUNT is updated "locally" in COMDAT until the subroutine returns to the calling program and then the value of COUNT is passed back to the calling program. Only at this time is the variable COMPAR actually changed. If the variables are passed by location, then TEST and COUNT correspond to the same actual variable and the subroutine does not work. Of course this depends on the order in which the values are passed back to the calling program, for if COUNT is passed back first, followed by TEST, then an incorrect answer results.

On the second call to COMDAT we have another problem. Here it makes no difference whether the variables are passed by location or value. The variable TEST is altered in COMDAT and it corresponds to a constant back in the calling program. By changing TEST in COMDAT we are actually changing the constant $-5.$ in the calling program to 0. When the constant $-5.$ is used later on in the calling program,

$$X = -5. + X$$

it gives a value of $X = 0!$ This is a very insidious error. These types of problems are avoided by observing two rules.

1. Identify the "input" and "output" dummy arguments of all subroutines. This is best done in comment statements at the beginning of the subroutine as we did earlier. Never change the value of an "input" dummy variable. If it has to be modified, set it equal to a local variable and modify the local variable.

2. Never use the same variable for more than one argument in the subroutine CALL statement.

Thus far we have only shown data passing between two levels of subprograms: a main program, where the arguments are local variables to the main program, and a subroutine. However, data can be passed between many different levels of subroutines by using dummy arguments from the calling program as arguments in a CALL statement to yet another subroutine. An example of this is shown in Figure 4.5. However, it is important to remember what is actually done in the computer. This is shown conceptually in Figure 4.6.

This example reinforces the notion that subroutines are completely independent of one another. Local variables in one subroutine can have the same name as a local variable in another subroutine but this does not mean that they are related in any way. An element of a vector in the argument list can be associated with a scalar in the dummy argument list. Yet at all levels the actual memory words associated with the data are in the main program. Each subsequent call simply passes along the address in memory where the data resides.

```
C  A PROGRAM TO SORT DATA INTO ASCENDING ORDER

      PARAMETER (NIN=5, NOUT=6)
      DIMENSION VECT(25)
      READ(NIN,*)    (VECT(I), I=1,25)
      WRITE(NOUT,100) (VECT(I), I=1,25)
  100 FORMAT('1 THE RAW DATA IS THE FOLLOWING'/(5E12.4))

C  SORT THE DATA INTO ASCENDING ORDER USING THE SUBROUTINE BUBBLE

      CALL  BUBBLE ( VECT,25 )
      WRITE(NOUT,101) (VECT(I), I=1,25)
  101 FORMAT('0 THE SORTED DATA IS THE FOLLOWING'/(5E12.4))
      STOP
      END

      SUBROUTINE BUBBLE( VECTOR,LENGTH )

C  THIS SUBROUTINE PERFORMS A BUBBLE SORT OF DATA INTO ASCENDING
C  ORDER
C  INPUT   — VECTOR - RAW DATA (REAL VECTOR)
C          — LENGTH - NUMBER OF ELEMENTS IN THE VECTOR OF RAW
C                     DATA
C  OUTPUT — VECTOR - SORTED DATA
C
      DIMENSION VECTOR(LENGTH)
      LOGICAL DONE

C  SET THE DONE SWITCH TO .TRUE. TO START
      DONE = .TRUE.

C  MAKE A PASS THROUGH THE DATA AND INTERCHANGE ELEMENTS THAT
C  ARE OUT OF ORDER
    5 DO 10 I = 1,LENGTH-1
        IF( VECTOR(I) .GT. VECTOR(I+1) ) THEN
          CALL SWITCH(VECTOR(I), VECTOR(I+1))
          DONE = .FALSE.
        END IF
   10 CONTINUE

C  CHECK TO SEE IF ANY CHANGES WERE MADE ON THIS PASS, IF NO
C  CHANGES WERE MADE THEN THE DATA IS SORTED
      IF( DONE ) RETURN

C  CHANGES WERE MADE, RESET THE SWITCH AND TRY AGAIN
      DONE = .TRUE.
      GOTO 5
      END

      SUBROUTINE SWITCH( VAR1, VAR2 )

C  THIS SUBROUTINE SWITCHES THE VALUES OF VAR1 AND VAR2
C  INPUT      VAR1   — VALUE TO BE SWITCHED WITH VAR2
C             VAR2   — VALUE TO BE SWITCHED WITH VAR1
C  OUTPUT     VAR1
C             VAR2

      TEMP = VAR1
      VAR1 = VAR2
      VAR2 = TEMP

      RETURN
      END
```

Figure 4.5 Dummy variables as arguments in a subroutine call.

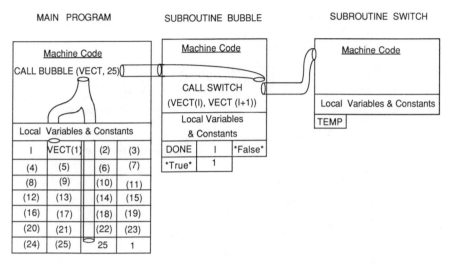

Figure 4.6 Conceptual picture of argument passing between three subroutines.

We have learned how subprograms pass information to one another through argument lists and corresponding dummy argument lists. These argument lists contain either local variables or dummy arguments of the calling subroutine. Next we look at another method of sharing information between subroutines.

4.2. GLOBAL VARIABLES—COMMON BLOCKS

In this section we explore *global variables*. Sometimes it is inconvenient to treat all variables as local and share them between subroutines by passing them through argument lists. This is true when very large numbers of variables must be passed to a subroutine. This is particularly true when many variables are passed into a subroutine to allow them to be subsequently passed to lower subroutines. Such situations increase the likelihood of programming errors in the lengthy argument lists that must be written for each subroutine call. In these cases it is preferable to allow all subroutines to access a common store of global variables. In FORTRAN, global variables reside in a *COMMON block*. This "common" memory region is shared or accessed by any of the subroutines in a multimodule program. Our previous example of the bubble sort subroutine is rewritten by putting the variables in a COMMON block as shown in Figure 4.7. The variable storage is shown conceptually in Figure 4.8. Both the main program and the subroutine have access to the variables in the COMMON block. Any subroutine in the program with a COMMON statement has access to these variables.

The use of the COMMON block to share information between the main

```
C  A PROGRAM TO SORT DATA INTO ASCENDING ORDER
      LOGICAL DONE
      COMMON VECTOR(25), LENGTH, DONE, TEMP, IMAX
      PARAMETER (NIN=5, NOUT=6)

      READ(NIN,*)     (VECTOR(I), I=1,25)
      WRITE(NOUT,100) (VECTOR(I), I=1,25)
 100  FORMAT('1 THE RAW DATA IS THE FOLLOWING'/(5E12.4))

C  SORT THE DATA INTO ASCENDING ORDER USING THE SUBROUTINE BUBBLE
      LENGTH = 25
      CALL  BUBBLE
      WRITE(NOUT,101) (VECTOR(I), I=1,25)
 101  FORMAT('0 THE SORTED DATA IS THE FOLLOWING'/(5E12.4))
      STOP
      END
      SUBROUTINE BUBBLE

C  THIS SUBROUTINE SORTS DATA INTO ASCENDING ORDER USING A BUBBLE
C  SORT ALGORITHM.  THE DATA MUST BE IN COMMON VECTOR(25)
      LOGICAL DONE
      COMMON VECTOR(25), LENGTH, DONE, TEMP, IMAX

C  SET THE DONE SWITCH TO TRUE TO START
      DONE = .TRUE.

C  MAKE PASS THROUGH THE DATA AND REVERSE ANY PAIRS OF DATA THAT
C  ARE OUT OF ORDER
   5  DO 10 I = 1,LENGTH-1
         IF( VECTOR(I) .GT. VECTOR(I+1) ) THEN
            TEMP = VECTOR(I)
            VECTOR(I) = VECTOR(I+1)
            VECTOR(I+1) = TEMP
            DONE = .FALSE.
         END IF
  10  CONTINUE
      IF( DONE ) RETURN

C  RESET THE SWITCH AND TRY AGAIN
      DONE = .TRUE.
      GOTO 5
      END
```

Figure 4.7 Subprograms sharing global variables.

program and the subroutine BUBBLE has changed the character of the sub-routine from its original intent. The program in Figure 4.1 sorts floating point numbers in any vector passed to BUBBLE through its argument list. With information passed through the COMMON block, BUBBLE only sorts float-ing point numbers in the subscripted global variable VECTOR. Any list of data to be sorted must be first copied into the global variable VECTOR. This is therefore an inappropriate situation to pass data through a COMMON block. In this case, the BUBBLE subroutine should be left in its original form. Global variables from the COMMON block can still be passed to it to sort. This program is shown in Figure 4.9 and the conceptual picture is given in Figure 4.10. (In this simple example program it might seem foolish to be so concerned with such details. However, the intent is to demonstrate the princi-ples for application in large-scale programs where there may be hundreds of subroutines, some of which are best called with argument lists and some with

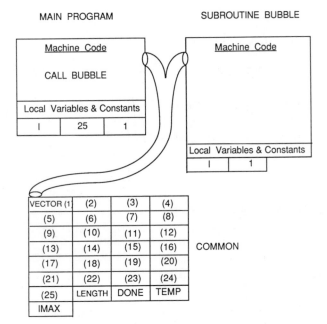

MAIN PROGRAM   SUBROUTINE BUBBLE

Figure 4.8 Conceptual picture of COMMON.

```
C  THIS PROGRAM PASSES GLOBAL VARIABLES AS ARGUMENTS TO
C  A SUBROUTINE TO SORT THEM

      PARAMETER( NIN=5, NOUT=6)
      COMMON VECTOR(10), VEC1(10), VEC2(10),
     1       IMAX, IMAX1, IMAX2

C  READ THE INPUT
      READ(NIN,*) IMAX
      READ(NIN,*) (VECTOR(I), I=1,IMAX)
      READ(NIN,*) IMAX1
      READ(NIN,*) (VEC1(I), I=1,IMAX1)
      READ(NIN,*) IMAX2
      READ(NIN,*) (VEC2(I), I=1,IMAX2)

C  SORT THE DATA
      CALL BUBBLE( VECTOR,IMAX )
      CALL BUBBLE( VEC1,IMAX1 )
      CALL BUBBLE( VEC2,IMAX2 )

C  PRINT THE RESULTS
      WRITE(NOUT,100) (VECTOR(I), I=1,IMAX)
      WRITE(NOUT,101) (VEC1(I), I=1,IMAX1)
      WRITE(NOUT,102) (VEC2(I), I=1,IMAX2)
  100 FORMAT('0 SORTED VECTOR IS'/ (5E12.4))
  101 FORMAT('0 SORTED VEC1   IS'/ (5E12.4))
  102 FORMAT('0 SORTED VEC2   IS'/ (5E12.4))
      END

      SUBROUTINE BUBBLE( VECTOR,LENGTH )
          .
          .
          .
      (Same as in Figure 4.1)
```

Figure 4.9 Global variable passed as argument to subroutine.

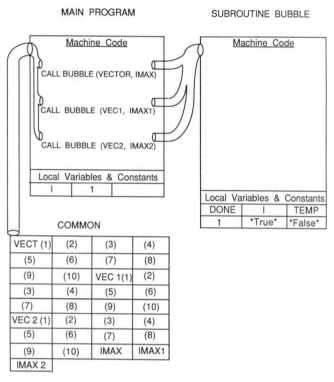

Figure 4.10 Conceptual picture of global variable passed through argument list.

COMMON access to global variables.) Global variables "in COMMON" can be passed between subroutines through argument lists, just as local variables can be passed. In Figure 4.9 the subroutine BUBBLE does not include a COMMON statement, thus there is no conflict in variable names between the global variable VECTOR and the dummy argument VECTOR.

Global variables can be passed through argument lists even though the called subroutine also has a COMMON statement so long as the dummy argument name is different from the name of the global variable in the COMMON block. Such a program is shown in Figure 4.11. This is shown conceptually in Figure 4.12.

This multiple access to global data through both COMMON and argument lists is emphasized by the somewhat contrived program in Figure 4.13. What happens here? X is 0.0 because X and A refer to the same variable. This of course makes no sense from a programming point of view (although it is a legitimate FORTRAN program). There are circumstances where access by one subroutine to global variables through both COMMON and dummy arguments is important. This is discussed in Section 4.3.

```
C   THIS PROGRAM COMPUTES PRESSURES USING AN IDEAL GAS LAW.   IT
C   DEMONSTRATES HOW SUBROUTINES CAN BE PASSED VARIABLES IN
C   COMMON WHILE STILL HAVING ACCESS TO COMMON THEMSELVES

      COMMON PRESS(3), DENS(3), TEMP(3), GASCON
      PARAMETER (NIN=5, NOUT=6)

      READ(NIN,*) GASCON
      READ(NIN,*) (DENS(I), I=1,3)
      READ(NIN,*) (TEMP(I), I=1,3)

C   COMPUTE THE PRESSURE ASSOCIATED WITH EACH OF THE THREE
C   DENSITIES AND TEMPERATURES USING AN IDEAL GAS LAW

      DO 10 I = 1,3
         CALL IDLGAS( DENS(I), TEMP(I), PRESS(I) )
   10 CONTINUE

C   OUTPUT THE RESULTS
      WRITE(NOUT,100) (DENS(I), TEMP(I), PRESS(I), I=1,3)
  100 FORMAT('0 DENSITY     TEMPERATURE PRESSURE'/(3E12.4))
      STOP
      END

      SUBROUTINE IDLGAS( D, T, P )

C   THIS SUBROUTINE COMPUTES THE PRESSURE USING AN IDEAL GAS
C   LAW.   IT GETS THE DENSITY AND TEMPERATURE FROM ITS DUMMY
C   ARGUMENT LIST AND GETS THE GAS CONSTANT FROM COMMON
C   INPUT     D       - DENSITY
C             T       - TEMPERATURE
C   OUTPUT    P       - PRESSURE

      COMMON PRESS(3), DENS(3), TEMP(3), GASCON

      P = D * GASCON * T
      RETURN
      END
```

Figure 4.11 Global variable passed to subroutine with access to same COMMON.

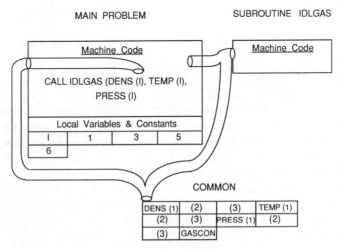

Figure 4.12 Conceptual picture of global variable passed to a subroutine with access to same COMMON.

```
C  THIS PROGRAM DEMONSTRATES HOW THE SAME GLOBAL DATA CAN BE
C  ACCESSED BY A SUBROUTINE THROUGH BOTH ITS DUMMY ARGUMENT LIST
C  AND THROUGH COMMON

      COMMON A, B, C
      PARAMETER (NOUT=6)

C  SET SOME VALUES
      A = 10.
      B = 20.
      C = 30.

C  CALL THE SUBROUTINE WITH GLOBAL VARIABLES AS ARGUMENTS
      CALL TAFFY(A,B)

C  WRITE THE RESULTS
      WRITE(NOUT,100) A, B, C
  100 FORMAT('0 A, B, AND C ARE',3E12.4)
      STOP
      END

      SUBROUTINE TAFFY(X,Y)

C  THIS SUBROUTINE PERFORMS ARITHMETIC OPERATIONS ON A
C  COMBINATION OF DUMMY ARGUMENTS AND GLOBAL VARIABLES

      COMMON A, B, C

C  THIS STATEMENT CHANGES A TO ONE BECAUSE THE DUMMY ARGUMENT
C  X IS ASSOCIATED WITH A IN THE ARGUMENT LIST OF THE CALLING
C  PROGRAM
      X = X - A + 1.

C  THUS THE VALUE OF Y IS INCREMENTED BY ONE IN THIS STATEMENT
C  BECAUSE Y IS ASSOCIATED WITH B IN THE ARGUMENT LIST OF THE
C  CALLING PROGRAM
      Y = B + A

      RETURN
      END
```

Figure 4.13 Access to same global variable through both COMMON and dummy argument list.

The global variable approach has advantages and disadvantages. Already mentioned is the simplification of the argument lists in subroutine calls. We will see later in the discussion of software design that this is not necessarily a strong advantage. A disadvantage is that global variables must have unique names. They cannot have the same names as any local variables or dummy arguments in subroutines with access to the global variables. Now, several people working on the same program must coordinate their choice of variable names to avoid duplication. We already have seen that this is not a problem with local variables. In the example in Figure 4.7 all variables are global except the variable I. There is a local variable with this name in both the main program and the subroutine. Use of global variables opens the possibility of a subroutine inadvertently modifying the value of a variable that it was not meant to change. Such errors with global variables are difficult to find because the whole program is open to suspicion.

4.2.1. Named Common Blocks

Thus far only a single common area for storing global variables has been discussed. This is called *unnamed or blank COMMON*. The FORTRAN language also provides a means to group global variables into so-called *named COMMON blocks*. Any number of named COMMON blocks can be defined. The notation for a named COMMON block is

```
COMMON/REALS/ VECTOR(25), TEMP
COMMON/INTRS/ IMAX, LENGTH
```

where REALS and INTRS are the names of the two different COMMON blocks. By using named COMMON blocks, global variables that are related and are used only by a subset of the subroutines in a program can be grouped together. This is advantageous because fewer variables are exposed to unintended modification by a subroutine that really has no need to access them. It also improves the organization of large-scale software. The same rules apply to global variables in named and unnamed COMMONs. The variable names must be unique. The same variable name cannot be used in two named COMMONs that are used in the same subroutine and the names must be different from any local variables or dummy arguments used by a subroutine.

4.2.2. Sequential Nature of Common Blocks

All of our examples have shown COMMON statements with the same global variable names in each subroutine where access is needed. This is the situation in most applications. However, the variable names appearing in the COMMON statement in different subroutines need not be the same. Actually, the COMMON area of memory is treated by the FORTRAN language as just a block of words with sequential addresses. Variables are stored sequentially and whatever variable name that corresponds to the memory word that is a given offset past the beginning of the COMMON block is associated with the data in that word. This is demonstrated by the program listing in Figure 4.14. This is shown conceptually in Figure 4.15.

Using this feature a COMMON block can be created to serve as temporary working storage for different independent (they don't call one another) subroutines in a large program. This is important if many different subroutines need large numbers of temporary variables. The program fragment shown in Figure 4.16 demonstrates this. In this example the subroutine DECIDE is independent from COMPUT. Each subroutine uses the memory words associated with COMMON/WORK/ to save temporary values used during their respective computations. Each time a subroutine uses COMMON/WORK/ it must assume that it initially contains "garbage." It just overwrites the garbage to temporarily save results. This example also shows that a COMMON block need not be defined with the same number of words in each subroutine. Sub-

```
C   PROGRAM TO CONVERT CELCIUS TO FARENHEIT AND VISE VERSA

       PARAMETER (NIN=5,NOUT=6)
       COMMON/TEMPER/ CT, FT

    10 READ(NIN,*) ITEST, TEMP

       IF( ITEST .EQ. 1 ) THEN
          FT = TEMP
          CALL CELSUS
       ELSE
          CT = TEMP
          CALL FAREN
       ENDIF

       WRITE(NOUT,*) 'CELSIUS=', CT, '  FARENHEIT=', FT
       GOTO 10
       END

       SUBROUTINE CELSUS

C   COMPUTE THE CELSIUS TEMPERATURE FROM THE FARENHEIT VALUE

       COMMON/TEMPER/ CT, FT

       CT = (5./9.) * (FT - 32.)

       RETURN
       END

       SUBROUTINE FAREN

C   COMPUTE THE FARENHEIT TEMPERATURE FROM THE CELSIUS VALUE

       COMMON/TEMPER/ CELTMP, FARTMP

       FARTMP = (9./5.) * CELTMP + 32.

       RETURN
       END
```

Figure 4.14   Same COMMON with different variable names.

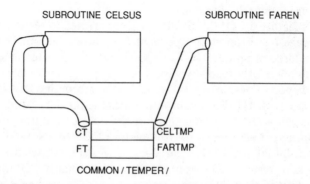

Figure 4.15   Conceptual picture of COMMON with different variable names.

```
C   MAIN PROGRAM
        COMMON/WORK/ A(10000)
        .
        .
        .
        END

        SUBROUTINE COMPUT(X,Y,Z)
C
C   COMPUTE Z GIVEN X AND Y
        COMMON/WORK/ TEMP1(2000), TEMP2(2000), TEMP3(2000)
        REAL X(2000), Y(2000), Z(2000)
        .
        .
        DO 10 I = 1,2000
            TEMP1(I) = Y(I) + X(I)
            TEMP2(I) = Y(I) - X(I)
            TEMP3(I) = Y(I) * X(I)
            Z(I) = TEMP1(I) / TEMP2(I) * TEMP3(I)
     10 CONTINUE
        .
        .
        END
        SUBROUTINE DECIDE
C
C   DECIDE ON SOMETHING OVER AND OVER AGAIN
        COMMON/WORK/ DEC1(4000), DEC2(4000)
        LOGICAL DEC1, DEC2
        .
        .
        END
```

Figure 4.16 COMMON block holding different temporary variables for different subroutines.

routine COMPUT uses 6000 words while subroutine DECIDE uses 8000 words. The main program initially defined the COMMON block with 10,000 words. The linker appropriates the number of words corresponding to the definition with the maximum length. The maximum size need not come in the main program.

4.2.3. Common Initialization—Block Data

Initialization of COMMON block variables is done using the BLOCK DATA routine. This is somewhat analogous to the DATA statement used to initialize local variables. An example of COMMON block initialization is shown in Figure 4.17. Often large tables of static data (physical properties as functions of temperature, for instance) are required by a program. These can be stored in COMMON blocks and initialized by BLOCK DATA routines in the manner shown. In this way the same data is easily shared by different subroutines.

4.3. PSEUDODYNAMIC VARIABLE DIMENSIONING

Consider a large engineering applications program that has 100 subroutines. Each subroutine has about 200 statements and there are 100 subscripted vari-

```
      SUBROUTINE LOOKUP(X,Y)

C  A  LOOK UP THE VALUE OF Y CORRESPONDING TO  Y(X) IN THE TABLE
C  YVAL
      DIMENSION XVAL(10)
      DIMENSION YVAL(10)

C  INITIALIZE LOCAL VARIABLES XVAL AND YVAL
      DATA XVAL/0.0,1.5,2.0,3.0,4.0,5.5,7.0,8.0,12.,20./
      DATA YVAL/0.0,15.,20.,30.,40.,55.,70.,80.,120.,200./

C  FIND THE INDEX IN THE XVAL TABLE
      DO 10 I = 2,10
        IF( X .LT. XVAL(I) ) GOTO 20
10 CONTINUE
20 CONTINUE

C  INTERPOLATE IN THE TABLES
      SLOPE = (YVAL(I) - YVAL(I-1)) / (XVAL(I) - XVAL(I-1))
      Y = SLOPE * (X - XVAL(I-1)) + YVAL(I-1)

      RETURN
      END
```

This could also have been written as the following.

```
      SUBROUTINE LOOKUP(X,Y)

C  LOOK UP THE VALUE OF Y CORRESPONDING TO  Y(X) IN THE TABLE
C  YVAL
      COMMON/TABLE/ XVAL(10), YVAL(10)

C  FIND THE INDEX IN THE XVAL TABLE
      DO 10 I = 2,10
        IF( X .LT. XVAL(I) ) GOTO 20
10 CONTINUE
20 CONTINUE

C  INTERPOLATE IN THE TABLES
      SLOPE = (YVAL(I) - YVAL(I-1)) / (XVAL(I) - XVAL(I-1))
      Y = SLOPE * (X - XVAL(I-1)) + YVAL(I-1)

      RETURN
      END

      BLOCK DATA INIT
      COMMON/TABLE/ XVAL(10), YVAL(10)
C  INITIALIZE THE GLOBAL VARIABLES XVAL AND YVAL
      DATA XVAL/0.0,1.5,2.0,3.0,4.0,5.5,7.0,8.0,12.,20./
      DATA YVAL/0.0,15.,20.,30.,40.,55.,70.,80.,120.,200./
      END
```

Figure 4.17 Block data initialization of COMMON blocks.

ables that these subroutines operate on. Depending on the complexity of the problem to be solved, each subscripted variable may require 10–10,000 elements. Small test problems might require 10 vector elements while full-blown design problems might require 10,000 vector elements. This program could be a finite element program to solve stress problems, a finite difference program to solve for temperature distributions in materials, a neutron transport program to solve for the neutron flux in a three-dimensional duct, or a circuit solver to design electrical networks. In order to solve problems up to the maximum size, the program would have to have vector dimensions of

```
DIMENSION A(10000), B(10000), ...
```

This wastefully ties up tremendous amounts of memory for problems where a short vector length of 10 or 100 is required. Since users are usually charged for both CPU time and memory use, this could substantially increase the cost of solving these very simple problems. What can be done to solve this dilemma? There are three possible solutions.

1. Have 100 versions of the program with variable dimensions of 100, 200, 300, . . . , 10,000 and then use the one that is just larger than the problem to be solved. The disadvantages of this scheme are that it is wasteful of disk space and it is error-prone because any change to the source program would have to be made to all of the versions.

2. Edit the source file and change all dimensions to the exact length required for the given problem and then recompile the program each time it is used. Recompilation of large programs every time they are used can be expensive.

3. Use *pseudodynamic storage allocation* and recompile only the main program each time the program is used. Or possibly call a system routine to dynamically allocate at execution time just the amount of memory needed by the program once the size of the problem is determined.

The third approach is the best method and is used by many large software products to handle the problem of widely varying vector dimensions for problems of differing complexity.

Pseudodynamic vector dimensioning is accomplished using a combination of COMMON variables and variables passed through argument lists. It is quite complex, but its advantages are so great that most large-scale applications software written in FORTRAN use it. The program fragment in Figure 4.18 demonstrates how it works. The main program is as short as possible. It defines a single parameter—the length of the long vector VAR—sets it equal to a variable LENGTH, and then calls COMPUT to perform the remainder of the calculation.

Each vector variable in the program is associated with a sequence of elements (subvector) of the long vector VAR. The index of the element in VAR corresponding to the first element of each subvector is saved in an INTEGER variable IPn called a *pointer*. Thus,

```
VAR(IP1) THROUGH VAR(IP100)
```

```
C  MAIN PROGRAM - JUST TO SET THE COMMON LENGTHS
C  LENTOT IS THE ONLY PARAMETER THAT NEED BE CHANGED TO
C  CHANGE ALL VECTOR DIMENSIONS
       PARAMETER (LENTOT=XXXXXX)
       COMMON/VARBLS/ LENGTH, VAR(LENTOT)
       LENGTH = LENTOT
       CALL COMPUT
       STOP
       END

       SUBROUTINE COMPUT
       COMMON/SCALAR/ .....
       COMMON/VARBLS/ LENGTH, VAR(1)
       COMMON/LNGTHS/ L1, L2, L3, L4, L5, L6, L7, L8, L9, L10,
      1              L11,L12,L13,L14,L15,L16,L17,L18,L19,L20,
      2              L21,L22,L23,L24,L25,L26,L27,L28,L29,L30,
      3              L31,L32,L33,L34,L35,L36,L37,L38,L39,L40,
      4              L41,L42,L43,L44,L45,L46,L47,L48,L49,L50,
      5              L51,L52,L53,L54,L55,L56,L57,L58,L59,L60,
      6              L61,L62,L63,L64,L65,L66,L67,L68,L69,L70,
      7              L71,L72,L73,L74,L75,L76,L77,L78,L79,L80,
      8              L81,L82,L83,L84,L85,L86,L87,L88,L89,L90,
      1              L91,L92,L93,L94,L95,L96,L97,L98,L99,L100

       COMMON/POINTS/
      1       IP1, IP2, IP3, IP4, IP5, IP6, IP7, IP8, IP9, IP10,
      1       IP11,IP12,IP13,IP14,IP15,IP16,IP17,IP18,IP19,IP20,
      2       IP21,IP22,IP23,IP24,IP25,IP26,IP27,IP28,IP29,IP30,
      3       IP31,IP32,IP33,IP34,IP35,IP36,IP37,IP38,IP39,IP40,
      4       IP41,IP42,IP43,IP44,IP45,IP46,IP47,IP48,IP49,IP50,
      5       IP51,IP52,IP53,IP54,IP55,IP56,IP57,IP58,IP59,IP60,
      6       IP61,IP62,IP63,IP64,IP65,IP66,IP67,IP68,IP69,IP70,
      7       IP71,IP72,IP73,IP74,IP75,IP76,IP77,IP78,IP79,IP80,
      8       IP81,IP82,IP83,IP84,IP85,IP86,IP87,IP88,IP89,IP90,
      1       IP91,IP92,IP93,IP94,IP95,IP96,IP97,IP98,IP99,IP100

C  SET UP THE VECTOR LENGTHS
       L1 =
       L2 =
       L3 =
       .
       .
       .
       L98 =
       L99 =
       L100 =

C  SET UP THE VECTOR POINTERS IN THE LARGE VECTOR VAR
       IP1 = 1
       IP2 = IP1 + L1
       IP3 = IP2 + L2
       .

       IP98 = IP97 + L97
       IP99 = IP98 + L98
       IP100 = IP99 + L99
       LEN = IP100 + L100
       IF( LEN .GT. LENGTH ) THEN
         WRITE(NOUT,100) LEN, LENGTH
         RETURN
       ENDIF

C  NOW COMPUTE SOMETHING TO DEMONSTRATE HOW SUBSCRIPTED
C  VARIABLES ARE PASSED TO SUBROUTINES
       CALL STATE(VAR(IP6),VAR(IP27),VAR(IP12),VAR(IP92))

       .
       .
       RETURN
100 FORMAT(' NOT ENOUGH MEMORY - WORDS REQUIRED =', I6/
      1        '                     WORDS AVAILABLE=', I6)
       END

       SUBROUTINE STATE(DENSTY,TEMPER,PRESS,VISCOS)

       COMMON/SCALAR/ ...
       COMMON/VARBLS/ LENGTH, VAR(1)
       COMMON/POINTS/
      1       IP1, IP2, IP3, IP4, IP5, IP6, IP7, IP8, IP9, IP10,
      1       IP11,IP12,IP13,IP14,IP15,IP16,IP17,IP18,IP19,IP20,
```

Figure 4.18 Pseudodynamic variable dimensioning.

```
      2      IP21,IP22,IP23,IP24,IP25,IP26,IP27,IP28,IP29,IP30,
      3      IP31,IP32,IP33,IP34,IP35,IP36,IP37,IP38,IP39,IP40,
      4      IP41,IP42,IP43,IP44,IP45,IP46,IP47,IP48,IP49,IP50,
      5      IP51,IP52,IP53,IP54,IP55,IP56,IP57,IP58,IP59,IP60,
      6      IP61,IP62,IP63,IP64,IP65,IP66,IP67,IP68,IP69,IP70,
      7      IP71,IP72,IP73,IP74,IP75,IP76,IP77,IP78,IP79,IP80,
      8      IP81,IP82,IP83,IP84,IP85,IP86,IP87,IP88,IP89,IP90,
      1      IP91,IP92,IP93,IP94,IP95,IP96,IP97,IP98,IP99,IP100

C   DEFINE THE DUMMY ARGUMENTS AS SINGLY SUBSCRIPTED
      REAL DENSTY(*), TEMPER(*), PRESS(*), VISCOS(*)
               .
               .
               .

C   CALL ANOTHER SUBROUTINE TO DEMONSTRATE HOW DUMMY ARGUMENTS
C   FOR STATE CAN BE USED IN THE ARGUMENT LIST ALONG WITH
C   POINTERS INTO THE LONG VECTOR FOR VARIABLES THAT WERE NOT
C   PASSED INTO STATE
      CALL GETVEL(DENSTY,PRESS,VAR(IP60))
               .
               .
      RETURN
      END

      SUBROUTINE GETVEL(DENSTY,PRESS,VELOC)
      COMMON/VARBLS/ LENGTH, VAR(1)
      COMMON/SCALAR/ ...
      COMMON/POINTS/ IP1, IP2, IP3, ...

C   DEFINE THE DUMMY ARGUMENTS AS SINGLY SUBSCRIPTED
      REAL DENSTY(*), PRESS(*), VELOC(*)
               .
               .
      RETURN
      END
```

Figure 4.18   (*Continued*)

represent the first elements of all of the 100 vector variables used by the program. The length of each vector variable is recorded in the corresponding length variable, L1–L100. This is shown conceptually in Figure 4.19. Documentation must be kept to record the associations between the subvectors in VAR and the actual vectors to be used by the program. This can be done in the listing of the program as well as externally.

When a subroutine is called, *we use the "pointers" into the long vector VAR in the argument list:*

```
CALL STATE(VAR(IP6),VAR(IP27),VAR(IP12),VAR(IP92))
```

where these are all of the vector variables that will be used by the subroutine. In the subroutine dummy argument list *we use actual variable names to correspond to each of the pointers in the call statement:*

```
SUBROUTINE STATE (DENSTY,TEMPER,PRESS,VISCOS)
```

In this way, we "assign" variable names to the subvectors.

The trivial main program is edited to set the long vector length to the proper value for the problem. It is then recompiled, linked to the subroutines, loaded,

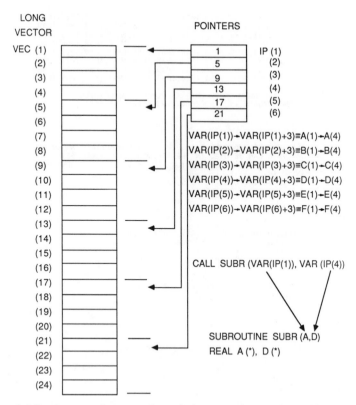

Figure 4.19 Conceptual picture of pseudodynamic subscripted variable assignment.

and executed. This scheme depends on the fact that the space reserved for a COMMON block is always the largest requested. All subroutines gain access to the vector variables that they need through argument lists. Scalars are accessed through COMMON/SCALAR/. This method of handling variables through a combination of COMMON blocks and argument lists is quite sophisticated and yet is entirely within the FORTRAN 77 standard.

A variation of this approach is to utilize system routines to request additional memory at execution time, once the size of the problem is determined from input. This method usually requires that the COMMON block that is to be expanded be loaded at the end of the executable file so that memory can be extended beyond the original end boundary of the code. This is shown schematically in Figure 4.20. This approach removes the necessity to recompile the main program and relink it to the subroutines before execution. The disadvantage is that it is not standard FORTRAN 77 because it depends on the call to a system routine.

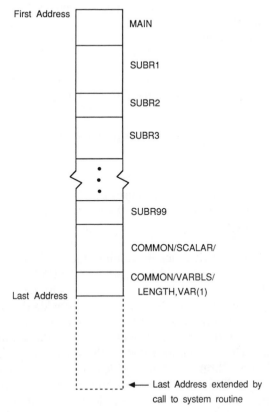

Figure 4.20 Extension of a COMMON block by calling a system routine.

4.4. USING SUBROUTINE NAMES AS ARGUMENTS AND DUMMY ARGUMENTS

It is sometimes necessary to provide a subroutine with the name of another subroutine which it in turn will call. This is most often done when using subroutine libraries for useful mathematical operations such as integration, matrix equation solution, etc. Because subroutine names look the same as variable names to the FORTRAN compiler, there must be a way to identify them as the names of subroutines. This is done with the EXTERNAL statement. An example follows.

Suppose that a set of coupled first order differential equations are to be solved. There are many numerical analysis subroutine libraries that have routines to perform this task. It is more efficient to use these routines than to take the time to write one for yourself (unless you are in a numerical analysis class and this is meant to be an educational experience). We will assume that you are most interested in solving an engineering problem and have already taken the appropriate numerical analysis class and know how such routines work. The differential equations are

$$\frac{dX_1}{dt} = \sin(t)\, X_1(t) + X_2(t)$$

$$\frac{dX_2}{dt} = X_1(t) + \sin^2(t)\, X_2(t)$$

These equations are solved numerically using the DVERK routine in the IMS library.[1] This DVERK subroutine requires that a subroutine to evaluate the right-hand side of the equations be supplied by the user. The IMSL documentation gives a specific format for the dummy argument list for this subroutine. This is because the DVERK subroutine calls the subroutine as part of the solution algorithm. But the IMSL documentation does not require that this subroutine have any special name. After all, what if the DVERK routine is called to solve two different sets of differential equations within the same program? Then there must be two different subroutines to provide the right-hand sides of the differential equations. The DVERK routine knows the name of the subroutine to call because the name is provided through the argument list in the CALL statement. This is demonstrated in the program fragment in Figure 4.21. The subroutine library routine DVERK then has statements similar to those at the bottom of Figure 4.21. Again, there is the need for an EXTERNAL declaration in the called subroutine to identify the dummy argument as a subroutine name. Notice that the dummy argument need not have the same name as the argument. This in fact is the whole point of passing subroutine names as arguments. This ability to call a subroutine that appears in a dummy argument list is critical to the use of libraries in the FORTRAN language. In this way, only the object code needs to be supplied with the library and the library only participates in the linking step. If this were not the case, then only two less general approaches are available:

1. User provided subroutine called by the library subroutine must have the same name as the one in the CALL statement in the library subroutine.
2. Library subroutine source program must be provided and the CALL statement modified to correspond to the subroutine names chosen by the user.

In the first of these cases the user would be restricted to the subroutine name specified by the library documentation. In the second case the library subroutine would be recompiled along with the user program. Neither of these options is as attractive as passing the subroutine name through the argument list.

```
            EXTERNAL RHSIDE
                   .
                   .
            CALL DVERK( N,RHSIDE,T,DISP,TEND,TOL,IND,C,NW,W,IER )
                   .
                   .
            END
            SUBROUTINE RHSIDE( N,T,DISP,DERIV )

C   THIS SUBROUTINE IS WRITTEN BY THE USER BUT CALLED BY
C   THE IMSL LIBRARY ROUTINE DVERK

            REAL T, DISP(N), DERIV(N)

C   COMPUTE THE RIGHT HAND SIDES OF THE EQUATIONS TO BE
C   SOLVED BY DVERK
            DERIV(1) = SIN(T) * DISP(1) + DISP(2)
            DERIV(2) = DISP(1) + SIN(T) ** 2 * DISP(2)
            RETURN
            END


     Representative statements in the DVERK routine (not the
     actual DVERK source program)

            SUBROUTINE DVERK(N,FCN,X,Y,XEND,TOL,IND,C,NW,W,IER)

            EXTERNAL FCN
                   .
                   .
            CALL FCN(N,X,Y,YPRIME)
                   .
                   .
            RETURN
            END
```

Figure 4.21 Using a subroutine name in the argument list of a call to the IMSL subroutine DVERK.

4.5. ENTRY POINTS IN SUBROUTINES

Subroutines are "entered" at different positions within the body of the subroutine by using the ENTRY statement. The ENTRY statement looks very much like the initial SUBROUTINE statement with an entry point name and a dummy argument list. ENTRY points are useful when related calculations rely on the same data. However, entry points are not essential and can always be replaced with separate subroutines.

Consider interpolation in a one-dimensional table. This requires two steps. First, the two tabulated values of the independent variable that lie on each side of the interpolant are found, and then the interpolation is done. Using a subroutine with an entry point, as shown in Figure 4.22, allows one to perform this two-step process by calling the subroutine. If one has already determined the position in the table and just wishes to perform a linear interpolation, then the entry point is called.

The use of entry points makes program development confusing because

```
C  THIS PROGRAM CALLS TABLE TO INTERPOLATE.  IT WILL EXTRAPOLATE
C  BELOW THE TABLE LOWER BOUNDARY BUT WILL NOT EXTRAPOLATE ABOVE
C  THE TABLE UPPER BOUNDARY

      DIMENSION XTAB(10), YTAB(10)
      DATA XTAB/1.,2.,3.,4.,5.,6.,7.,8.,9.,10./
      DATA YTAB/1.,4.,9.,16.,25.,36.,49.,64.,81.,100./

    5 READ(5,*,END=999) X
      CALL TABLE(YTAB,XTAB,X,Y,NINT,IERR)
      IF(IERR .EQ. 0) THEN
        WRITE(6,100) X, Y
      ELSE IF(IERR .EQ. 1) THEN
        CALL INTERP(YTAB,XTAB,X,Y,NINT)
        WRITE(6,100) X, Y
      ELSE
        WRITE(6,101) X
      ENDIF
      GOTO 5
  999 STOP
  100 FORMAT('0 X-VALUE=',E12.4,'  Y-VALUE=',E12.4)
  101 FORMAT('0 X-VALUE=',E12.4,'  EXCEEDS TABLE MAXIMUM')
      END

      SUBROUTINE TABLE( YTAB, XTAB, NTAB, X, Y, NINT, IERR )

C  THIS SUBROUTINE FINDS THE INDEX IN A VECTOR OF TABULATED
C  X-VALUES THAT FALLS JUST BELOW THE INTERPOLANT X AND THEN
C  INTERPOLATES TO OBTAIN THE VALUE Y.  SHOULD X FALL OUTSIDE
C  THE BOUNDS OF THE TABLE, CONTROL IS RETURNED TO THE CALLER.
C  SHOULD THE CALLER WISH TO EXTRAPOLATE THEN A CALL TO THE
C  ENTRY POINT INTERP WILL DO THIS.
C  INPUT    YTAB   - VECTOR OF DEPENDENT TABULATED VALUES
C           XTAB   - VECTOR OF INDEPENDENT TABULATED VALUES
C           NTAB   - DIMENSION OF THE TABLE VECTORS
C           X      - INDEPENDENT VARIABLE TO INTERPOLATE
C  OUTPUT   Y      - DEPENDENT INTERPOLATED VALUE
C           NINT   - INDEX IN TABLE BELOW INTERPOLANT X
C           IERR   - ERROR FLAG =0 OKAY, =1 X BELOW SMALLEST
C                    TABLE VALUE, =2 X ABOVE HIGHEST TABLE VALUE

      REAL XTAB(*), YTAB(*)

C  SET THE ERROR FLAG TO ZERO
      IERR = 0

C  FIND THE INDEX
      DO 10 N = 2,NTAB
        IF( X .LT. XTAB(N) ) THEN
          NINT = N - 1
          GOTO 20
        ENDIF
   10 CONTINUE
C  IF WE REACH HERE, X IS GREATER THAN THE MAX TABLE VALUE
C  XTAB(NTAB).  SET ERROR FLAG AND RETURN
      IERR = 2
      RETURN

C  CHECK FOR X BELOW LOWEST TABLE VALUE
   20 CONTINUE
      IF( X .LT. XTAB(1) ) THEN
        IERR = 1
        RETURN
      ENDIF

C  ALL IS WELL, GO ON TO INTERPOLATE
      GOTO 100

      ENTRY INTERP( YTAB, XTAB, NTAB, X, Y, NINT, IERR )

C  THIS ENTRY INTERPOLATES IN A TABLE, GIVEN THE INDEX CLOSEST
C  TO THE INDEPENDENT VARIABLE

  100 CONTINUE

C  USE A SIMPLE LINEAR INTERPOLATION
      SLOPE = (YTAB(NINT+1) - YTAB(NINT)) /
     1        (XTAB(NINT+1) - XTAB(NINT))
      Y = YTAB(NINT) + SLOPE * (X - XTAB(NINT))

      RETURN
      END
```

Figure 4.22 Subroutine with an ENTRY point.

they are like separate subroutines yet are not associated with a SUBROUTINE statement. Therefore they do not "show up" when scanning source program files for SUBROUTINE statements with a text editor for instance. Two searches must always be done to find all subroutines and entry points. This is annoying when working on a very large program. On the other hand, entry points are convenient for applications like the one in Figure 4.22.

4.6. ALTERNATE RETURN POINTS

Program execution normally starts again with the statement following the call to a subroutine. For the case of a call to the TABLE subroutine in Figure 4.22, one would have

```
CALL TABLE(YTAB,XTAB,NTAB,X,Y,NINT,IERR)
                              control returns to this point
```

This normal return point is altered by use of an alternate return specification in the subroutine call. The subroutine returns to different statements in the calling routine, depending on conditions determined by the called subroutine. This is shown in the program listing in Figure 4.23. In this case the subroutine returns control to the statement following the calling statement if the value of X is within the bounds of the table. It returns to statement label 10 if X is less than the minimum table value and returns to statement label 20 if X is greater than the maximum table value.

Although alternate return points are part of standard FORTRAN 77, the concept of alternate returns violates the principles of structured design outlined in Chapter 9. Alternate return points make a program obscure and do not exemplify the qualities of well-structured programming. This is mainly because the decision-making process is done in a subordinate subroutine (the one called) when the guiding principle of structured design is to make decisions in the highest level subroutines while the lower level ones make fewer decisions but do more of the work.

4.7. SAVING LOCAL VARIABLES
BETWEEN SUBROUTINE CALLS

When a subroutine is entered for the first time, all of the local variables to that subroutine are *undefined* unless they are initially defined using a DATA statement. (An undefined variable is one whose value has not yet been set by appearing on the left side of an assignment statement. On many computer systems, undefined variables have a value of zero, but this is not true of all systems and FORTRAN 77 has no specification for this value.) Upon exiting a subroutine, all local variables become undefined unless they are initially defined and have not been changed by the subroutine. This is demonstrated in

```
C   THIS` PROGRAM CALLS TABLE TO INTERPOLATE.  IT WILL EXTRAPOLATE
C   BELOW THE TABLE LOWER BOUNDARY BUT WILL NOT EXTRAPOLATE ABOVE
C   THE TABLE UPPER BOUNDARY.  IT USES ALTERNATE RETURNS TO DECIDE

        DIMENSION XTAB(10), YTAB(10)
        DATA XTAB/1.,2.,3.,4.,5.,6.,7.,8.,9.,10./
        DATA YTAB/1.,4.,9.,16.,25.,36.,49.,64.,81.,100./

      5 READ(5,*,END=999) X
        CALL TABLE(YTAB,XTAB,X,Y,NINT,&10,&20)
        WRITE(6,100) X, Y
        GOTO 5
     10 CALL INTERP(YTAB,XTAB,X,Y,NINT)
        WRITE(6,100) X, Y
        GOTO 5
     20 WRITE(6,101) X
        GOTO 5
    999 STOP
    100 FORMAT('0 X-VALUE=',E12.4,'  Y-VALUE=',E12.4)
    101 FORMAT('0 X-VALUE=',E12.4,'   EXCEEDS TABLE MAXIMUM')
        END
        SUBROUTINE TABLE( YTAB, XTAB, NTAB, X, Y, NINT, *, * )

C   THIS SUBROUTINE FINDS THE INDEX IN A VECTOR OF TABULATED
C   X-VALUES THAT FALLS JUST BELOW THE INTERPOLANT X AND THEN
C   INTERPOLATES TO OBTAIN THE VALUE Y.  SHOULD X FALL OUTSIDE
C   THE BOUNDS OF THE TABLE, CONTROL IS RETURNED TO THE CALLER.
C   SHOULD THE CALLER WISH TO EXTRAPOLATE THEN A CALL TO THE
C   ENTRY POINT INTERP WILL DO THIS.
C   INPUT    YTAB    - VECTOR OF DEPENDENT TABULATED VALUES
C            XTAB    - VECTOR OF INDEPENDENT TABULATED VALUES
C            NTAB    - DIMENSION OF THE TABLE VECTORS
C            X       - INDEPENDENT VARIABLE TO INTERPOLATE
C   OUTPUT   Y       - DEPENDENT INTERPOLATED VALUE
C            NINT    - INDEX IN TABLE BELOW INTERPOLANT X

        REAL XTAB(*), YTAB(*)

C   FIND THE INDEX
        DO 10 N = 2,NTAB
          IF( X .LT. XTAB(N) ) THEN
            NINT = N - 1
            GOTO 20
          ENDIF
     10 CONTINUE

C   IF WE REACH HERE, X IS GREATER THAN THE MAX TABLE VALUE
C   XTAB(NTAB).  RETURN TO SECOND ALTERNATE RETURN POINT
        RETURN 2

C   CHECK FOR X BELOW LOWEST TABLE VALUE.  IF BELOW, RETURN TO
C   FIRST ALTERNATE RETURN POINT
     20 CONTINUE
        IF( X .LT. XTAB(1) ) RETURN 1

C ALL IS WELL, GO ON TO INTERPOLATE
        GOTO 100

        ENTRY INTERP( YTAB, XTAB, NTAB, X, Y, NINT )

C   THIS ENTRY INTERPOLATES IN A TABLE, GIVEN THE INDEX CLOSEST
C   TO THE INDEPENDENT VARIABLE - NINT

    100 CONTINUE

C   USE A SIMPLE LINEAR INTERPOLATION
        SLOPE = (YTAB(NINT+1) - YTAB(NINT)) /
       1        (XTAB(NINT+1) - XTAB(NINT))
        Y = YTAB(NINT) + SLOPE * (X - XTAB(NINT))

        RETURN
        END
```

Figure 4.23 Alternate returns from a subroutine.

the program listing in Figure 4.24. The local variables TWO and FOUR remain defined after exiting the subroutine because they were initially defined by the DATA statement and are not changed anywhere in the subroutine (i.e., they do not appear on the left side of the " = " in any assignment statement). However, the local variables NREAL, NOTREL, ARG, and ARGSQ become undefined once the subroutine is exited because they are redefined in the body of the subroutine. On the next call to the subroutine they do not necessarily have the value that they had upon exiting from the previous call. This makes no difference for the variables ARG and ARGSQ since they are redefined without regard to their previous values. But the variables NREAL and NOTREL are meant by the programmer to retain their previous values in order to accumulate the numbers of real and nonreal root equations processed by this subroutine. This problem is overcome by using the SAVE statement. The SAVE statement is a nonexecutable statement appearing at the head of a subroutine that specifies which variables should be made to retain their values for a subsequent call. The inclusion of

```
SAVE NOTREL, NREAL
```

at the head of the subroutine ensures that the variables NOTREL and NREAL retain their values on the next call to the subroutine QUADR.

The fact that the FORTRAN 77 standard does not guarantee the retention of local variable values in a subroutine from one invocation of it to the next

```
      SUBROUTINE QUADR(A,B,C,X1,X2)

C  COMPUTE ROOTS OF A QUADRATIC EQUATION IF THE ROOTS ARE REAL
C  AND RECORD THE NUMBER OF OCCASIONS WHEN THE ROOTS ARE REAL
C  AND THE NUMBER OF OCCASIONS WHEN THEY ARE NOT REAL.  IF 100
C  NON-REAL ROOTS ARE ENCOUNTERED WRITE A MESSAGE

      DATA TWO/2./, FOUR/4./, NREAL/0/, NOTREL/0/

C  DETERMINE WHETHER THE EQUATION HAS REAL ROOTS
         ARG = B ** 2 - FOUR * A * C
         IF( ARG .GE. 0. ) THEN
            ARGSQ = SQRT(ARG)
            X1 = (-B + ARGSQ) / TWO
            X2 = (-B - ARGSQ) / TWO
            NREAL = NREAL + 1
         ELSE
            X1 = 0.
            X2 = 0.
            NOTREL = NOTREL + 1
            IF( NOTREL .GE. 100 ) THEN
               WRITE(6,100) NOTREL, NREAL
            ENDIF
         ENDIF
      ENDIF
      RETURN
  100 FORMAT('  NUMBER OF NON-REAL ROOT EQUATIONS', I4/
     1           NUMBER OF REAL ROOT EQUATIONS    ', I4)
      END
```

Figure 4.24 Status of local variables upon exiting a subroutine.

is not widely recognized. Most FORTRAN 77 compilers in fact generate machine code that *does retain* local variable values. This has in turn left FORTRAN users with the expectation that such retained values are available on all computers. This ambiguity about the function of any particular compiler is removed by using a SAVE statement with no arguments at the head of each subroutine. Such a statement saves all variables that might otherwise not have their values retained between calls to the subroutine. A final question is, why would the FORTRAN 77 standard be written in such a way?

The answer to this question comes from the many different ways that memory space can be defined for an executable program. One way is simply to associate the memory words required to hold all of the local variables for a subroutine with the object module for that subroutine. This is the way that most FORTRAN compilers do it and is the way that we have used to represent object files in all of our discussions thus far. But another way is to have a "pool" of memory available that the subroutines can share as a place to store local variables. This area of memory is called a *stack* or sometimes a *pushdown stack*. The linker sets the addresses of the local variables so that they reference the words in this special block of memory. Hence, the subroutines share memory yet they do not really know that they are doing so. This is shown schematically in Figure 4.25 for our familiar bubble sort. When the main program is executing, only its local variables are defined on the stack. When the BUBBLE subroutine is called, its local variables are "pushed onto the stack." When the SWITCH subroutine is called, its local variable is also pushed onto

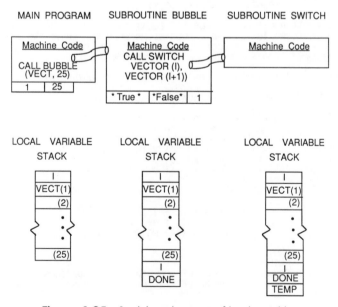

Figure 4.25 Stack-based storage of local variables.

the stack. Once SWITCH is exited, its variable disappears from the stack and likewise for BUBBLE once it is exited. This stack approach to storing local variables has the advantage of allowing recursive subroutine calls.

4.8. FORTRAN FUNCTIONS AND INTRINSIC FUNCTIONS

FORTRAN function subprograms are similar to subroutine subprograms. They both have an interface and a body. They have local variables, dummy arguments, and access to global variables through COMMON. They differ in the way that functions are invoked and the way that functions pass results back to the caller. Functions pass back only a single scalar value. The use of functions is demonstrated in Figure 4.26. Function names must be typed just like variable names:

```
A-H,O-Z   are real values
I-N       are integer values
```

This default typing is changed by including the function name in an INTEGER or REAL declaration. If desired, functions are always replaceable with subroutines as shown in Figure 4.27.

```
      FUNCTION SPEED(DENS,TEMP)

C  THIS FUNCTION COMPUTES THE SOUND SPEED OF A NONIDEAL GAS WITH
C  DENSITY DENS AND TEMPERTURE TEMP

      SPEED = SQRT(PRESS(DENS,TEMP) / DENS)
      RETURN
      END

      FUNCTION PRESS(D,T)

C  THIS FUNCTION COMPUTES THE PRESSURE OF A NONIDEAL GAS BY
C  CORRECTING THE IDEAL GAS FORMULA WITH A VALUE OBTAINED FROM
C  A TABLE LOOKUP PROCEDURE

      COMMON/GASDAT/ XTAB(100), YTAB(100), GASCON

C  GET THE CORRECTION TERM. IF OUT OF TABLE BOUNDS, USE
C  EXTRAPOLATION

      CALL TABLE(YTAB,XTAB,NTAB,X,CORREC,NINT,IERR)
      IF( IERR .NE. 0 ) CALL INTERP(YTAB,XTAB,NTAB,X,CORREC,NINT)
      PRESS = D * GASCON * T * CORREC
      RETURN
      END

      SUBROUTINE TABLE( YTAB, XTAB, NTAB, X, Y, NINT, IERR )
            .
            .
            .

          (Same as in Figure 4.22)
```

Figure 4.26 Use of FORTRAN functions.

```
      SUBROUTINE SPEED(DENS,TEMP,SNSPED)

C  THIS SUBROUTINE COMPUTES THE SOUND SPEED OF A NONIDEAL GAS WITH
C  DENSITY DENS AND TEMPERATURE TEMP

      CALL PRESS(DENS,TEMP,PRESR)
      SNSPED = SQRT(PRESR / DENS)
      RETURN
      END

      SUBROUTINE PRESS(D,T,P)

C  THIS SUBROUTINE COMPUTES THE PRESSURE OF A NONIDEAL GAS BY
C  CORRECTING THE IDEAL GAS FORMULA WITH A VALUE OBTAINED FROM
C  A TABLE LOOKUP PROCEDURE

      COMMON/GASDAT/ XTAB(100), YTAB(100), GASCON

C  GET THE CORRECTION TERM. IF OUT OF TABLE BOUNDS, USE
C  EXTRAPOLATION

      CALL TABLE(YTAB,XTAB,NTAB,X,CORREC,NINT,IERR)
      IF( IERR .NE. 0 ) CALL INTERP(YTAB,XTAB,NTAB,X,CORREC,NINT)
      P = D * GASCON * T * CORREC
      RETURN
      END
```

Figure 4.27 Using subroutine rather than function subprograms.

Intrinsic functions are supplied with the FORTRAN compiler in a library that is used during the linking stage of program development. Intrinsic functions include most common mathematical functions. They are listed in Figure 3.5. A new feature of FORTRAN 77 is the inclusion of generic intrinsic functions. For instance, the logarithm function has three forms: ALOG, DLOG, and LOG. The ALOG function only operates on real arguments, the DLOG function only operates on double-precision arguments, whereas the LOG function allows the compiler to determine the type of argument and to choose the correct function to specify. In this way, the LOG function is *context-sensitive* because the compiler makes a decision depending on the context in which the function appears.

4.9. SUBROUTINE ARGUMENT ASSOCIATION CONVENTIONS

The material in this section is intended for individuals with assembly language programming experience. No attempt is made to explain the machine characteristics of these particular computers. The reader is referred to the appropriate reference manual. Because these three computer types represent a large fraction of the machines that are used for scientific computation, we use them as specific examples of subroutine argument association conventions.

4.9.1. IBM "360-Like" Computers

All IBM 30xx and 43xx series computers use the "IBM 360" architecture with general-purpose registers used as pointers to lists of the addresses of arguments to subroutines. The general registers are saved by the called subroutine in a save area that resides in the calling routine. The save areas of different levels of subroutines are connected by a double-linked list for subroutine traceback. This is shown in the program fragment in Figure 4.28. In the calling program general register one (grl) is loaded with the address of the list of addresses of the arguments in the call. This list of addresses is called PARLIST. General

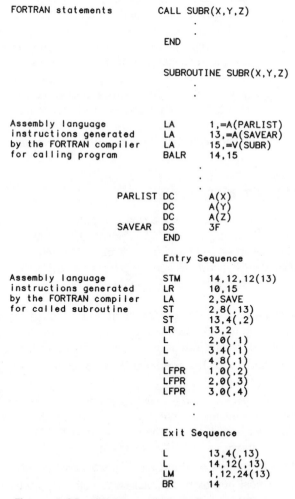

Figure 4.28 IBM 30xx and 43xx subroutine linking.

register 13 is loaded with the address of the save area called SAVEAR where the called subroutine will save the contents of the general registers once it is entered. General register 15 is loaded with the address of the subroutine to be called and the call is done with the branch-and-link register BALR instruction where the return address is put into gr14. In the called subroutine all general registers except gr13 are stored in the save area provided by the calling subroutine, starting with the fourth word (12 bytes from the address pointed to by gr13). The address of the called subroutine is shifted from gr15 to gr10 so that gr15 can be used for subsequent calls. General register 2 is loaded with the address of the save area in the called subroutine and this address is saved in the third word of the save area in the calling routine. This provides a forward link between save areas. Then the address of the save area in the calling routine, which is in gr13, is saved in the second word of the save area in the called subroutine, thus providing a backward link between save areas. Finally, the address of the save area in the called subroutine is moved from gr2 to gr13 in preparation for a possible subsequent call to another subroutine. The first word of the save area can be used for keeping special information. Next the address of the first argument is loaded into gr2, the address of the second argument is loaded into gr3, and the address of the third argument is loaded into gr4. Then the actual values of the arguments are loaded into floating point registers 1, 2, and 3. They can then be used for computation.

4.9.2. DEC VAX Architecture

The DEC VAX is a so-called stack-based computer, where subroutine arguments are "pushed" onto a stack and "popped" off of the stack by the called subroutine. This process, along with the branch and return addresses, is all handled by a single instruction as shown in Figure 4.29. The CALLG machine instruction accomplishes all of the following functions:

1. It puts the address of the next instruction into the fifth word of the call frame on the stack so that the RET instruction executed by the called subroutine will return execution to the instruction following the call.

2. It puts the address of the argument list into the argument pointer (AP), which is register 12.

3. It selectively saves only the registers in the range R0-R11 that will be needed by the subroutine. The registers to be saved are specified by the procedure-entry mask that is the first word of the called subroutine. In the example above, R2 and R3 are saved.

4. It stacks information so that nested subroutine calls are possible.

5. It marks critical points in the stack which allows traceback.

6. It completely restores the stack during the return operation so that there is no risk of unwanted debris being left on the stack.

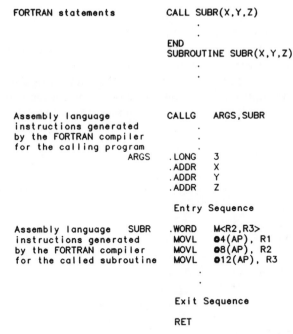

```
FORTRAN statements          CALL SUBR(X,Y,Z)
                                 .
                                 .
                            END
                            SUBROUTINE SUBR(X,Y,Z)
                                 .
                                 .


Assembly language           CALLG    ARGS,SUBR
instructions generated           .
by the FORTRAN compiler          .
for the calling program          .
                    ARGS    .LONG    3
                            .ADDR    X
                            .ADDR    Y
                            .ADDR    Z

                            Entry Sequence

Assembly language    SUBR   .WORD    M<R2,R3>
instructions generated      MOVL     04(AP), R1
by the FORTRAN compiler     MOVL     08(AP), R2
for the called subroutine   MOVL     012(AP), R3
                                 .
                                 .

                            Exit Sequence

                            RET
```

Figure 4.29 DEC VAX subroutine linking.

7. It cleans up the stack in a way that allows an argument list to be put on the stack and automatically removed at return.

In the called subroutine the first word is actually the procedure-entry mask that tells the CALLG instruction which registers to save on the stack. Registers R12–R15 are always saved because these are special-purpose registers that must be saved in order to call further subroutines. The next three instructions in the called subroutine move the actual values of the arguments into the registers R1–R3 by doing an indirect reference through the words that hold the addresses of these arguments.

Clearly, CALLG is a very powerful subroutine linkage instruction in comparison to the IBM instruction. The VAX linkage allows recursive subroutine calls if desired whereas the IBM approach does not.

4.9.3. Cray XMP Architecture

The subroutine linkage convention on Cray XMP computers is not as "fixed" as those on IBM and VAX computers. There are in fact two different conventions in use today with the possibility that these could be changed in the future. Therefore care must be taken when using the following descriptions. However, it is useful to review the concepts used by the Cray FORTRAN compilers to link subroutines on the Cray XMP architecture.

The two different conventions available on the Cray XMP are a static memory environment where reentrant or recursive subroutines are not allowed and a stack-based method of argument passing and register saving that allows reentrancy. These two options correspond roughly to the concepts introduced by the IBM and DEC VAX conventions. The nonreentrant form is shown in Fig-

```
Calling Program

   .
   .
   A6       ARGLIST
   A0       X
   +1,A6    A0
   A0       Y
   +2,A6    A0
   A0       Z
   +3,A6    A0
   R        SUBR
   .
   .


Entry Sequence

   *     =      3+BU         * Number of B's to save
   NB    =      0+TU         * Number of T's to save
         CON    'SUBR'       * ASCII entry name
   TNB   VWD    32/0         * mandatory zero
         VWD    whatever
         CON
         CON
          .
          .
   SAVELOC BSS  NB+NT
   SUBR  =      *
         A0     W.TNB        * Save B's
         B77    A0
         A0     SAVELOC
         A1     NB
         0,A0   B77,A1
         B01    A6           * Base of argument list
         B02    A0           * Reference base (traceback)
         A0     SAVELOC+NB   * IFF NT > 0, Save T's
         A1     NT           * IFF NT > 0
         0,A0   T00,A1       * IFF NT > 0

Return Sequence

         A0     B02          * Restore B's
         A1     NB
         B77,A1 0,A0
         A0 SAVELOC+NB   * IFF NT > 0, Restore T's
         A1     NT           * IFF NT > 0
         T00,A1 0,A0        * IFF NT > 0
         J      B00
```

Figure 4.30 Cray XMP subroutine linking (nonreentrant).

ure 4.30. Argument addresses are put into a list in the calling program and register A6 points to this list of addresses. Register B00 contains the return address. Specified B and T registers are saved in a region in the called routine. The A, S, and V registers are not saved. The VL, VM, B70–77, and T70–77 registers are also not saved.

Figure 4.31 shows the situation for a reentrant subroutine. This assumes a stack-based environment where the stack grows from low addresses to high

```
        Entry Sequence

        *
        CON      'SUBR'          * ASCII entry point name
TNB     VWD      32/0            * mandatory zero
        VWD      whatever
        CON
        CON

          .
          .
EXT     $STKOFEN
NB      =        4+BU            * Number of B's to save
NT      =        0+TU            * Number of T's to save
NL      =        ...             * Number of locals

SUBR    =        *
        A0       W.TNB           * Word address of entry point
        B77      A0
        A0       B66             * Current stack top
        A1       NB
        ,A0      B77,A1          * Saves B77 through B.NB
        A2       B66             * Current stack top
        A2       A2+A1           * Computing new stack top
        B02      A0              * New reference base
        A1       NT              * IFF NT > 0, Save T's
        A0       A2              * IFF NT > 0
        A2       A2+A1           * IFF NT > 0,Computing new stack top
        A0       T00,A1          * IFF NT > 0
        A1       NL              * IFF NL > 0,Computing new stack top
        A2       A2+A1           * IFF NL > 0
        B01      A6              * Address of argument list
        A1       B67             * Stack limit
        A0       A1-A2
        B66      A2              * New stack limit
        JAP      *+4
        R        $STKOFEN        * Resets stack base possibly

        Return Sequence

        A0       B02
        A1       NB
        B77,A1   ,A0
        B66      A0              * Cut stack top back
        A2       B66             * IFF NT > 0, Restore T's
        A0       A2+A1           * IFF NT > 0
        A1       NT              * IFF NT > 0
        T00,A1   ,A0             * IFF NT > 0
        J        B00
```

Figure 4.31 Cray XMP subroutine linking (reentrant).

addresses. In the calling routine register B00 contains the return address, register A6 contains a pointer to the argument list header. It is the responsibility of the called routine to save the B and T registers. The A, S, and V registers are not saved. The VL, VM, B70–77, and T70–77 registers are also not saved. In the called routine register B00 contains the return address, register B01 contains a pointer to the argument list header of the called routine, register B02 contains a pointer to the base of the current stack frame (or to the register save area in the case of static memory mode), register B66 contains a pointer to the top of the current stack frame, register B67 contains a pointer to the absolute top of the stack, and B70–77 are scratch registers. The stack frame has no specific layout except for the first four words. The first word of the stack frame is a pointer to the traceback name block (TNB), the second word is the return address, the third word is a pointer to the argument list (in the stack frame), and the fourth word is a pointer to the base of the current stack frame. These four words are followed by anything else that is needed. The traceback name block precedes the entry point of the called routine and permits language processors to put names longer than eight characters in the traceback information. Traceback information is used by the error traceback routines, by the flow trace routines, and by debug programs.

REFERENCES

1. DVERK subroutine, IMSL Library, Vol. 1, June 1982.

EXERCISES

1. What is wrong with the following subroutine? What would you expect to happen if this subroutine were executed as shown? Execute it and explain what you see.

```
B = 3.
C = 2.
CALL SUBR(A,B,C)
WRITE (*, *) A,B,C
END
SUBROUTINE SUBR(A,B,N)
A = B + N
RETURN
END
```

2. What is wrong with the following program segments? How would you correct them?

```
(a) C MAIN PROGRAM
      DIMENSION A(10,10)
```

```
          .
          .
      CALL SUBR(A,10)
          .
          .
      END
      SUBROUTINE SUBR(X,10)
      DIMENSION X(10,10)
          .
          .
      END
```

(b)
```
C MAIN PROGRAM
      DIMENSION A(N)
      N = 10
      CALL SUBR(A,N)
          .
          .
      END
      SUBROUTINE SUBR(B,M)
      DIMENSION B(M)
          .
          .
      END
```

(c)
```
C MAIN PROGRAM
      DIMENSION A(100,100)
      N = 10
      CALL SUBR(A,N)
          .
          .
      END
      SUBROUTINE SUBR(B,M)
      DIMENSION B(M,M)
          .
          .
      END
```

(d)
```
C MAIN PROGRAM
      DIMENSION A(10,10)
      READ(*,*) NMAX
      READ(*,*) ((A(I,J), I=1,NMAX),J=1,NMAX)
      CALL SUBR(A,NMAX)
          .
          .
      END
      SUBROUTINE SUBR(B,N)
      DIMENSION B(N,N)
          .
          .
      END
```

3. Identify the local and global variables and the dummy arguments in the following program. What values will be printed for X(I) and Y(I) in SUB2?

```
C MAIN PROGRAM
      DIMENSION A(10),B(10),C(10),D(10)
      COMMON C, D, E(10), F(10)
      DO 10 N = 1,10
      A(N) = 1.
      B(N) = 2.
      C(N) = N
      D(N) = C(N)
      E(N) = D(N-1)
      F(N) = N * N
   10 CONTINUE
      CALL SUB1(A,B,C,D,E,F,N)
         .
         .
      END
      SUBROUTINE SUB1(D,B,C,N,X,Y,Z,H)
      DIMENSION D(*), B(*), C(*), X(*), Y(*), Z(*)
      REAL N(*)
      INTEGER H
      COMMON A(10), W(10), E(10), F(10)
      CALL SUB2(D,A,H)
         .
         .
      END
      SUBROUTINE SUB2(X,Y,N)
      DIMENSION X(N), Y(N)
      WRITE(*,*) (X(I),Y(I), I=1,N)
      RETURN
      END
```

4. Write a main program and two subroutines to solve the linear equations in problem 5 of Chapter 3. The main program should read the input from a disk file and call a subroutine JACOBY with the following arguments:

```
CALL JACOBY(N,A,X,B,EPS,IMAX,ITER)
```

where A is the coefficient matrix of dimension $A(N,N)$, X is the solution vector of dimension $X(2*N)$, B is the right-hand side of the equations of dimension $B(N)$, EPS is the tolerance that must be met to terminate the iteration, IMAX is the maximum number of iterations allowed before giving up, and ITER is the number of iterations required for the converged solution.

The subroutine JACOBY calls another subroutine SOLVE to perform a single iteration. One half of the vector X (dimensioned $2*N$) is used to save the previous iteration and the other half is used for the solution of the current iteration. The subroutine JACOBY tests for convergence using these two vectors.

The call to SOLVE should be done in such a way that values of the solution need not be moved from one half of X to the other before the next iteration. In other words, the first and last half of X should be alternated in the argument list in the call to SOLVE. (This can be accomplished with a single CALL statement if the arguments and their indices are cleverly chosen. See if you can do it this way.) The final converged solution should always be returned by JACOBY to the main program in the first half of X.

5. Use a numerical subroutine library such as IMSL to solve the following set of differential equations. You must write a main program to call the library routine and you must write a subroutine to evaluate the right-hand sides of the differential equations.

$$Y'_1 = Y_2 \qquad\qquad Y_1(0) = 0$$
$$Y'_2 = 2(e^{2x} - y_1^2)^{1/2} \qquad Y_2(0) = 1$$
$$x = 0 \rightarrow 1$$

6. The linker is generally the least appreciated step in the FORTRAN program development process. Write a short report on the linker used on your computer system. Include a discussion of its options, the format of the object file, etc.

7. In the following program fragment, identify those statements or parts of statements associated with the subroutine interface and those parts associated with the subroutine body.

```
   SUBROUTINE EXAM(VAR1,VAR2,IVAR,VAR3)
   DIMENSION VAR1(IVAR), VAR4(100), VAR2(100)
   COMMON A(200), B(200), C(200), D(200)
   DIMENSION VAR6(100), VAR3(100), VAR5(100)
   DO 10 I = 1,IVAR
      A(I) = VAR6(I) * VAR3(I)
10 CONTINUE
```

5

FORTRAN Input and Output

Input and output, or I/O, refers to the communications between a FORTRAN program (or any program for that matter) and its surrounding environment. The surrounding environment includes (1) the user's terminal, (2) disk files, (3) magnetic tapes, (4) other peripheral devices such as printers and card readers, and (5) other computers via networks. This input and output is coded in different ways depending on the application.

In recent years there has been increasing emphasis on the way that computer programs interact with the user. This new emphasis is called *user friendliness* and refers to input and output that is understandable to users that are not familiar with computer programming. In others words, user-friendly input does not require that numbers be aligned in specific columns on the input line. Input files are often filled with comments to guide the user in preparing the input. Input is often read directly from the keyboard while the user is prompted by messages on the CRT screen of the terminal. Input is processed by the program to ensure its correctness or at least consistency before using it in the execution of the calculations. In this way the user is not confronted by error comments such as:

FLOATING POINT OVERFLOW AT LOCATION 074352

when the actual problem was an input error. Such messages are not "friendly," particularly to users with no understanding of computer programming.

User-friendly output is self-explanatory. It is filled with textual information in addition to the actual data to allow the user to understand the data without reference to computer documentation and, again, without an understanding

117

of computer programming. Options are often provided to allow the user to customize the output to appear in a variety of formats depending on the application. Graphical output is a common feature in today's scientific programs. The introduction of low-cost laser printers makes graphical output as easy to produce as printed output.

The FORTRAN 77 language has a sophisticated set of formatting instructions for reading and writing lines of text and converting data from text to binary format and vice versa. The input is most easily managed if it is sequential and record-oriented. In other words, the input is read one line at a time. This is of course a carryover from the days when input was read from a card reader and each card was a record. The expression *card image* is still often used to refer to a record. The sequential textual output is intended for a line printer. The format *control instructions* are skip a line, skip to the top of the next page, overprint the same line, and so on. These are in contrast to a CRT screen-oriented output which positions a cursor in the *X-Y* plane and then writes text starting at this point. The FORTRAN language has no output instructions suitable for CRT interaction. For this reason it is impossible to create user-friendly programs with only FORTRAN statements if extensive CRT terminal interaction is required. Programs must call system-dependent subroutines to accomplish this.

The FORTRAN 77 language has a number of file manipulation commands that allow the programmer to create standard, portable programs that use disk files to communicate between programs. There is a temptation to use the file manipulation commands on the local computer system rather than the standard FORTRAN commands because the system-dependent commands are often much more powerful and useful. This is always a trade-off between convenience and portability.

Magnetic tapes allow information to be transferred between one computer and another. This is facilitated by a standard tape format that has been established through the overwhelming use of IBM equipment in the world marketplace. While each computer manufacturer has a tape format that is used between its own machines, they also support the "IBM standard" to allow transfer between different computer types. The FORTRAN language supports the positioning and reading and writing of magnetic tapes.

5.1. FORMATTED INPUT AND OUTPUT

The most common method for the user to communicate with a FORTRAN program is through formatted input and output. In formatted input the data is in the form of ASCII or EBCDIC characters. Upon reading the data, the strings of characters are converted into floating point or fixed point numbers. The same is true of formatted output. Floating or fixed point data are converted into strings of characters under the control of formatting instructions in the WRITE statement and are sent to the output device. This formatted input and output can be either *free* or *fixed* format depending on the extent to which the user wants to control the formatting. With the near extinction of cards and card readers, it is customary to use free format input from disk files and fixed format output to disk files or a line printer. These are discussed in the following sections.

5.1.1. Free Format Input and Output

Free format I/O is called *list-directed I/O*. We have been using this in the programming examples in earlier chapters. For input, we use one of the statements

```
      READ(*,*)      variable list
      READ(u,*,END=mmm,ERR=nnn)   variable list
        .
        .
        .
mmm  CONTINUE
        .
        .
nnn  CONTINUE
```

The first form reads from the *default input device,* often the user's terminal. In the past, the default input device was the card reader. The last form reads input from a *logical I/O unit* designated by the integer "u", which must be associated with some specific device or file by either an operating system command or with the FORTRAN OPEN statement (see Section 5.3.1). Historically, the card reader was associated with unit 5. Today the terminal keyboard is often designated as unit 5. The "*" identifies this as a list-directed read operation (i.e., there are no format instructions). The END= and ERR= fields are optional. Should the READ statement try to read records past the end of a file, then control is returned to the statement label mmm. Should there be some error condition encountered during the read operation, then control is returned to the statement label nnn. If these alternate return points are not included in the READ statement and such an error occurs, control is usually returned to the operating system, a message is printed on the user's terminal, and execution is terminated.

The list-directed form of input is well suited to input from the terminal. List-directed input is also convenient for disk files where input data is mixed with explanatory comments about the input. In the discussion we assume that the input data comes from a disk file.

The data items to be read by list-directed input should be separated by spaces or commas. Each READ statement continues to read records until all variables in the variable list are given values. The next READ statement starts reading from the following record even though there may be unread data on the last record. This is demonstrated in Figure 5.1. This feature of list-directed

FORTRAN statements

```
READ(2,*) I, A, B, (S(K), K=1,3)
READ(2,*) J, C, D, (T(K), K=1,3)
```

Input data file

```
7 5.4 2.E-6 .167E-23 3.E-11 4.375E-12 2.223E-5 4.826E-7
2 3.5 4.E-7
7.67E10 4.33E3
8.997E2 5.924E4
```

Variables are assigned the following values

```
I      <— 7
A      <— 5.4
B      <— 2.E-6
S(1)   <— .167E-23
S(2)   <— 3.E-11
S(3)   <— 4.375E-12

J      <— 2
C      <— 3.5
D      <— 4.E-7
T(1)   <— 7.67E10
T(2)   <— 4.33E3
T(3)   <— 8.997E2
```

Figure 5.1 List-directed input (read records until variable list is satisfied, then skip the remainder of the last record).

input is useful for allowing the placement of comments in the file to describe the data. An empty file can be prepared with all of the comments in it and used as a "template" for the creation of input to the program. In this way the input file is self-documenting. In Figure 5.2 each READ statement reads a single number into the specified variable. The remainder of that input line is then ignored because each READ statement starts reading from a new record (line) in the file. Hence, the comments at the end of the lines are ignored by the FORTRAN program. The user must be careful that each line has enough data items to satisfy the number of entries in the variable list for that READ statement. If not, the program tries to read the comment characters and convert them to a fixed or floating point number. This generates an error condition. A general subroutine to read data files in this format is given in Figure 5.3. This subroutine can be used in any FORTRAN program to handle the list-directed input.

For list-directed output, FORTRAN has the statements

```
PRINT ,      variable list
WRITE(*,*)   variable list
WRITE(u,*)   variable list
```

The first two forms are the same. They write data in free format to the default output device, usually the user's terminal. In past years the default output device was the line printer. The third form writes data to the file attached to

FORTRAN statements to read file

```
      CHARACTER*10 COLOR
             .
             .
      READ(5,*) NCASE
      READ(5,*) IUTAPE
      READ(5,*) IOUT
      READ(5,*) IGRAPH
      READ(5,*) XMASS
      READ(5,*) XVOLUM
      READ(5,*) XTEMP
      READ(5,*) COLOR
```

Input data file

```
12                      ;Number of cases to evaluate
3                       ;Unit number for properties data tape
6                       ;Unit number for output
8                       ;Unit number for graphical output info
735.                    ;Mass of widget(grams)
792.                    ;Volume of widget(cm**3)
293.                    ;Temperature of widget(kelvin)
'BLACK'                 ;Color of widget
  .                           .
  .                           .
  .                           .
```

Figure 5.2 List-directed input with comments in the file.

```
      SUBROUTINE LDI( NIN, NREC, NLINE, A, IERR )
C  THIS SUBROUTINE READS LIST DIRECTED INPUT, WHERE COMMENTS CAN
C  BE PLACED AT THE END OF EACH LINE FOR DOCUMENTATION
C  INPUT    NIN    - UNIT SPECIFIER FOR LOGICAL INPUT DEVICE
C           NREC   - NUMBER OF RECORDS TO READ
C           NLINE  - NUMBER OF DATA ITEMS ON EACH RECORD
C  OUTPUT   A      - VECTOR OF DATA ITEMS THAT WERE READ
C           IERR   - CONDITION CODE 0=OKAY, 1=END OF FILE
C                    2=ERROR

      DIMENSION A(*)

C  IFIRST COUNTS THE NUMBER OF DATA ITEMS THAT ARE READ
      IFIRST = 1

C  LOOP OVER THE NUMBER OF RECORDS TO BE READ.  READ FROM EACH
C  AND PUT THE RESULTS SEQUENTIALLY IN THE VECTOR A.
      DO 10 N = 1,NREC
         READ(NIN,*,END=99,ERR=999)
     1      (A(I), I=IFIRST,IFIRST+NLINE-1)
         IFIRST = IFIRST + NLINE
   10 CONTINUE

C  NORMAL RETURN
      IERR = 0
      RETURN

C  END OF FILE RETURN
   99 IERR = 1
      RETURN

C  ERROR RETURN
  999 IERR = 2
      RETURN
      END
```

Figure 5.3 Subroutine to read list-directed input.

the unit specifier "u". Historically the lineprinter was associated with unit 6. Unit 6 is now the user's terminal. The output format is determined by the FORTRAN output routine and cannot be changed by the user. The list-directed form of output is not very desirable because the user has no control of the format that the output takes. This makes user-friendly output difficult. List-directed output is useful for printing output used for debugging purposes by the programmer because floating point numbers are written with enough decimal digits to cover the full precision of the mantissa. An example of list-directed output is shown in Figure 5.4 where the value of pi is printed in both single and double precision.

5.1.2. Fixed Format Input and Output

The most convenient form of output in FORTRAN is fixed format output. In this case the user specifies exactly how the data is written to the line printer or disk file using *formatting instructions*. The WRITE statement has the general form

```
      WRITE(UNIT=u,FMT=label,END=mmm,ERR=nnn) variable list
label FORMAT(...)
```

or, in a more common abbreviated form,

```
      WRITE(u,label,END=mmm,ERR=nnn) variable list
```

The WRITE statement includes the logical I/O unit specifier u and the statement label of a FORMAT statement that holds the formatting instructions. Again, the END= and ERR= alternate return points are optional. The variable list includes the variables that are written by this statement. While the WRITE statement is quite straightforward, the associated FORMAT statement

```
C  THIS PROGRAM DEMONSTRATES THE FORMAT OF LIST DIRECTED OUTPUT
C  BOTH A AND AA SHOULD BE EQUAL TO PI

      REAL A
      DOUBLE PRECISION AA

      A = 2. * ASIN(1.0)
      AA = 2.D0 * ASIN(1.D0)

      WRITE(6,*) A, AA

      STOP
      END

The output from this program executed on a DEC VAXstation 2000 is

   3.141593        3.141592653589793
```

Figure 5.4 List-directed output.

is complex. The formatting instructions are coded in a language of their own. To develop user-friendly, well-documented output, the syntax of this language must be mastered.

The FORMAT statement controls

1. The number of significant digits printed for each variable
2. Textual information, and
3. Carriage control and line formatting

The syntax of the FORMAT statement is elaborate. For all of the details the reader is referred to a text on FORTRAN 77 programming. A few examples that highlight common format options follow.

The simplest format to understand is the one for INTEGER variables. It has the form:

$$I\,n$$

where n is the number of decimal digits to print. Leading zeroes are printed as blanks. Figure 5.5a shows an example of this.

REAL variables are formatted in several different ways. The most common is the *E-type format* that looks like scientific notation. The format syntax for E-type format is

$$E\,n.m$$

where n is the number of characters to be used for the entire number and m is the number of decimal digits to print from the mantissa. For proper spacing n must be greater than or equal to $m + 7$ because the printed number takes the form

$$s0.xxxxxxEsyy$$

where the leftmost "s" is the sign of the number, xxxxxx is the mantissa, "E" designates the E-type format, the next "s" is the sign of the exponent, and yy is the exponent. Notice that there are 7 characters in addition to the mantissa and thus $n \geq m + 7$. If n is greater than $m + 7$, then the number is printed with leading blanks to make up the extra characters. An example of the E-type format is given in Figure 5.5b. Double-precision numbers are printed the same way, only using the D-type format:

$$D\,n.m$$

where all the same rules apply.

(a) INTEGER format

```
    J = 24
    WRITE(6,100) J
100 FORMAT(I6)
```

Appears as | 24

(b) REAL E—type format

```
    A = 1024.42
    WRITE(6,200) A
200 FORMAT(E12.5)
```

Appears as | 0.10244E 04

(c) Repeated formats

```
    I = 2457
    J = 9987
    WRITE(6,200) I,J
200 FORMAT(2I6)
```

Appears as | 2457 9987

(d) REAL E—type format with "P" modifier

```
    A = 1024.42
    WRITE(6,201) A
201 FORMAT(1P1E12.5)
```

Appears as | 1.02442E 03

(e) Text interspersed with numerical data

```
    J = 24
    A = 1024.42
    WRITE(6,300) J, A
300 FORMAT(' INDEX =', I6, ' RESULT=', 1P1E12.5)
```

Appears as | INDEX =   24   RESULT= 1.02442E 03

(f) Each WRITE starts a new line

```
    J = 24
    A = 1024.42
    WRITE(6,300) J
    WRITE(6,301) A
300 FORMAT(' INDEX =', I12)
301 FORMAT(' RESULT=', 1P1E12.5)
```

Appears as | INDEX =   24
          | RESULT= 1.02442E 03

(g) End—line—sentinel to start new line

```
    J = 24
    A = 1024.42
    WRITE(6,300) J, A
300 FORMAT(' INDEX =', I12/ ' RESULT=', 1P1E12.5)
```

Appears as | INDEX =   24
          | RESULT= 1.02442E 03

Figure 5.5 Different variable formats.

(h) Blank-space-sentinel to hold spaces

```
      J = 24
      A = 1024.42
      WRITE(6,300) J, A
  300 FORMAT(2X,'INDEX =', I12/ 2X, 'RESULT=', 1P1E12.5)
```

Appears as │ INDEX =   24
           │ RESULT= 1.02442E 03

(i) Carriage control characters

```
      J = 24
      A = 1024.42
      WRITE(6,300) J, A
  300 FORMAT('0  INDEX =', I12/ '0  RESULT=', 1P1E12.5)
```

│ ────Previous line of output────

Appears as │ INDEX =   24
           │
           │ RESULT= 1.02442E 03

(j) Multiple WRITEs to print columns of numbers

```
      DIMENSION A(3), B(3), C(3)
      DO 5 I = 1,3
        B(I) = ARCSIN(1.)
        A(I) = 2. * B(I)
        C(I) = B(I) / 2.
    5 CONTINUE
      WRITE(6,100)
      DO 10 I = 1,3
        WRITE(6,101) I, A(I), B(I), C(I)
   10 CONTINUE
  100 FORMAT(' #       PI        PI / 2     PI / 4'/' ')
  101 FORMAT(I2,1P3E12.4)
```

	#	PI	PI / 2	PI / 4
Appears as	1	3.1416E 00	1.5708E 00	7.8540E-01
	2	3.1416E 00	1.5708E 00	7.8540E-01
	3	3.1416E 00	1.5708E 00	7.8540E-01

(k) Single WRITE and FORMAT to print columns of numbers

```
      DO 10 I = 1,3
        WRITE(6,100) I, A(I), B(I), C(I)
   10 CONTINUE
  100 FORMAT(' #       PI        PI / 2     PI / 4'/' '/
     1       (I2,1P3E12.4))
```

	#	PI	PI / 2	PI / 4
Appears as	1	3.1416E 00	1.5708E 00	7.8540E-01
	2	3.1416E 00	1.5708E 00	7.8540E-01
	3	3.1416E 00	1.5708E 00	7.8540E-01

Figure 5.5 (*Continued*)

A series of INTEGER or REAL variables are printed with the same format by including a *repeater prefix* on the variable format:

$$rIn \quad \text{or} \quad rEn.m$$

where *r* is the number of times that the format should be repeatedly applied. An example is shown in Figure 5.5c.

The leading zero in the E-type format carries no information and is a slight deviation from standard scientific notation where a significant digit is usually put ahead of the decimal point. The number of digits appearing before the decimal point in an E-type format is controlled using the "P"-format modifier. This is shown in Figure 5.5d.

Textual information can be interspersed with numerical data. In the format instructions, textual information appears within apostrophes. This is shown in Figure 5.5e. The FORTRAN output routines format the output by moving sequentially through the format instructions, printing the text within the apostrophes, and printing the next variable in the variable list according to the format specification that comes next. The programmer must ensure that the variables in the list are matched with the variable formats in the format instructions. Each new WRITE statement starts on a new line as shown in Figure 5.5f.

The end of a line within a format instruction is designated with an end-of-line sentinel "/" as demonstrated in Figure 5.5g. Blank spaces are inserted using the text within apostrophes, by overspecifying the number of digits to print in an INTEGER format, or by overspecifying the number of spaces for a REAL E-type format (i.e., 1P1E15.5). Blank spaces are also specified using the blank-space-sentinel

$$nX$$

where n is the number of spaces to reserve. This is shown in Figure 5.5h.

The so-called *carriage control characters* are a holdover from the days when only line printers were available for printed output. The carriage control is the first character on each line. If this character is a blank, then this line is printed. If this character is a zero in ASCII (octal 60) or EBCDIC (octal 360), then a line is skipped before printing. If this character is a one in ASCII (octal 61) or EBCDIC (octal 361), then the line printer skips to the top of the next page before printing the line. This first character of each line is not printed on the line printer but is interpreted as a format instruction. This is demonstrated in Figure 5.5i.

A particularly difficult aspect of line formatting is the *implicit repeated format*. As discussed earlier, the FORTRAN write routines scan through the format instructions associated with a WRITE statement, printing the text and variables in the list according to the format specification. There are times when one wishes to repeat the same format, line after line. This is true when columns of subscripted variables are printed under column headings. This is accomplished by using the feature that each WRITE statement will start with a new line (Figure 5.5j). This same format is specified with a single WRITE and FORMAT statement combination by using the implicit repeated format feature as shown in Figure 5.5k. When the variable list in a WRITE statement has more variables than are specified in the associated format instructions, the

FORTRAN output routine repeats the format instructions that are contained within the deepest nested parentheses.

The use of all of these format instructions is demonstrated in Figure 5.6. Formatting output in this way is frustrating because errors are easily made in writing the format instructions. The FORTRAN I/O system routines have a *format interpreter* that evaluates the format specification every time it is used. The syntax of format instructions is often not inspected by the FORTRAN compiler for correctness and errors are therefore uncovered at execution time by the output routine rather than at compile time. For instance, it is the responsibility of the programmer to ensure that the first character in each line is correctly specified. The FORTRAN statements shown in Figure 5.7 would have the unintended effect displayed there. Implicit repeated formats must be within nested parentheses. The example in Figure 5.8 shows the unintended result of neglecting this rule.

5.1.3. Namelist Input and Output

The READ and WRITE statements discussed in the previous sections adhere strictly to the FORTRAN 77 standard. There is another important form of free format input and output called *NAMELIST input and output* that is not part of the FORTRAN 77 standard. Yet nearly all FORTRAN compilers support this versatile and useful feature. It is used in many large-scale FORTRAN programs and therefore it is necessary to discuss it. Because it is not part of the standard, it differs slightly for different computers. The examples used here are for the DEC VAX.

An example of the NAMELIST READ and WRITE is given in Figure 5.9. The variables to be inputted or outputted in a NAMELIST READ or WRITE are declared in a NAMELIST declaration at the head of the subprogram where the READ or WRITE appears. This list of variables is given a name as part of the NAMELIST declaration. This declaration has no effect on any other declaration involving the same variables. The variables can be local or in COMMON. The WRITE statement simply outputs all of the variables in the associated NAMELIST declaration in a free format determined by the FORTRAN output routine. The difference between the NAMELIST WRITE and

```
      WRITE(6,2020) R1A(1), U1B(1),
     1              (INDEX(J),R1A(J),DR2A(J),T3(J),COMPR(J),U1B(J),
     1              TR2A(J),TN2A(J),T38(J),PN2A(J),Q2B(J),  J=2,JMAX)
 2020 FORMAT('0'/'    #   ',
     1 'RADIUS     ZONE WIDTH   MASS DENS    COMPRESSION VELOCITY    ',
     2 'R TEMP     ION TEMP     MAG PRESS    ION PRESS   ART VISC'/
     3 '          ',
     3 '(CM)       (CM)         (G/CM3)      (V0/V)      (CM/S)     ',
     4 '(EV)       (EV)         (J/CM3)      (J/CM3)     (J/CM3) '/
     4 '  '/  0',1P1E12.4,36X,1P1E12.4/(I4,10E12.4))
```

Figure 5.6 Elaborate format statement and output generated by it.

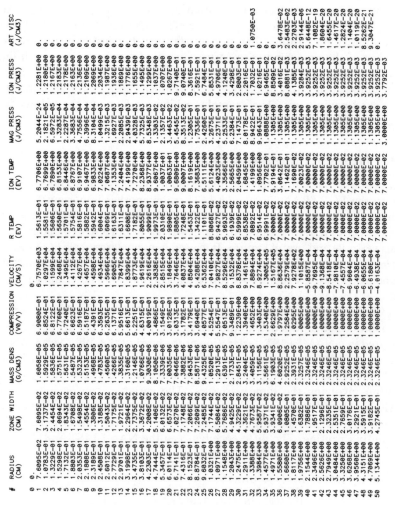

Figure 5.6 (*Continued*)

```
      I = 100
      J = 200
      WRITE(6,100) I,J
  100 FORMAT(2I3)
```

```
     |———top of a new page———
     |00 200
     |
```

Figure 5.7 Carriage control error.

the standard list-directed WRITE is that the NAMELIST WRITE also writes the names of the variables appearing in the NAMELIST declaration along with their values. Thus the output is self-documenting, albeit not very well formatted. The READ statement reads values for the variables in the NAMELIST declaration. However, it differs from the standard list-directed READ in the format of the input file. In the case of the NAMELIST READ the actual variable names are included along with the values to be assigned for them, much in the same way as an assignment statement. Notice that all variables in the NAMELIST declaration need not be included in the NAMELIST input file. Those that are not included retain their values from before the READ. In this way variables can be assigned *default values* before the READ and only those variables that need to be changed are included in the input file. This important feature is demonstrated in Figure 5.9.

This feature of allowing default values and only reading changes to these values makes the NAMELIST READ statement very useful for large-scale programs. Actual variable names appearing in the input may seem foreign to a user with no programming experience and this could be considered a draw-

```
      DIMENSION A(3), B(3), C(3)
      DO 5 I = 1,3
        B(I) = ARCSIN(1.)
        A(I) = 2. * B(I)
        C(I) = B(I) / 2.
    5 CONTINUE
      DO 10 I = 1,3
        WRITE(6,100) I, A(I), B(I), C(I)
   10 CONTINUE
  100 FORMAT(' #      PI       PI / 2      PI / 4'/' '/
     1        I2,1P3E12.4)
```

```
            |  #      PI       PI / 2      PI / 4
            |
Appears as  |  1  3.1416E 00  1.5708E 00  7.8540E-01
            |  #      PI       PI / 2      PI / 4
            |
            |  2  3.1416E 00  1.5708E 00  7.8540E-01
            |  #      PI       PI / 2      PI / 4
            |
            |  3  3.1416E 00  1.5708E 00  7.8540E-01
```

Figure 5.8 Implicit repeated format error.

```
C  A PROGRAM TO DEMONSTRATE THE FEATURES OF NAMELIST INPUT AND
C  OUTPUT.  INPUT VARIABLES ARE SET TO DEFAULT VALUES AND ONLY
C  THOSE REQUIRING DIFFERENT VALUES NEED BE INPUT.  NAMELIST
C  VARIABLES ARE EITHER LOCAL OR IN COMMON.

      PARAMETER( NIN=5, NOUT=6 )
      COMMON A(10), B, C, I

C  NAMELIST VARIABLES CAN BE BOTH LOCAL AND IN COMMON
      NAMELIST/VARS/ A, B, C, D, E, F, G, H ,I, J

C  SET DEFAULT VALUES
      DO 10 I = 1,10
      A(I) = 1.
   10 CONTINUE
      B = 10.
      C = 10.
      D = 10.
      E = 10.
      F = 10.
      G = 10.
      H = 10.
      I = 1
      J = 1

C  READ CHANGES TO DEFAULT VALUES
      READ(NIN,VARS)

C  WRITE ALL OF THE VARIABLES
      WRITE(NOUT,VARS)

      STOP
      END
```

```
Input file attached to unit specifier 5

 $VARS
   A(1)=3.,4.,5., B=2., J=8
 $END
```

```
Output file attached to unit specifer 6

 $VARS
 A     =   3.000000   ,   4.000000   ,  5.000000   ,  7*1.000000
 B     =   2.000000   ,
 C     =   10.00000   ,
 D     =   10.00000   ,
 E     =   10.00000   ,
 F     =   10.00000   ,
 G     =   10.00000   ,
 H     =   10.00000   ,
 I     =          1,
 J     =          8
 $END
```

Figure 5.9   NAMELIST READs and WRITEs.

back. However, most users of engineering applications software have some computer literacy and for them this represents a very convenient way to self-document the input so long as the variable names have some meaning.

The NAMELIST WRITE statement is not useful for general output because the formatting cannot be controlled by the programmer. However, it is useful for debugging purposes because it prints the maximum number of significant digits for each floating point variable, is easy to implement, and is self-documenting for the programmer familiar with the variable names.

5.1.4. Conversion From ASCII to Binary and Vice Versa

The character representation of a number in ASCII codes that the user types in from the terminal or that the computer sends back to the terminal is different from the binary representation of the number that the computer uses to perform arithmetic. Thus the computer must convert back and forth between these two representations. This conversion is done by the FORTRAN input and output system subroutines that are invoked when the program executes a formatted READ or WRITE statement. The FORMAT statement gives these subroutines guidelines to use for the conversion.

To demonstrate this explicitly we will work through an example. Suppose that the user executes the program in Figure 5.10. The following characters are transferred and conversions are made as the program is executed.

Step 1: `WRITE(6,*) 'INPUT MAXIMUM'`

These bits (in octal) are sent from the computer to the terminal.

```
111 116 120 125 124 040 115 101 130 111 115 125 115 015 012
 I   N   P   U   T       M   A   X   I   M   U   M   cr  lf
```

Step 2: The user types 2

These bits (in octal) are sent from the keyboard to the computer.

```
062 015
 2   cr
```

Step 3: The FORTRAN I/O routine converts the character 2 (octal 062) into the integer representation for 2. On a 32-bit computer integer 2 in two's complement notation is

00000000000000000000000000000010

```
      DIMENSION A(4)
      WRITE(6,*) 'INPUT MAXIMUM'
      READ(5,*) NMAX
      IF( NMAX .LE. 4 ) THEN
        WRITE(6,100) NMAX
        READ(5,*) (A(I), I=1,NMAX)
        WRITE(6,101) (A(I), 1,NMAX)
100     FORMAT( 'INPUT ',I1, ' ELEMENTS OF A')
101     FORMAT('0A='/(2E12.5))
      ENDIF
      STOP
      END
```

Figure 5.10 Program to demonstrate conversion from ASCII to binary and vice versa.

Step 4: The test is performed to compare the input to 4 and the test succeeds. Thus the computer sends to the terminal:

```
111 116 120 125 124 040 062 040 105 114 105 115 105 116 124 123
 I   N   P   U   T       2       E   L   E   M   E   N   T   S
                         |
                         |____NMAX
040 117 106 040 101 015 012
 O   F       A   cr  lf
```

where the FORTRAN I/O routines convert NMAX from

```
00000000000000000000000000000010   (binary)
```

to the equivalent ASCII code

```
00110010  or  062  in octal
```

Step 5. The user then types

```
12. 5.
```

and the following is transmitted from the keyboard to the computer:

```
061 062 056 040 065 056 015
 1   2   .       5   .   cr
```

Step 6: The FORTRAN I/O routines convert these two character representations of numbers into their binary floating point equivalents.

```
12. --> 01000010011000000000000000000000
        ||        ||
        ||_exp__||____mantissa_____|
        |
        |_sign
 5. --> 01000001110100000000000000000000
```

The exponent is 8 bits and the mantissa is 23 bits, biased by 128.

Step 7:

```
WRITE(*,100) (A(I), I=1,NMAX)
100 FORMAT('0A=' /(2E12.5))
```

Execution of this statement results in the conversion of the floating point binary representation of the first two elements of A into the character representation as specified in the FORMAT statement that is referenced in the WRITE statement. The following characters are transmitted to the terminal from the computer:

```
060 101 075 015 012
 0   A   =  cr  lf
060 056 061 062 060 060 060 105 040 060 061 040 060 056 065 060 060
 0   .   1   2   0   0   0   E       0   1       0   .   5   0   0
... 060 060 105 040 060 060 015 012 ...
     0   0   E       0   0  cr  lf
```

Notice that the first zero in the FORMAT statement is not interpreted as a carriage control but is printed. Terminals used to communicate with the computer generally do not interpret the first character of each line as a carriage control. Were the output sent to a disk file, the zero would again be retained. Only line printers interpret the leading character as a carriage control. Thus, if the line were sent to a line printer, it would be converted to

```
012 101 075 015 012
 lf  A   =  cr  lf
```

This rather extended example emphasizes the conversion from ASCII to binary and binary to ASCII that automatically occurs during communications with a FORTRAN program through formatted input and output. This conversion process is transparent to the user but should be kept clearly in mind by the programmer. More complex features of FORTRAN input and output require an understanding of the distinction between representing a number as a sequence of ASCII characters and the internal binary code for the number in either fixed or floating point notation. This conversion does not come for free. For programs with extensive I/O and few computations, a large fraction of their execution time is spent in the formatted input and output routines.

5.1.5. Using Character Variables as Format Instructions and Internal Files

A powerful feature of FORTRAN 77 is the CHARACTER variable. This data type was not available in earlier versions of FORTRAN. The CHARACTER variable is used to hold character information in the form of ASCII codes. These *character strings* are compared, concatenated, and separated into substrings. These features are generally discussed in beginning courses on FORTRAN programming. The CHARACTER variable is also useful in performing sophisticated input and output. It does this through two applications. The first is FORMAT definitions and the second is *internal files.*

The FORTRAN 77 language allows the specification of input and output formats through CHARACTER variables as well as FORMAT statements. Recall that in Section 5.1.2 we stated that format instructions are untouched by the FORTRAN compiler but are stored as character strings in the program and passed to the READ and WRITE routines where they are processed by an interpreter to control the input or output format. This processing of format instructions at execution time allows them to be stored in CHARACTER variables as an alternative to FORMAT statements. The contents of the FORMAT statement is fixed at compile time and cannot be changed, even though it is not used until execution time. The contents of CHARACTER variables can be changed at execution time, prior to their use as format instructions. This is demonstrated in Figure 5.11. The character string assigned to the CHARACTER variable FMT must be enclosed in apostrophes. The apostrophes within the character string must therefore be distinguished from the delimiters. This is done by using double apostrophes within the string to signify an actual single apostrophe. The format instructions are in exactly the same form in the CHARACTER variable as they are in the FORMAT statement, including the outer parentheses. When character strings are inputted using free format input, they must be enclosed within apostrophes to distinguish which characters are part of the string. Blanks cannot be used as delimiters for character strings because blanks are characters themselves. The versatility of specifying format instructions at execution time has endless possibilities for elaborate output formatting.

The use of CHARACTER variables as internal files allows a FORTRAN program to perform formatted input or output in two steps. For input, the program first reads a record in the form of ASCII characters from an input device and puts them into a CHARACTER variable called an internal file. Then a READ is done using this internal file as the "input device" and converts the character string into fixed and floating point numbers according to format instructions. For output the reverse is done. Using a formatted WRITE statement, fixed and floating point numbers are converted into an ASCII character string and are put into an internal file. Then a formatted WRITE statement writes the character string to an actual output device such as a disk file. Input and output using internal files are demonstrated in Figure 5.12. When writing to or reading from an internal file, the internal file name (CHARAC-

```
The three program fragments will give identical results.

(a)  Conventional static FORMAT statement

     WRITE(6,100) (A(I), I=1,100)
 100 FORMAT(' THE A VECTOR IS'/(1P10E12.4))

(b)  Fixed CHARACTER variable value

     CHARACTER*34 FMT
     FMT = '('' THE A VECTOR IS''/(1P10E12.4))'
     WRITE(6,FMT) (A(I), I=1,100)

(c)  Inputted CHARACTER variable value

     CHARACTER*34 FMT
     READ(5,*) FMT
     WRITE(6,FMT) (A(I), I=1,100)

where the user inputs from logical I/O unit 5

'('' THE VECTOR A IS''/(1P10E12.4))'
```

Figure 5.11 CHARACTER variables as format instructions.

```
      CHARACTER*80 CHARS
      CHARACTER*10 COUT

C  READ A LINE OF CHARACTERS INTO THE CHARACTER VARIABLE CHARS
      READ(5,'(A)') CHARS

C  READ CHARS AS AN INTERNAL FILE TO CONVERT ITS CONTENTS INTO
C  A FIXED POINT NUMBER
      READ(CHARS,*) NUM

C  PERFORM A COMPUTATION
      NUMSQ = NUM * NUM

C  CONVERT THE FIXED POINT RESULT INTO CHARACTERS BY WRITING
C  IT TO AN INTERNAL FILE
      WRITE(COUT,'(I4)') NUMSQ

C  ADD A COMMENT TO THE RESULT BY CONCATENATING A CHARACTER
C  STRING TO COUT
      CHARS = ' THE VALUE OF NUM SQUARED IS ' // COUT

C  WRITE THE CHARACTERS TO UNIT 6
      WRITE(6,100) CHARS
  100 FORMAT(A)
      STOP
      END
```

Figure 5.12 Using internal files for READs and WRITEs

TER variable name) is substituted for the unit specifier in the WRITE or READ statement. In Figure 5.12 we have also used another option for the format specification. Rather than referencing a FORMAT statement or using a CHARACTER variable in the WRITE statement, a character string is used in the position for the format specification. The format specification for reading or writing a CHARACTER variable is simply "A".

The input files for large-scale applications programs are often thousands of records in length. These files must be annotated with comment cards in order to be understandable to the user. Such files should also have two other features. There should be few rules regarding the order in which data values are entered in the file and *update records* should be allowed to overwrite values previously entered in the file. In this way a "base case" is established and modifications to it are simply entered as updates at the end of the file. Along with comment cards, this makes a complex input file self-documenting. In such a scheme each input record (or line in the file) usually begins with a character field that identifies the data that appears in the record. Hence, the record must be read once to ascertain the value of the identifier field and then read again to transfer the data to the variables where it belongs. An example of such an input file and the subroutine that reads it are given in Figures 5.13 and 5.14.

5.2. UNFORMATTED OR BINARY INPUT AND OUTPUT

A second general category of input and output is *unformatted* or *binary I/O*. Unformatted output, as the name suggests, does not translate numerical data

```
*  INPUT DECK FOR A COMPLICATED SIMULATION PROGRAM — A FLUID
*  DYNAMICS SOLVER PERHAPS.  PREPARED BY GAM ON 6/6/87 BUT WITH
*  UPDATES AT THE END
*
*               NUMBER OF      NUMBER OF     FIRST TIME    MAXIMUM
*               MESH POINTS    TIME STEPS    STEP          TIME
*
CONSTANT001     2000           1000          1.0           1000.0
*
*  BOUNDARY CONDITIONS ON EACH OF THE SURFACES, 1=REFLECTING AND
*  2=FREE SURFACE
*
*               LEFT BD.       RIGHT BD.     TOP BD.       BOTTOM BD.
*
CONSTANT0005    1              2             2             1
*
*  REGION DEFINITIONS WITH INITIAL DENSITY, PRESSURE, ETC.
*
*               LOWER LEFT INDICES      UPPER RIGHT INDICES
*               X    Y                  X    Y
*
REGION   0001   1    1                  20   25
*
DENSITY 0001    2.E-3
PRESSURE0001    0.1E6

                                  .
                                  .
                                  .

*  UPDATE 12/7/87  INCREASE THE PROBLEM TIME
CONSTANT0004     2000.0
*  UPDATE 12/8/87  INCREASE PROBLEM TIME AGAIN
CONSTANT0004     3000.0
```

Figure 5.13   Input file for large-scale software using internal files.

from its internal (or binary) form to ASCII characters using a format instruction. The same is true for unformatted input; the data is not converted to binary format when read by the program, but must already be in binary format. The form of these statements is

```
WRITE(u)    variable list
READ(u)     variable list
```

where "u" is a unit specifier and "variable list" is a list of variables. Unformatted I/O is useful when large amounts of data are saved and read back at a later point in the program or by a subsequent program. A program fragment that demonstrates this is shown in Figure 5.15.

Unformatted WRITEs save CPU time and space on disk files in comparison to formatted WRITEs. Converting binary numbers to ASCII characters using the FORMAT statement requires a substantial amount of CPU time. The FORTRAN I/O routines have an interpreter within them that interprets the FORMAT statements every time formatted I/O is done. A number in character format can take up more space on the disk than a binary number. The floating point number 474.5382 written in 1P1E14.7 format requires 14 characters to be represented.

```
      SUBROUTINE INPUT(
     1                  IN,
     3                  NRECRD)

C   THIS SUBROUTINE READS RECORDS FROM I/O UNIT SPECIFIER 'IN'
C   AND PUTS THE RESULTS INTO THE APPROPRIATE VARIABLES.   IT
C   RETURNS THE TOTAL NUMBER OF RECORDS READ IN 'NRECRD'

      COMMON
     1       CONST(1000), REGION(1000), XLL(1000), YLL(1000),
     2       XUR(1000), YUR(1000), DENSTY(1000), PRESS(1000)
                            .
                            .
                            .

      CHARACTER*80 INLINE

C   READ THE INPUT LINE INTO AN INTERNAL FILE

   10 READ(IN,'(A)',END=999) INLINE

C   IGNORE COMMENT LINES

      IF(INLINE(1:1) .EQ. '*') GOTO 10

C   DETERMINE THE INPUT LINE IDENTIFIER AND RETURN AN INTEGER
C   INDEX ASSIGNED TO THAT IDENTIFIER

      CALL TYPE(
     1          INLINE(1:8),
     3          IDENT)

C   CONVERT THE LINE IDENTIFIER NUMBER TO INTEGER BY READING
C   THE INTERNAL FILE SUBSTRING

      READ(INLINE(9:12),'(I4)') LNUMB

C   PROCESS EACH INPUT LINE TYPE DIFFERENTLY

      GOTO (100,200,300), IDENT

C   PROCESS 'CONSTANT' LINE

  100 CONTINUE

C  .DETERMINE THE NUMBER OF CONSTANTS AND THE LINE LENGTH
C   THEN READ THE LINE INTO THE APPROPRIATE VARIABLES USING A
C   FORMATTED READ OF THE INTERNAL FILE

      CALL PARSE(
     1          INLINE(13:80),
     3          NN,MEND)
      READ(INLINE(13:MEND),'(E12.4)') (CONST(LNUMB-1+L), L=1,NN)

      GOTO 900

C  PROCESS 'REGION  ' LINE

  200 CONTINUE
                    .
                    .
                    .
```

Figure 5.14 Subroutine segment to read data file with identifiers at the beginning of each record and with comments.

```
WRITE(11) NMAX
WRITE(11) AVE, STDEV, (DATA(I), I=1,NMAX)
        .
        .
REWIND 11
READ(11) NMAX
READ(11) X, Y, (Z(J), J=1,NMAX)
        .
        .
```

Figure 5.15 Using unformatted WRITEs and READs to save and retrieve data.

```
040 064 056 067 064 065 063 070 062 060 105 040 060 062
  4   .   7   4   5   3   8   2   0   E       0   2
```

These 14 characters require 14 bytes in a disk file. On a computer with a 32-bit word, this represents 3.5 words. If stored in binary format,

```
01000011111011010100010011100100 (IEEE Format)
```

it requires only four bytes, the number required to store one single-precision floating point number. Furthermore, the binary format ensures that the number does not lose any of its precision when read from the file and reused. Using formatted output the binary number is converted to a character string of the *decimal equivalent* of the number. The reverse is true when the number is read back into the program. Unless the format allows enough decimal digits to capture the full precision of the binary number, there will be a slight error in its value when read back into the program.

Unformatted information is almost never created directly by the user. Instead, it is created by a program through an unformatted WRITE, to be subsequently read by the same program or a different program. Each execution of a binary WRITE statement creates a *record* in the file that receives the information. This is shown schematically in Figure 5.16. When this information is read back into a program by binary READ statements, there must be a correspondence between the amount of information requested on the execution of the READ statement and the amount of information in the record to be read. Each READ statement reads back less than or the equivalent of the amount of information in the next record in the file. Should the READ statement request more information than is in the next record, an error message will result. In other words, a single READ statement does not read more than one record. If the READ statement requests less than the amount of information in the next record, this information is read and the remainder of the record is discarded. The next READ statement reads from the following record. This is again shown schematically in Figure 5.16. This is in contrast to formatted READs where records continue to be read until all of the variables in the variable list are provided values.

Unformatted output and input have the advantage of efficiently transfer-

```
WRITE(15) LENTH1, LENTH2, LENTH3, LENTH4, LENTH5
WRITE(15) (DATA1(I), I=1,1000)
WRITE(15) (DATA2(I), I=1,1050)
WRITE(15) (DATA3(I), I=1,400)
WRITE(15) (DATA4(I), I=1,800)
WRITE(15) (DATA5(I), I=1,650)
                .
                .
C  READ BACK DATA SETS DATA2 AND DATA5 INTO WORK2 AND WORK5
C  SKIPPING OVER DATA SETS DATA1, DATA3, AND DATA4
       REWIND 15
       READ(15) LENTH1, LENTH2, LENTH3, LENTH4, LENTH5
       READ(15) DUMMY
       READ(15) (WORK2(I), I=1,LENTH2)
       READ(15) DUMMY
       READ(15) DUMMY
       READ(15) (WORK5(I), I=1,LENTH5)
```

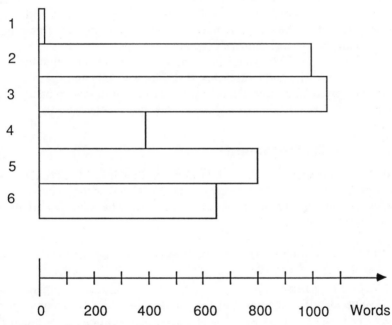

Figure 5.16 Using unformatted READs and WRITEs to skip over records.

ring information from program to disk file or magnetic tape and back again to a program. They have the disadvantage of not allowing the user to "see" the information, since it is coded in binary format and is unrecognizable if printed out at the terminal or on the line printer. For this reason it is best to use binary format for static information, such as tables of properties of materials, steam tables for instance, or for intermediate results that only have a short lifetime, such as data to be processed by a graphical postprocessor. Binary information is of course not transferrable between different types of computers and so is normally restricted to use on the one computer on which it is created.

5.3. DISK FILES

FORTRAN 77 programs are best suited to solving large-scale scientific problems on mainframe computers. The most common method of input and output in large-scale computation is through disk files. The user, with the aid of a screen editor, types input into a disk file. This disk file is then associated with a logical unit specifier in the FORTRAN program and all READ statements that reference this I/O unit will read from the associated file. The same is true for output. The FORTRAN program writes to a I/O unit specifier that is associated with a disk file. This disk file can be later viewed with a screen editor. The FORTRAN program may write directly to the line printer, but this is not common on most modern computer systems.

The FORTRAN 77 language has a number of statements that are used to manipulate disk files and to associate disk files with I/O unit specifiers. These statements often have equivalents in the operating system command language and are therefore not used to the extent they might otherwise be.

5.3.1. OPEN Statement

A disk file is associated with a I/O unit specifier in a FORTRAN program through use of the OPEN statement. The OPEN statement contains information concerning the characteristics of the disk file. The following are the arguments in the OPEN statement:

UNIT=*u*. The unit identifier specifies the I/O unit number to be associated with the disk file.

FILE=*filename*. Where *filename* is a character expression whose value identifies the name of the file to associate with the unit specifier.

STATUS=*sta*. Where *sta* is a character expression whose value is OLD, NEW, SCRATCH, or UNKNOWN. OLD is used if the file already exists, NEW is used if the file does not yet exist, SCRATCH is used if the file is to be destroyed after the program execution, and UNKNOWN is used if the status is unknown. If STATUS is not given the default is UNKNOWN.

ACCESS=*acc*. Where *acc* is a character expression whose value is SEQUENTIAL or DIRECT. This specifier establishes the access method. More discussion about sequential and direct access files comes later. If ACCESS is not given, then the default is SEQUENTIAL.

FORM=*fm*. Where *fm* is a character expression whose value is FORMATTED or UNFORMATTED. It specifies whether the file is to hold formatted or unformatted (binary) information. Notice that a file cannot hold a combination of these in FORTRAN 77. If FORM is omitted, then FORMATTED is assumed for SEQUENTIAL files and UNFORMATTED is assumed for DIRECT files.

RECL=`length`. Where *length* is an integer expression with positive value that specifies the record length for direct access files.

To connect an existing formatted sequential-access file named INPUT to I/O unit 3, the following statement is used:

```
OPEN(UNIT=3, FILE='INPUT', STATUS='OLD',
1 ACCESS='SEQUENTIAL', FORM='FORMATTED')
```

To connect a new unformatted sequential-access file named OUTPUT to I/O unit 4, one uses

```
OPEN(UNIT=4, FILE='OUTPUT', STATUS='NEW',
1        FORM='UNFORMATTED')
```

5.3.2. REWIND Statement

If a sequential file must be read more than once during a program execution, then the file is "rewound" back to the beginning using the REWIND statement. This is quite obviously a carryover from the old days when magnetic tapes were more commonly used. However, the same concept holds for a sequential file. The form of this statement is very simple.

```
REWIND (UNIT=u) or REWIND u
```

where u is the I/O unit specifier.

5.3.3. CLOSE Statement

After a file is used, it is detached from a I/O unit specifier by using the CLOSE statement. The CLOSE statement has a list of arguments just as the OPEN statement does.

UNIT=*u*. Where *u* is the I/O unit specifier associated with the file to be detached.

ERR=*s*. Where *s* is a statement label in the subroutine where the CLOSE statement is executed. Control is transferred to this statement label if an error condition exists.

STATUS=*sta*. Where *sta* is a character expression whose value is KEEP or DELETE. If the value is KEEP, then the file is retained after detachment. If the value is DELETE, then the file is deleted after detachment. In the case of a SCRATCH file, it is always deleted. For other files the default value is KEEP.

To close the file attached to unit 2, we use

```
CLOSE (UNIT=2)
```

5.3.4. Sequential Access and Direct Access Files

The FORTRAN 77 language supports two different types of disk files: sequential and direct access files. Sequential access files, as the name implies, must be read and written one record at a time. To read the tenth record in the file, the first nine records must first be read. The example in Figure 5.16 is an unformatted sequential file. Sequential access files have records of varying length and contain either formatted or unformatted information. This is all specified in the OPEN statement that assigns the file to the logical I/O unit specifier in the FORTRAN program.

```
$ ASSIGN 3 = INFILE.DAT
$ ASSIGN 9 = OUTFILE.DAT
$ RUN PROG.EXE
                .
                .
                .
        READ(3,*) A, B, C
        READ(3,*) (DATA(I), I=1,100)
                .
                .
        WRITE(9,100) X, Y, Z
        WRITE(9,101) (DATA(I), RESULT(I), I=1,100)
    100 FORMAT(' THE VALUES OF X, Y, AND Z ARE'/1P3E12.4)
    101 FORMAT(' THE RESULTS ARE'/' '/(1P2E12.4,5X,2E12.4))
                .
                .
                .
$RUN PROG
                .
                .
                .
        OPEN( UNIT=3, FILE='INFILE.DAT' )
        OPEN( UNIT=9, FILE='OUTFILE.DAT' )
                .
                .
        READ(3,*) A, B, C
        READ(3,*) (DATA(I), I=1,100)
                .
                .
        WRITE(9,100) X, Y, Z
        WRITE(9,101) (DATA(I), RESULT(I), I=1,100)
    100 FORMAT(' THE VALUES OF X, Y, AND Z ARE'/1P3E12.4)
    101 FORMAT(' THE RESULTS ARE'/' '/(1P2E12.4,5X,2E12.4))
                .
                .
                .
```

Figure 5.17 Using equivalent operating system commands in place of OPEN statements.

Record #

1	297	64	0	5627	38
2	374	50	2249	5	750
1096	1020	3521	47	3740	4121
4	2422	7	874	13	97
502	23	594	199	75	186

Figure 5.18 Schematic picture of a direct access file.

Sequential access files are the default file type for FORTRAN programs. Consequently, OPEN statements for sequential access files are usually unnecessary because files are assigned to I/O unit specifiers through operating system commands. The two sequences shown in Figure 5.17 produce identical results on the Digital Equipment Corporation VAX VMS Operating System.

Direct access files allow FORTRAN programs to reference any record in the file without reading all of the records that precede it. To allow this, all records are the same length and each record is given a *record number* to reference it. Direct access files require an explicit declaration using an OPEN statement. The record length is specified in the OPEN statement for the file. The FORTRAN READ statement specifies the record to be read using the record number. A schematic picture of a direct access file is shown in Figure 5.18.

Direct access files are a very powerful feature when specific data must be selected from a large quantity of data in a file (i.e., data base applications). Records need not be written with sequential record numbers because they are read back by reference to the record number and not their relative position in the file. Example of direct access WRITEs and READs are given in Figure 5.19. The record length is 25 because each number is written in I5 format (with five characters) and there are five numbers in each record. If the direct access file in Figure 5.18 were read by the program fragment in Figure 5.19, then the vector ITEM1 would contain the data

23 594 199 75 186

```
        .
        .
   OPEN( UNIT=3, FILE='INFILE.DAT', ACCESS='DIRECT',
  1       FORM='FORMATTED', RECL=25 )
        .
        .
   READ(UNIT=3,FMT='(5I5)',REC=502) (ITEM1(I), I=1,5)
        .
        .
   READ(UNIT=3,FMT='(5I5)',REC=1096) (ITEM2(I), I=1,5)
```
Figure 5.19 Reading from a direct access file.

and the vector ITEM2 would contain the data

1020 3521 47 3740 4121

EXERCISES

1. Discuss the default input and output unit specifiers on the computer system that you are using. Are they the terminal keyboard and screen? What numbers are designated for them? Does the operating system have commands to "attach" files to user-defined I/O unit specifiers? What are these commands? Is a file automatically created if an output unit specifier is referenced? If so, what name is the file given?

2. Write a main program that calls the subroutine written in problem 4 of Chapter 4. This main program should prompt the user for the name of a file. The name is then inputted from the keyboard and this file is used as the input to the same problem solved in problem 4 of Chapter 4. Use an OPEN statement to attach the file name to the I/O unit specifier.

3. Using the WRITE statement and the output given below determine the FORMAT statement that produces this output.

```
   WRITE(6,100)   A, B, C, (I,D(I),E(I),F(I),G(I),
1                  I=1,3)
```

```
|                   A.............1.2E 02
|                   B.............3.2E 02
|                   C.............6.7E 02
|         D           E            F            G
| 1    4.67E-03    7.54E-04    1.21E-01    2.22E-04
| 2    9.48E 03    6.28E 02    5.19E 01    3.39E 00
| 3    3.82E 01    8.40E 02    3.96E 02    1.18E 00
```

4. Write a program that reads the following set of data using free format input. Then write the data into different sequential files using formatted output, unformatted (binary) output, and NAMELIST output. Write the data into a direct access file using binary output. Write a second program that reads each of these four files and writes the output in formatted form to show that each data set remains identical to its initial value. Use the same I/O unit specifier for all of the READs and WRITEs and use OPEN and CLOSE statements to reassign it to different files.

```
   5.    10.    15.    20.    25.
   1.     2.     3.     4.     5.
  -5.   -10.   -15.   -20.   -25.
 1.E4   1.E5   1.E6   1.E7   1.E8
```

5. What is wrong with the following program segments? How would you fix them?

(a)
```
        WRITE(6,100) A, B, (C(I), I=1,100)
    100 FORMAT(' THE MEAN IS                      ',E12.4/
      1         ' THE STANDARD DEVIATION IS',E12.4/
      2         ' THE DATA IS                    ',10E12.4)
```

(b)
```
        DIMENSION A(100), B(25), C(10,2),
        DIMENSION X(100), Y(25), Z(20)
            .
            .
        WRITE(8) (A(I), I=1,100)
        WRITE(8) (B(I), I=1,25)
        WRITE(8) (C(I,1), I=1,10)
        WRITE(8) (C(I,2), I=1,10)
            .
            .
        REWIND 8
        READ(8) (X(I), I=1,100)
        READ(8) (Y(I), I=1,25)
        READ(8) (Z(I), I=1,20)
```

▬ 6

Programming Style

In recent years, with the increased emphasis on structured computer languages such as Pascal and C, there has also been an emphasis on well-written programs. Programs are no longer judged only on the basis of their execution performance. The source program must also have *style*. Good programming style leads to improvements in three areas:

1. Readability of the program
2. Error-free program writing, and
3. Modification of the existing program

Readability of the program is obvious. A well-documented program with meaningful variable names, indentation, and liberal use of spaces in line formatting is easier to understand than one with no comments, obscure variable names, and no spaces. The subroutine in Figure 4.1 is shown again in Figure 6.1 with all of the line formatting and comments removed. The variable names have also been changed. The difference in readability is striking.

Consistent programming style also leads to more error-free program writing. This connection is not quite so obvious. If statements are always written in exactly the same format, then the programmer makes fewer syntax errors when originally writing the program. This idea is analogous to the professional golfer who always goes through exactly the same routine before hitting each shot. Consistent repetition leads to fewer errors because the programmer automatically knows what is to be written next. In Figure 6.2 we have modified the program in Figure 4.1 to show the effects of inconsistent line formatting.

```
                    SUBROUTINE BUBBLE(V,L)
                    DIMENSION V(L)
                    LOGICAL XX
                    XX=.TRUE.
          50        DO 10 I=1,L-1
                    IF( V(I).GT.V(I+1)) THEN
                    X =V(I)
                    V(I)=V(I+1)
                    V(I+1)= X
                    XX=.FALSE.
                    END IF
          10 CONTINUE
                    IF(XX)RETURN
                    XX=.TRUE.
                    GOTO 50
                    END
```

Figure 6.1 Subroutine with no comments or line formatting and with poor variable name choices.

The program is less "attractive" than the original version. The real difference cannot be fully seen because it comes in the thoughts of the programmer as the source program is written.

Consistent style also makes the program easier to modify. This is a practical consequence of writing the same expressions in exactly the same way on each

```
           SUBROUTINE BUBBLE( VECTOR,LENGTH)

   C  THIS SUBROUTINE PERFORMS A BUBBLE SORT OF DATA INTO ASCENDING
   C  ORDER
   C  INPUT   — VECTOR – RAW DATA (REAL VECTOR)
   C            LENGTH – NUMBER OF ELEMENTS IN THE VECTOR
   C  OUTPUT — VECTOR – SORTED DATA

           DIMENSION VECTOR(LENGTH)
           LOGICAL DONE

   C.....SET THE DONE SWITCH TO .TRUE. TO START
                    DONE=.TRUE.

   C  MAKE A PASS THROUGH THE DATA AND INTERCHANGE ELEMENTS THAT
   C     ARE OUT OF ORDER
           5 DO 10 I=1,LENGTH-1
                IF( VECTOR(I).GT.VECTOR(I+1) ) THEN
                TEMP= VECTOR(I)
                    VECTOR(I)=VECTOR(I+1)
                    VECTOR(I+1) =TEMP
                    DONE=.FALSE.
                END IF
           10                   CONTINUE

   C  CHECK TO SEE IF ANY CHANGES WERE MADE ON THIS PASS, IF NO
   C  CHANGES WERE MADE THEN THE DATA IS SORTED
                IF(DONE)RETURN

   C.....CHANGES WERE MADE, RESET THE SWITCH AND TRY AGAIN
           DONE = .TRUE.
                        GOTO 5
           END
```

Figure 6.2 Subroutine with inconsistent line formatting.

occurrence. Suppose that all calls to the bubble sort subroutine must be changed from

```
CALL BUBBLE(...
to
CALL SORT(...
```

If the CALL statements are written in different ways, such as

```
CALLBUBBLE(...
CALL   BUBBLE(...
CALL BUBBLE(...
```

then a search and replace for "CALL BUBBLE(" using a file editor will not find all occurrences of the subroutine call. In a large program this leads to time-consuming multiple searches and makes modification inefficient. An undetected occurrence of CALL BUBBLE(is not recognized until link time when an "unresolved external reference" error is issued by the linker.

Structured programming uses the available language features to construct a logically well-structured program. Programming style involves how this source program appears to the programmer and other programmers who might have to maintain or modify it. Programming style is unique to each individual. There is no "correct" style. Each person must develop a style that they are most comfortable with. In the following sections we offer suggestions of style rules for FORTRAN 77. Some subset of these suggestions and perhaps other personal ones should be those used by a given individual.

6.1. VARIABLE NAMES AND DEFAULT VARIABLE TYPES

In the FORTRAN 77 standard, variables, parameters, subprogram names, and COMMON block names may have up to six alphanumeric characters and must start with A–Z. Lower case letters are not allowed. Many FORTRAN compilers allow more than six characters for a variable or subroutine name and most allow lower case letters. The temptation to use more than six characters for a variable name is great since this enhances the readability of the program. It is unfortunate that FORTRAN 77 does not allow longer names. Modern languages like Pascal do allow longer names such as Bubble_sort. The short names in FORTRAN are a holdover from the days when cards were used and long names resulted in more cards to carry around.

There are six different variable types in FORTRAN 77. These are given in Table 6.1. All scalar variables default to either INTEGER or REAL depending on the first character in their name. Other variable types and all subscripted variables must be explicitly declared. Notice that FORTRAN 77 does *not* in-

TABLE 6.1 Variable Types in FORTRAN 77

Variable	Initial Character
Integer	I–N
Real	A–H, O–Z
Logical	—
Character	—
Double-precision	—
Complex	—

clude the variable types REAL*4, REAL*8, INTEGER*2, INTEGER*4, and the like. These variable types are common in DEC and IBM FORTRAN languages and are almost universally recognized by other compilers but are not part of the standard. The *n refers to the number of bytes in each variable. Thus REAL*4 is single precision and REAL*8 is double precision. INTEGER*4 is equivalent to INTEGER and INTEGER*2 is a *half-word integer* that has no equivalent in FORTRAN 77.

The feature of default variable typing is unique to FORTRAN. In Pascal all variables must be explicitly declared. In BASIC there is no distinction between integer and real. There is a difference of opinion about the use of the default-naming conventions for real and integer variables. Some say adherence to the convention is good. An extra character placed at the head of the name forces the proper default typing for real and integer variables that would not otherwise have the correct type specification.

```
IMPED   --> AIMPED or XIMPED     impedance
INDUCT  --> AINDUC or XINDUC     inductance
COUNT   --> ICOUNT or NCOUNT     counter
```

If this is done it is recommended that the same character always be used for this purpose.

This approach has the advantage of *localizing* the understanding of the variable type. The programmer knows the variable type immediately from the name of the variable and need not infer it from the context in which the variable is used. There is no need to scan back in the program listing to the head of the subroutine to look at the declaration. Localization of understanding is thought to be important to productive, error-free programming.

Another school of thought says that names should be chosen without regard to default types and declarations should be used when necessary to modify the typing.

```
REAL IMPED, INDUCT
INTEGER COUNT
```

The last approach dictates that all variables be explicitly declared regardless of their default type. This is called *strong typing* and is mandatory in Pascal, for example.

```
REAL VOLTAG, CURENT, RESIST, IMPED, INDUCT
INTEGER I, J, COUNT
```

The difficulty with this approach is that one cannot "turn off" the default conventions in the FORTRAN compiler. Thus, if one forgets to declare a variable, the FORTRAN compiler does not flag this as an undeclared variable as the Pascal compiler would. It simply assigns it the default type that it deserves. This problem is partially circumvented by tricking the compiler. This is done by initially declaring all variables to be a type that is not used in the program using the IMPLICIT declaration statement and then declaring all variables used in the program in explicit declarations.

```
IMPLICIT COMPLEX (A-Z)
REAL VOLTAG, CURENT, RESIST, IMPED, INDUCT
INTEGER I, J, COUNT
```

Here we are assuming that the program uses no complex variables. By using this IMPLICIT COMPLEX statement the compiler is told that all variables beginning with the letters A–Z are to be complex unless overridden by an explicit declaration. At the end of the compiler listing, where the variables are all listed and assigned addresses, any undeclared variables "stick out" as COMPLEX and are thus identified as undeclared. An editor can be used to scan the compiler listing file for occurrences of the character string printed for complex variables. A better approach would of course be to have a compiler option that required all explicit declarations, but again FORTRAN 77 does not have this.

Since the purpose of programming style is to make the program more understandable, we suggest that consistency is the key in the case of variable declarations. Either forcing the name to be of the correct default type or the strong typing with all variables declared is the best approach. The worst method is using declarations only when the variable does not match the default type.

The choice of variable names is extremely important. Variable names should mean something.

Good Names		*Bad Names*	
TEMPER	VOLTAG	A	BB
VELOC	CURRNT	A1	X
DENSTY	RESIST	O	I
VISCOS	STRESS	AO	II

One should always be very careful about zero's and oh's. They are confusing and lead to many errors. There may be thousands of different variables in a large application program. To keep track of these variables they should be named in some *systematic* way.

The variable names may be related to the algorithm or numerical method used to solve the engineering problem. Suppose the program is solving partial differential equations with the independent variables being time (t) and one spatial dimension (x). These quantities are discretized in finite difference solutions as shown in Figure 6.3. Quantities on the boundaries of the finite difference cells are denoted with the character 1 and those at the centers of the cells are labeled with the character 2. Quantities evaluated at time ($n + 1$) are labeled with A, those at time ($n + 1/2$) are labeled with B, those at time (n) with C, and so on. Thus, the appearance of

$$\text{TEMP2B(J)}$$

can easily be recognized as the temperature evaluated at the jth cell center at time ($n + 1/2$). No matter what the application, the variable names should be assigned in a systematic way. Careful planning of this before any programming is done is important.

6.2.   SUBSCRIPTED VARIABLE DECLARATIONS

The FORTRAN language offers several ways to declare subscripted variables. Consistent use of each of these declarations for different purposes provides better self-documentation of the program. As an example, always use the DIMENSION statement to define actual storage for variables. Use the REAL and INTEGER statements to define the variable as a vector in the dummy argument list of a subroutine. This is demonstrated in Figure 6.4. This distinc-

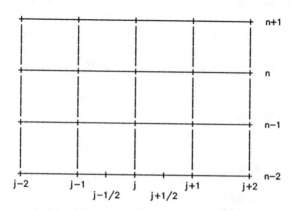

Figure 6.3   Finite difference space-time mesh.

tion of using different statements for variable storage definition and declaration of dummy arguments is a powerful way of explicitly showing for which subroutine the variables are local. It is also a reminder that dummy arguments are not true variables, but only aliases for actual variables in the calling subprogram.

6.3. STATEMENT FORMATTING

Use of blanks and indentation makes the source program more readable. The examples used throughout this text make this point. Consistent use of indentation aligns the various levels of nesting in the program. It always looks better to right-justify the statement labels rather than starting them in column 1. In any event, it is best to keep statement labels out of column 1 since this column is used to hold the line printer carriage control characters in some processors. So if your program is in a file that is listed by one of these processors, it can send the line printer wild. Blanks in a statement make it easier to read. Blank lines are allowed in FORTRAN 77 and can be used to set apart blocks of statements.

Blank spaces have a different meaning in FORTRAN than they do in most other modern languages. Blank spaces are usually thought to delimit expressions or *keywords* in most programming languages. In FORTRAN, blank spaces play no such role. They are totally superfluous to the syntax. The expression

```
DO10I=1,100
```

```
C  MAIN CALLING PROGRAM
C  DEFINE LOCAL VECTORS WITH LENGTH OF 100 USING "DIMENSION
C  STATEMENT"
       DIMENSION VAR1(100)
       DIMENSION VAR2(100)
       DIMENSION VAR3(100)
          .
          .
       CALL VMULT(VAR1,VAR2,VAR3,100)
          .
          .
       END

       SUBROUTINE VMULT(VEC1,VEC2,VEC3,LENGTH)
          .
C  DECLARE DUMMY ARGUMENTS AS VECTORS USING "REAL STATEMENT"
       REAL VEC1(*)
       REAL VEC2(*)
       REAL VEC3(*)
          .
          .
```

Figure 6.4 Use subscripted variable declarations consistently to identify true variables and dummy arguments.

is a legitimate FORTRAN statement. In fact, variable names may have blanks within them. The expressions

```
DO10IN DEX=1,100   and   DO 10 INDEX = 1,100
```

are treated the same by the FORTRAN compiler. Therefore blanks may be used wherever necessary to make the program more readable.

Just as with variable naming, consistent statement format style is important. One should choose a style for spacing each type of FORTRAN statement and always use this same format. Use the same format to

1. Indent IF-THEN-ELSE constructs
2. Indent statement labels
3. Place blanks within the statement
4. Signify continuation lines, and
5. Tabulate variable names in COMMON blocks

6.4. SUBROUTINE FORMAT STYLE

6.4.1. Argument List Structure

Argument lists for subroutine calls and dummy argument lists at the head of subroutines must match in the number and type of arguments. This is shown in Figure 6.5. One good way to identify which variables in argument lists are "input" variables and which are "output" variables is to group them together as shown in Figure 6.5. One might use a continuation line character of *one* for all arguments whose value is used by the subroutine but should not be changed (input arguments), use a value of *two* for arguments that enter the subroutine

```
C  CALLING SUBPROGRAM
            .
         CALL TABLE(
        1 YTAB, XTAB, NTAB, X,
        2
        3 Y, NINT, IERR)
            .
            .
         END
            .
         SUBROUTINE TABLE(
        1 YTAB, XTAB, NTAB, X,
        2
        3 Y, NINT, IERR)
            .
            .
```

Figure 6.5 Argument and dummy argument list formats for self-documentation of input and output arguments.

with one value and leave with another value (updated arguments), and use *three* for arguments that enter the subroutine with values that make no difference but return with computed values (output arguments). This format allows the programmer to easily distinguish which dummy variables in the subroutine correspond to the actual variables in the calling argument list. This is a good example of how programming style helps make the program self-documenting.

6.4.2. Overall Subroutine Structure

The overall subroutine structure, especially the placement of nonexecutable statements, should be consistent for all subroutines. An extreme example of this is shown in Figure 6.6. Declarations appear in a specific order and each kind of declaration is headed by a comment statement. In this way the programmer knows exactly where to look for each type of statement. If one is not seen, then it is safe to assume that there are no other occurrences of the statement somewhere else in the subroutine. The comment statement headers could be put into a file and a copy of this file could be used as the starting point for the creation of each new subroutine.

Another good practice is to use the SAVE statement at the beginning of each subroutine, just to be sure that local variables are saved in the way that they were intended to be. This also helps others who might be implementing the program on some other computer where local variables are not saved.

6.5. COMMENT STATEMENTS

Comment statements document the source program and provide information for the programmer. The content of comments is more important than the number of them, although a rule of thumb is that roughly 20–30% of the source program lines should be comments. Comments are divided into two kinds: those at the beginning of a subprogram that describe the function of the subprogram and its inputs and outputs, and those in the body of the subprogram that describe the computation. Comments at the beginning of the subprogram should be in a standard format that is agreed on by all members of the software development team before programming is begun. An example is shown in Figure 6.6. This block of comments should include:

1. A concise description of the function of the subprogram
2. A list of the input and output dummy arguments with definitions

Other information that often appears in this comment block is as follows:

3. All subprograms that call this subprogram
4. All subprograms that this subprogram calls

```
      SUBROUTINE GLGAS(
    1 DENSTY, TEMP, JMAX,
    2
    3 PRESS, ENERGY)

*********************************************************************
*
*   THIS SUBROUTINE COMPUTES THE EQUATION OF STATE OF A GAMMA
*   LAW GAS FOR A VECTOR OF DENSITY AND TEMPERATURE POINTS
*
*   DESCRIPTION OF DUMMY ARGUMENTS:
*
*   INPUT — DENSTY — VECTOR OF DENSITIES (KG/M3)
*            TEMP   — VECTOR OF TEMPERATURES (K)
*            JMAX   — NUMBER OF VECTOR ELEMENTS TO EVALUATE
*
*   OUTPUT— PRESS   — VECTOR OF PRESSURES (PA)
*            ENERGY — VECTOR OF SPECIFIC ENERGY (J/KG)
*
*   PROGRAMMED BY:  G.A. MOSES   AUGUST 10, 1987
*********************************************************************

*************** DECLARE DUMMY ARGUMENTS ************************

      REAL DENSTY(*)
      REAL TEMP(*)
      REAL PRESS(*)
      REAL ENERGY(*)

*************** DECLARE NAMED COMMON BLOCKS ********************

      COMMON/CONST/ RGAS, GAMMA

******************* DECLARE PARAMETERS ************************

      PARAMETER (ONE = 1.)

*************** DECLARE AND SAVE LOCAL VARIABLES ***************

      INTEGER J
      SAVE

*************** START BODY OF SUBROUTINE **********************

      DO 10 J = 1,JMAX
         PRESS(J) = DENSTY(J) * RGAS * TEMP(J)
         ENERGY(J) = PRESS(J) / ((GAMMA-ONE) * DENSTY(J))
   10 CONTINUE
      RETURN

*************** END BODY OF SUBROUTINE ************************

      END
```

Figure 6.6 Overall subroutine structure.

5. The name of the programmer(s)
6. The date when the subprogram was first written and the dates when it was modified
7. References to the literature or documentation for algorithms used in the subprogram

Comments within the body of the subprogram should guide the programmer through the logic of the computation. The decision making is the most difficult part of a program to understand upon first looking at it. Actual arithmetic statements are usually quite easy to interpret. Comments should explain the more obscure aspects of the program and not state the obvious. Blank lines add to the readability of the program. Again, consistency is very important. Comments should be formatted in a systematic way. Figure 6.7 shows the subroutine from Figure 4.1 with the comments removed but with the variable names and line formatting intact. The difference in readability and understanding is obvious.

An interesting test is to compare Figures 4.1, 6.1, 6.2, and 6.7. These are all the same subroutine but with different style features included. Decide for yourself which of the style features is most important to the readability of the program.

6.6. FORMAT STATEMENTS

FORMAT statements are nonexecutable statements and can appear anywhere in the subprogram along with the READ or WRITE statements that reference them. They should either be placed immediately after the READ or WRITE statement to which they correspond or should all be placed at the end of the subroutine in a group. There are advantages and disadvantages to each choice. If the FORMAT statement immediately follows the READ or WRITE statement, then the listing is cluttered with this nonexecutable statement, making the executable statements around it more difficult to read. If the FORMAT statements appear at the end of the subroutine, then they are nonlocal, making the programmer look elsewhere for the information to complete their understanding of the READ or WRITE statement. A recommendation is to position the FORMAT associated with an isolated READ or WRITE statement immediately after that statement. In a subprogram with many READ and WRITE statements, the associated FORMATs should be grouped at the end of the subprogram.

```
      SUBROUTINE BUBBLE( VECTOR,LENGTH )
      DIMENSION VECTOR(LENGTH)
      LOGICAL DONE
      DONE = .TRUE.
    5 DO 10 I = 1,LENGTH-1
         IF( VECTOR(I) .GT. VECTOR(I+1) ) THEN
            TEMP = VECTOR(I)
            VECTOR(I) = VECTOR(I+1)
            VECTOR(I+1) = TEMP
            DONE = .FALSE.
         END IF
   10 CONTINUE
      IF( DONE ) RETURN
      DONE = .TRUE.
      GOTO 5
      END
```

Figure 6.7 Subroutine with no comments.

6.7. CHOICE OF "STANDARD" FORTRAN

There is nothing more frustrating than working with a new program written somewhere else that is filled with FORTRAN "features" that are not part of the FORTRAN 77 standard. Again, remember that this program could be 20,000–100,000 lines long. Letting the compiler find all of these nonstandard features and then changing them, one by one, is a very time-consuming and expensive undertaking. However, one usually has very little choice.

When developing software one of the first questions to be answered is whether adherence to the FORTRAN 77 standard will be enforced. This depends on the expected lifetime of the software and the extent to which it will be executed on computers different from the one on which it was developed. Most FORTRAN compilers have numerous "extensions" to the FORTRAN 77 standard. However, the compiler can be executed in a mode that flags any nonstandard statements in the program. If the standard is being maintained, the compiler should always be executed with this option set to avoid problems with the portability of the program.

In any large-scale application, there are likely to be instances where the FORTRAN 77 standard cannot be maintained. This is frequently the case when system-dependent subroutines must be called to perform useful functions such as estimating the remaining CPU time during execution or getting the time and date when executed. These calls should be isolated to as few calling subroutines as possible and these subroutines should be well documented regarding the calls to nonstandard routines. Each call to a nonstandard routine should have comments that specify the information that is expected to be returned by the subroutine. In this way, alternative subroutines can be supplied so long as they return the appropriate information.

6.8. GOOD FORTRAN PROGRAMMING PRACTICES

A most important element of style is good programming practice, leading to machine code that is optimized for execution speed. All of the care put into comment statements, elaborate formats, and good variable names is tarnished if executable statements contain blunders that rob the program of execution speed. We emphasized in Chapter 1 that execution speed is not necessarily the most important feature of programs today if extra time is spent in obtaining it. However, good programming practice, leading to optimum coding as the program is written the first time, is valuable. Good programming practice is not a matter of individual taste. It can be stated in terms of rules. A set of these rules follows.

1. Avoid repeated intrinsic FORTRAN function evaluations of the same quantity. Functions such as EXP, SQRT, LOG, and especially DEXP, DSQRT, and DLOG take a great amount of time to execute. These functions of course

cannot be avoided, but they should be evaluated only once and the result saved for later use.

Poor programming:

```
DO 10 I = 1,IMAX
   .
   .
   .
A(I) = B(I) * DSQRT(C(I)) / DLOG(T(I))
   .
   .
   .
V(I) = W(I) * DLOG(T(I)) / A(I) * DSQRT(C(I))
10 CONTINUE
```

Good programming:

```
DO 10 I = 1,IMAX
CSQ(I) = DSQRT(C(I))
TLOG(I) = DLOG(T(I))
   .
   .
   .
A(I) = B(I) * CSQ(I) / TLOG(I)
   .
   .
V(I) = W(I) * TLOG(I) / A(I) * CSQ(I)
10 CONTINUE
```

Careless use of such FORTRAN intrinsic functions results in a surprisingly large fraction of CPU time spent in these routines.

2. Avoid using divides. The divide instruction always has the longest execution speed on any computer. It is often 3–10 times slower than the add and multiply instructions. Never divide by a constant. Always multiply by its inverse.

Poor programming:

```
A = B / C / D / 2.
DO 10 I = 1,IMAX
   X(I) = Y(I) / Z
10 CONTINUE
```

Good programming:

```
A = 0.5 * B / (C * D)
ZINV = 1. / Z
DO 10 I = 1,IMAX
   X(I) = Y(I) * ZINV
10 CONTINUE
```

Some FORTRAN compilers are clever enough to recognize division by a constant and will substitute multiplication by its inverse. Unless the machine code is inspected, there is no way to tell whether this has been done. Sometimes division by a number is clearer than multiplication by its inverse.

$$A \ / \ 3. \quad \text{as compared to} \quad 0.3333333 \ * \ A$$

Furthermore, the seven decimal digit constant 0.3333333 may be evaluated as the full-precision binary equivalent on computers with 24-bit mantissas, but on machines with greater precision such as the Cray it will be evaluated as

$$0.3333333000000000$$

which is of course not the full-precision value for 1/3. For compilers that evaluate constant expressions at compile time this can be remedied by using

$$(1./3.) \ * \ A$$

but again the intelligence of the compiler should be determined before this is done or else both a division and a multiplication will be executed to evaluate this expression. Another alternative is to use PARAMETERs to represent all often used constants (see item 8 below).

3. Use temporary variables to hold repeatedly used intermediate quantities.

Poor programming:

```
X1 = (-B + SQRT(B ** 2 - 4. * A * C)) / (2. * A)
X2 = (-B - SQRT(B ** 2 - 4. * A * C)) / (2. * A)
```

Good programming:

```
DENOM = 0.5 / A
SQUART = SQRT(B ** 2 - 4. * A * C)
X1 = (-B + SQUART) * DENOM
X2 = (-B - SQUART) * DENOM
```

Some compilers are intelligent enough to retain certain repeated arithmetic expressions in registers when generating machine code so that redundant calculations are not done. However, most are not really very sophisticated, so that temporary variables are still a good rule. To be sure of the compiler intelligence one must study the machine code generated by the compiler. For critical, CPU time-intensive subroutines, this may be required.

4. Try to avoid mixed mode arithmetic. Perform all computations in either single or double precision. Conversion from single to double and double to single precision takes CPU time on some computers. On other computers the single-precision floating point number is just the first half of the double-precision number.

Poor programming:

```
DOUBLE PRECISION DPVAR(100)
REAL SPVAR(100), RESULT(100)
      .
      .
      .
DO 10 I = 1,100
RESULT(I) = SPVAR(I) * DPVAR(I)
10 CONTINUE
```

First SPVAR(I) is converted to double precision and double-precision multiply with DPVAR(I) gives a double-precision result. This must then be converted to single precision to store in RESULT(I).

The conversion between integer and real variables is always time consuming. If indexes are *often* used in arithmetic expressions, it may be cost-effective to create a floating point vector of indexes.

Poor programming:

```
DO 10 I = 1,IMAX
   A(I) = B(I) * I
   C(I) = D(I) * I
10 CONTINUE
```

Better programming:

```
DO 1 I = 1,IMAX
   FI(I) = I
1 CONTINUE
      .
      .
      .
DO 10 I = 1,IMAX
   A(I) = B(I) * FI(I)
   C(I) = D(I) * FI(I)
10 CONTINUE
```

5. Avoid extraneous statement labels. Compilers try to optimize a program over segments of statements where the flow of control is uninterrupted. The flow of control is interrupted by statement labels because one could possibly jump to a statement label from somewhere else. The machine code generated by an optimizing compiler for the following two sequences of program would not necessarily be the same:

```
Y = A + B
X = W / (10. * G)
Z = Z * X
```

and

```
    Y = A + B
10  X = W / (10. * G)
    Z = Z * X
```

because in the first case the compiler might transpose the first two statements so that X could be evaluated sooner and be ready for the statement $Z = Z *$ X. This is particularly true on parallel processing computers where different arithmetic instructions can be executed simultaneously.

6. Avoid repetitive subroutine calls in DO loops to minimize subroutine entry overhead.

Poor programming:

```
    DO 10 I = 1,IMAX
    CALL COMPUT(X(I), Y(I), Z(I))
10  CONTINUE
         .
         .
         .
    SUBROUTINE COMPUT(A,B,C)
    C = A * B
    RETURN
    END
```

Good programming:

```
    CALL COMPUT(X,Y,Z,IMAX)
         .
         .
    SUBROUTINE COMPUT(A,B,C,IMAX)
    DIMENSION A(IMAX), B(IMAX), C(IMAX)
    DO 10 I = 1,IMAX
    C(I) = A(I) * B(I)
10  CONTINUE
    RETURN
    END
```

In the second case the subroutine is entered only once for each time that the vectors X and Y are multiplied together. In the first case the subroutine is entered IMAX times for each time that the vectors are multiplied. There is often a trade-off between the rigors of structured programming and optimization. The use of subroutines and particularly functions to evaluate small segments of program seems as though it is adhering to structured programming principles, and perhaps it actually is. However, the optimum machine code is often generated by eliminating these short subroutines and functions in favor of "in-line" coding of the expression or short segment of program. The place to be most concerned about this is in innermost nested DO loops.

7. Avoid multiple subscripted arrays if they are not required by the problem structure but are simply used as a convenience. Extra subscripts require extra computation because most computers have only a single index register to compute addresses of subscripted variables.

Poor programming:

```
DIMENSION ARRAY(1000,3)
DO 10 I = 1,1000
ARRAY(I,1) = A * B - C
ARRAY(I,2) = A / B - C
ARRAY(I,3) = A + B - C
10 CONTINUE
```

Good programming:

```
DIMENSION VEC1(1000), VEC2(1000), VEC3(1000)
DO 10 I = 1,1000
VEC1(I) = A * B - C
VEC2(I) = A / B - C
VEC3(I) = A + B - C
10 CONTINUE
```

However, if the problem structure calls for the use of multiple subscripted arrays, use them and do not explicitly compute the equivalent single subscript. The compiler can compute double indexes more optimally than can be done in the program.

Poor programming:

```
DO 10 I = 1,IMAX
   B(I) = 0.
   DO 10 J = 1,JMAX
      K = I + (J-1) * IMAX
      B(I) = B(I) + A(K) * X(J)
10 CONTINUE
```

Good programming:

```
DO 10 I = 1,IMAX
   B(I) = 0.
   DO 10 J = 1,JMAX
      B(I) = B(I) + A(I,J) * X(J)
10 CONTINUE
```

8. Evaluate constants to the full precision of the hardware. This often involves defining constants as PARAMETERs or explicitly evaluating them as ratios of *REAL integer numbers*.

Poor programming:

```
A = 0.333 * B
```

Good programming:

```
A = (1./3.) * B or PARAMETER( THIRD=1./3. )
                   A = THIRD * B
```

The first choice is acceptable if the compiler evaluates constant expressions at compile time and stores the result for execution time. Otherwise the second choice is necessary to avoid the undesired divide. Notice that the expression

```
A = (1/3) * B
```

would always give the result of zero! This is because the constant expression is interpreted by the compiler as the ratio of INTEGER fixed point constants and therefore fixed point arithmetic would be used to evaluate the expression. This is the proverbial circumstance where an omitted decimal point creates a bug that ruins the whole result. Numbers such as pi should also be defined to the full precision of the hardware. This is done by evaluating an expression that has pi as its value, such as

```
PARAMETER( PI = 2. * ASIN(1.) )
VOLUME = (4./3. * PI) * RADIUS ** 3
```

9. Avoid raising variables to fractional powers and, if necessary, save the results for repeated use.

Poor programming:

```
      DO 10 I = 1,IMAX
        A(I) = B(I) ** (2./3.) * C(I)
        D(I) = E(I) / B(I) ** (2./3.)
   10 CONTINUE
```

Good programming:

```
      DO 10 I= 1,IMAX
        B23 = B(I) ** (2./3.)
        A(I) = B23 * C(I)
        D(I) = E(I) / B23
   10 CONTINUE
```

Fractional powers are computed using logarithms and exponentials:

```
exp( 1n A ) = exp( 2/3 1n B )
        A   = exp( 2/3 1n B )
```

Thus, both a logarithm and an exponential function evaluation are used to raise a variable to a fractional power. This is of course costly. If a variable is always raised to the same integer power, use an INTEGER (fixed point) constant rather than a REAL (floating point) constant or variable. Most compilers evaluate low integer powers by just multiplying the number by itself the correct number of times. The compiler is optimized to switch to the logarithm-exponential algorithm when it is most efficient to do so. However, if a REAL variable is used as the power, then the compiler must always use the logarithm-exponential algorithm since it cannot determine the value of the power at compile time. If the power is a REAL constant, this may signal the compiler to again use the logarithm-exponential algorithm without regard to the actual value of the power.

Poor programming:

```
POWER = 2.
VAR1 = VAR2 ** 3.
VAR3 = VAR2 ** POWER
```

Good programming:

```
VAR3 = VAR2 ** 2
VAR1 = VAR3 * VAR2
```

6.9. HARDWARE-DEPENDENT OPTIMIZATION

A second level of optimization, tailoring a program to the architecture of the computer on which it executes, requires an understanding of the machine and the characteristics of the FORTRAN compiler that are used. There are two particular machine characteristics that can be discussed in general terms: virtual memory and vector computers. Most of the popular superminicomputers used today have virtual memories and the number-crunching supercomputers use vector operations to speed execution of FORTRAN DO loops. Efficient programming is briefly discussed for each of these features in the following sections.

6.9.1. Programming Rules for Virtual Memory Computers

When writing FORTRAN programs for virtual memory computers, there are some additional rules that should be followed to make optimum use of the hardware. The FORTRAN program should not access variables in such a way that each successive access is to a variable in a different page of memory.

Poor programming:

```
SUBROUTINE MULT(A,B,C)
DIMENSION A(1024,10), B(1024,10), C(1024,10)
```

```
      DO 10 I = 1,1024
      DO 10 J = 1,10
      A(I,J) = B(I,J) * C(I,J)
 10   CONTINUE
      RETURN
      END
```

Good programming:

```
      SUBROUTINE MULT(A,B,C)
      DIMENSION A(1024,10), B(1024,10), C(1024,10)
      DO 10 J = 1,10
      DO 10 I = 1,1024
      A(I,J) = B(I,J) * C(I,J)
 10   CONTINUE
      RETURN
      END
```

In the first case, the inner loop is accessing each 1024th word in memory (recall that the first index varies fastest in FORTRAN). Each of these words is in a different page of VM. Hence, to execute the inner loop requires that all 30 pages that span the variable storage for A, B, and C be present in real memory. If they are not, then page faults occur and the program suspends execution until the operating system can *page in* the needed page. In the second case, the inner loop can execute with only three pages of VM in real memory, a much more likely occurrence than 30 pages. Hence, by simply changing the order of the DO loop nesting, one is able to affect the turnaround time for program execution. (The CPU charge should be about the same unless the operating system charges for paging overhead.) So the rule is to always put the leftmost index in the middle of the DO loop nesting if at all possible. Note that the natural tendency is to do the opposite and vary the rightmost index the fastest.

Suppose that the following matrix operation is to be performed:

$$y = Ax$$

This is of course computed as

$$y_i = \sum_{j=1}^{j\max} a_{ij} x_j$$

Normally, matrix rows and columns are indexed in the following way and the natural choice is to label FORTRAN indices in the same way.

$$\begin{bmatrix} A_{11} & A_{12} & A_{13} & A_{14} \\ A_{21} & A_{22} & A_{23} & A_{24} \\ A_{31} & A_{32} & A_{33} & A_{34} \\ A_{41} & A_{42} & A_{43} & A_{44} \end{bmatrix} \longrightarrow \begin{bmatrix} A(1,1) & A(1,2) & A(1,3) & A(1,4) \\ A(2,1) & A(2,2) & A(2,3) & A(2,4) \\ A(3,1) & A(3,2) & A(3,3) & A(3,4) \\ A(4,1) & A(4,2) & A(4,3) & A(4,4) \end{bmatrix}$$

But this then forces the second index to be varied fastest. Instead, the indices of the FORTRAN program should be reversed in order, while maintaining their correspondence to i and j in the above algorithm.

$$\begin{bmatrix} A_{11} & A_{21} & A_{31} & A_{41} \\ A_{12} & A_{22} & A_{32} & A_{42} \\ A_{13} & A_{23} & A_{33} & A_{43} \\ A_{14} & A_{24} & A_{34} & A_{44} \end{bmatrix} \longrightarrow \begin{bmatrix} A(1,1) & A(2,1) & A(3,1) & A(4,1) \\ A(1,2) & A(2,2) & A(3,2) & A(4,2) \\ A(1,3) & A(2,3) & A(3,3) & A(4,3) \\ A(1,4) & A(2,4) & A(3,4) & A(4,4) \end{bmatrix}$$

This FORTRAN program segment performs the desired matrix operation while varying the leftmost index on the inner DO loop.

```
     DO 20 I = 1,4
       Y(I) = 0.
       DO 20 J = 1,4
         Y(I) = Y(I) + A(J,I)* X(J)
  20 CONTINUE
```

6.9.2. Programming Rules for Vector Computers

Vector computers gain their speed advantage when performing arithmetic operations on vectors of operands. In FORTRAN programs this operation occurs only in DO loops. Optimum programming results from clearing DO loops of any conditional tests (i.e., IF statements) and avoiding recursive references to previously evaluated vector elements.

Poor programming:

```
     DO 10 I = 1,IMAX
       A(I) = B(I) * C(I) + D(I)
       IF( A(I) .LT. 1.E−20 ) A(I) = 1.E−20
       X(I) = Y(I) / Z(I) * W(I)
       T(I) = (S(I) + R(I)) * U(I)
  10 CONTINUE
```

Better programming:

```
     DO 10 I = 1,IMAX
       A(I) = B(I) * C(I) + D(I)
       X(I) = Y(I) / Z(I) * W(I)
       T(I) = (S(I) + R(I)) * U(I)
```

```
   10 CONTINUE
      DO 20 I = 1,IMAX
         IF( A(I) .LT. 1.E-20 ) A(I) = 1.E-20
   20 CONTINUE
```

In the second case, the IF statement does not "poison" the DO loop that evaluates the arithmetic expressions that will be vectorized. Optimizing compilers on today's vector computers are able to recognize many situations where vectorization is possible even though the FORTRAN source program has not been explicitly written to do so. The compiler often generates machine code that has little correspondence to the source program lines that the programmer has written. For instance, the above so-called poor programming statements might in fact be compiled into machine code as if they had been written in the "better programming" form. The extent to which the compiler translates the source program into an equivalent vectorizable form is very dependent on the compiler and the machine architecture. For this reason, it is not possible to discuss optimized programming for vector computers without becoming very specific. This is beyond the scope of this text.

One other general rule for vector computers is to avoid references to previously evaluated vector elements.

```
      DO 10 I = 1,IMAX
      T(I) = A(I) * T(I-1) + B(I)
   10 CONTINUE
```

In this case $T(I-1)$ was defined on the previous pass through the DO loop. On vector computers operations are being performed simultaneously, and the value of $T(I-1)$ will not be available to use in the expression for $T(I)$. Thus the vectorizing compiler will determine that this DO loop cannot be vectorized and will generate machine code to execute it in the conventional but slower way. There is little that can be done by the programmer to avoid recursive references if the numerical algorithm calls for them. The problem must be carried back to the choice of the numerical algorithm. This is again beyond the scope of this text.

EXERCISES

1. Check your FORTRAN compiler to see whether it has an option to "flag" all nondeclared variables, thus enforcing strong variable typing. If so, use it for all subsequent programming exercises.

2. Select a programming exercise from Chapter 4 and rewrite it using the style suggestions from Chapter 6. Make a list of the style suggestions that you will use in all remaining programming exercises.

3. The proposed FORTRAN 8x standard would allow variables to have names with up to 31 characters including the underscore "_" that is often used as a "blank" in long names. Pick 20 entities from your field of engineering and create variable names for these entities using the six-character limit and then the 31-character limit. (Example: Total impedance might be given by "XIMPTL" using FORTRAN 77 and by "Total_impedance" using the new standard.)

4. Select a program from your field of engineering. Find 20 examples in the program that violate the style and good programming practice rules discussed in Chapter 6.

5. Select a programming exercise from Chapter 4 and trick your compiler to use strong typing by declaring all variables IMPLICIT COMPLEX (A–H,O–Z) and then explicitly declaring each one. Leave one undeclared and print the compiler output to see the result.

6. If you are using a virtual memory computer, what is the page size in bytes? Can you request the operating system to tell you the number of page faults encountered during execution? Execute the following loops within two different programs and request the number of page faults in each case.

```
    DO 10 I = 1,NWORDS
    DO 10 J = 1,10
    A(I,J) = B(I,J) * C(I,J)
10  CONTINUE

    DO 10 J = 1,10
    DO 10 I = 1,NWORDS
    A(I,J) = B(I,J) * C(I,J)
10  CONTINUE
```

where NWORDS is the number of words in a page.

7. If you are using a vector computer, does the optimizing compiler vectorize the summation operation?

```
    A = 0.
    DO 10 I = 1,IMAX
    A = A + VECTOR(I)
10  CONTINUE
```

If so, how does it do it? (*Note:* This is likely to be a difficult question that requires a discussion of the hardware features of the computer.)

7

Debugging

The most time-consuming step in software development is debugging and testing the program. Debugging and testing require twice as much effort as initially writing the program. Yet elementary programming courses give most attention to writing programs rather than to debugging and testing them. This is only natural since a language must first be learned before debugging has any relevance. However, once a language has been mastered, attention should be focused on debugging and testing to further improve software development efficiency. Much of the remainder of this text is devoted to discussions of programming methods and software development methods that improve the software development efficiency.

7.1. PRINCIPLES OF DEBUGGING

The underlying principles of efficient debugging are simply stated yet difficult to achieve. They are

1. Make few initial programming errors, and
2. Quickly find and correct the errors that are made.

Initial programming errors are minimized by starting with a good software development plan, following good structured programming practices, and developing a consistent programming style. The techniques for software development are discussed in Chapters 9 through 11, but they are briefly introduced here.

Finding errors is the subject of this chapter. This requires familiarity with defensive programming methods, compiler options, and debugging tools made available as part of the system software environment.

The rapid correction of errors, once they are found, again depends on the quality of the software development plan. Good software design isolates errors to a single subroutine and thus makes their correction easier than when several subroutines must be modified.

7.1.1. Well-Designed Software

Well-designed software refers to the overall structure of the program and how it relates to the structure of the problem it is solving. A large problem is solved by dividing it into smaller parts. The software to implement the solution to this problem must correspond to these same parts in the form of subroutines. If the software is designed properly, then debugging and testing of the individual subroutines can be done nearly independently (usually by different people). In this way, once a subroutine is debugged, it forever remains debugged. This is important for very large programs because every change to the program cannot be followed by a test of each subroutine.

7.1.2. Structured Programming

Structured programming refers to the logic and program flow within a subroutine. The use of IF-THEN-ELSE constructions and the avoidance of GOTO statements generally indicate good structured programming practices. These are stressed in elementary programming courses. Logic errors are common in large-scale software. While these errors can never be totally avoided, logic errors are minimized if clear logic constructs are used. Spaghetti code, so named because the execution flow is redirected forward and backward by many GOTO statements, is often debugged the first time because the programmer has in mind the "logic" of the mess. However, changing this program and testing it at a later date becomes a horrifying ordeal of unraveling the spaghetti before the change is made with confidence. Hence, the practice of structured programming helps to avoid logic errors, particularly when changes are made at a later time.

7.1.3. Programming Style

Consistent programming style leads to fewer syntax errors. Self-documenting style gives the programmer greater understanding of the source statements at a later time. Comment statements contribute to understanding of the source program and thereby lead to fewer errors from misunderstanding.

7.1.4. Psychology of Debugging

Psychology plays a large role in debugging. Despite the care put into program design and programming technique, mistakes will always be made. Programmers should be both enthusiastic and suspicious. Novice programmers expect that their program contains no errors when they first type it into a file. They are wrong. They then spend hours ridding the source program of FORTRAN syntax errors. After this they again expect that their program contains no more errors. They are disappointed to find that the debugging has just begun. Most of the time spent in debugging is spent on the execution of the program and not on the FORTRAN language errors. Debugging the executable program usually represents 90% of the debugging time for skilled programmers. This is because skilled programmers make few FORTRAN syntax mistakes and because execution errors are much more difficult to diagnose. No amount of preplanning eliminates all of the programming errors. This human fallibility must be faced every day by the programmer. Attempts to ignore it lead to disaster. The creed of the successful programmer is to *assume no program works properly until proven by rigorous tests.*

There are two types of programming errors: (1) lack of understanding errors and (2) oversight errors. The first type of error results from an incomplete understanding of the FORTRAN language and the computer hardware and system software. The only way to gain this understanding is through experience. These errors are completely eliminated with enough experience.

The second type of error is never completely removed. As experience is gained, the number of these errors diminishes to a certain level but does not drop below this level no matter how diligently one works at removing them. This is shown schematically in Figure 7.1. In fact, it is counterproductive to try to remove them. Once a subroutine is written, typed into a file, and reviewed for obvious mistakes, it is time to "run it through the compiler." The compiler will detect a forgotten statement label or a missing DIMENSION

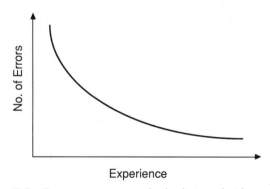

Figure 7.1   Errors are never completely eliminated with experience.

statement. At a cost of $40 per hour, the engineer is too expensive to spend time searching through a listing looking for potential mistakes. Good compilers are very helpful in uncovering such mistakes.

7.1.5. Defensive Programming

Once the program execution stage of debugging is reached, there are two rules:

1. Expect no part of the program to work properly, and
2. Always have access to the maximum amount of information.

The first of these is psychology again but it is related to the second rule. Novice programmers write a program, compile it, execute it, and look at the answer that it generates. It's wrong. So they stare at the listing for hours hoping that the error (or, more likely, errors) will jump out at them and scream, "Here I am, fix me." It never happens. The solution to this problem is to print out every piece of information that is part of the program (i.e., all of the variables and indications of program logic flow). *If a program is not giving the correct answer and if the course of action to correct this problem is not obvious within 10 minutes of first looking at the results and the program listing, then the programmer is not working with enough information.* Debugging is really diagnosis. Just as in medical diagnosis, more tests and more information gathered about the symptoms lead to a greater chance that the true problem will be found.

7.1.6. Subprogram and Integrated Debugging

Well-designed, large-scale software consists of many separate subprograms, each performing a specific function. If designed properly, these subprograms can be debugged independent of one another. The independent debugging requires that the inputs and outputs from a subprogram be concisely defined. Then a "driver" program is written to call a single subprogram with values of input passed into the subprogram through the argument list or a COMMON block. These input values need not be actual values from a computation but they should be legitimate so that the output computed by the subprogram can be checked against the correct values computed independently by the engineer.

Once the subprograms have been independently debugged and there is confidence that each performs its function for the full range of input values, they are combined into an integrated program and this is then debugged. If each subprogram body performs its function properly, this integrated debugging only involves the interfaces between the subprograms.

7.1.7. Testing

Once a large-scale software product has successfully executed its first full-scale calculation with no errors, there is a natural tendency to assume that it is fully debugged. This is usually incorrect. If the completion time for the software development effort has been underestimated and the users of the software are anxious to receive it, then there is a great desire to give it to them after this first successful test calculation. This is dangerous unless the users are veterans who realize that newly created software is always filled with unfound bugs. Before a software product is "ready for the streets" it should be subjected to both an "alpha" and a "beta" test.

An alpha test group usually consists of the original developers of the program. They are most familiar with the source program and can make changes to it quickly as errors are found. As the rate of error discovery goes from one per day to one per several weeks, the program is ready for testing by a beta test group.

A beta test group is usually not the original developers of the program. It is instead a group of knowledgeable users with an understanding of the source program. Very often this group is anxious to use the program to obtain results and is willing to participate in the testing process. Because the beta group did not write the software, they do not have the psychological block against seeing errors in it. They help to uncover more subtle errors and errors that appear when the program is extended beyond the bounds of its alpha testing. For instance, they identify input errors that the original development group hoped would never happen. Input errors cannot be predetermined by the software developers. After a software product has undergone both an alpha and a beta test, it is ready for use by the large community of users.

7.2.   DEBUGGING WITHIN THE FORTRAN 77 STANDARD

The FORTRAN 77 language itself offers no special features to help in the debugging process. This is unfortunate, but it is true of most programming languages. Very often, the FORTRAN compiler has debugging features as extensions of the FORTRAN 77 standard. Examples of these are given in the following sections. In this section, we discuss techniques that use only the FORTRAN standard.

Large-scale FORTRAN programs are divided into many subroutines that each perform a subtask within the total solution algorithm. With such a large-scale program, there are two levels of debugging: (1) subroutine interface and (2) subroutine body debugging.

7.2.1.   Subroutine Interface Debugging

All nonlocal variables used by a subroutine (whether dummy arguments or global variables) are identified in comment statements at the head of the subroutine. WRITE statements at the beginning of each subroutine announce the entry into that subroutine and then write *all* of the nonlocal variables. The same is true for the end of the subroutine. Before the return statement a

WRITE statement announces the exit from the subroutine and again writes *all* of the variables in the same format as at the beginning. The variables are grouped according to whether they are input that should not be changed by the subroutine or output that contains the results of the computations in the subroutine. In this way one traces the execution flow through the many subroutines and sees how the variables are changed by each subroutine. This level of debugging treats each subroutine as a black box. There is no attempt to understand how the subroutine performs a particular task but only a record of the inputs and results. An example of this is shown in Figure 7.2.

The debug output can be "hardwired" into the program or can be turned on and off through user control of input variables. Several different implementations are shown in Figure 7.3. These debug switch variables are put into a named COMMON block of their own so that they are less likely to contribute to any errors that one is seeking. Different options are built into the debug output selection switches. In subroutines with large amounts of input data, in the form of tables for instance, it is desirable to have a separate switch to print this data. Once the data has been checked and is found not to be the source of error, this switch is turned off for further debugging.

Once a program has been debugged and is operating in a relatively error-free mode, there may be occasion to modify the program. When this is done, the debug output is "turned on" for a test calculation to verify that the modification did not have any unexpected effects.

7.2.2. Subroutine Body Debugging

If the subroutine contains complex logic, then it is important to imbed WRITE statements announcing the execution of each different flow path. This "debug output" gives a clear picture of the program flow through the subroutines, program flow within the subroutines, and the operations of each subroutine on the variables. Never cut corners with debug output. The debug output internal to the subroutine body is controlled with a different switch variable than that at the subroutine entry and exit.

This idea of maximum information while debugging cannot be emphasized enough. Even experienced programmers who have followed these rules for years find themselves trying to cut corners in the interest of time because they have "confidence" that they won't make any mistakes. This so-called confidence is a very false sense of security.

This debugging technique is closely linked to the question, what is the optimum subroutine size? This is discussed more fully in Chapter 9 on structured design. However, the current discussion indicates the most practical answer to this question. A subroutine is the optimum size when it can be conveniently debugged by an engineer with (1) the debug output, (2) a listing of the source program, and (3) a calculator. A good test of the completeness of the debug output is the following. One should be able to work through the computations using values of the variables printed at the beginning of the subroutine in the

```
      SUBROUTINE RK4(
     1 XEND, NSTEP, RHS,
     2 X, Y,
     3 IERR )

C  THIS SUBROUTINE USES A FOURTH ORDER RUNGE-KUTTA ALGORITHM
C  TO SOLVE A FIRST ORDER DIFFERENTIAL EQUATION
C  INPUT    XEND  - END POINT OF INDEPENDENT VARIABLE
C           NSTEP - NUMBER OF STEPS
C           RHS   - EXTERNAL FUNCTION TO PROVIDE THE RIGHT HAND
C                   SIDE OF THE ODE
C  UPDATED  X     - INITIAL POINT OF INDEPENDENT VARIABLE
C                 - END POINT OF INDEPENDENT VARIABLE
C           Y     - INITIAL POINT OF DEPENDENT VARIABLE
C                 - END POINT OF DEPENDENT VARIABLE
C  OUTPUT   IERR  - ERROR CONDITION =0 OKAY, =1 XEND<X

      EXTERNAL RHS
      LOGICAL DEBUG
      COMMON/DEBBIE/ IDEB, DEBUG(100)
      PARAMETER( SIXTH=1./6., HALF=1./2. )

C  OPTIONAL DEBUG OUTPUT

      IF( DEBUG(4) ) THEN
        WRITE(IDEB,*) ' ENTERING RK4'
        WRITE(IDEB,1000) XEND, NSTEP, X, Y, IERR
      ENDIF

C  CHECK FOR SOME CONSISTENCY BEFORE STARTING

      IF( XEND .LE. X ) THEN
        IERR = 1
        RETURN
      ENDIF

C  DEFINE LOCAL VARIABLES AND GET THE STEP SIZE

      XLOCAL = X
      YLOCAL = Y
      XSTEP = (XEND - X) / NSTEP
      XSTEP2 = HALF * XSTEP

C  LOOP THROUGH THE NUMBER OF STEPS, SOLVING THE ODE

      DO 100 N = 1,NSTEP

C  GET THE R-K TERMS BY EVALUATING THE RHS OF THE ODE

        AK1 = XSTEP * RHS(XLOCAL, YLOCAL)
        AK2 = XSTEP * RHS(XLOCAL+XSTEP2, YLOCAL+0.5*AK1)
        AK3 = XSTEP * RHS(XLOCAL+XSTEP2, YLOCAL+0.5*AK2)
        AK4 = XSTEP * RHS(XLOCAL+XSTEP, YLOCAL+AK3)
C  UPDATE THE SOLUTION AND THE INDEPENDENT VARIABLE
        YLOCAL = YLOCAL + SIXTH * (AK1 + 2.*AK2 + 2.*AK3 + AK4)
        XLOCAL = XLOCAL + XSTEP

  100 CONTINUE

      X = XEND
      Y = YLOCAL
      IERR = 0

C  OPTIONAL DEBUG OUTPUT

      IF( DEBUG(4) ) THEN
        WRITE(IDEB,*) ' EXITING RK4'
        WRITE(IDEB,1000) XEND, NSTEP, X, Y, IERR
      ENDIF
      RETURN
 1000 FORMAT(' INPUT - XEND, NSTEP', 1P1E12.4, I12/
     1       ' UPDATE - X, Y', 2E12.4/
     2       ' OUTPUT - IERR', I12)
      END
```

Figure 7.2 Debug output at beginning and end of subroutine.

Hardwired debug output

```
    WRITE(IDEB,1000) (A(I), I=1,IMAX),
   1                 (B(I), I=1,IMAX),
   2                 (C(I), I=1,IMAX),
   3                  X, Y, Z
```

Output always printed when logical switch is true

```
    LOGICAL DEBUG
    COMMON/DEBBIE/ IDEB, DEBUG(100)
       .
    IF( DEBUG(6)) THEN
       WRITE(IDEB,1000) (A(I), I=1,IMAX),
   1                    (B(I), I=1,IMAX),
   2                    (C(I), I=1,IMAX)
    ENDIF
    IF( DEBUG(7) ) THEN
       WRITE(IDEB,1001) X, Y, Z
    ENDIF
```

Output printed every n'th time where N counts the number of cycles

```
    COMMON/DEBBIE/ IDEB, NDEBUG(20)
       .
    IF( N / NDEBUG(6) * NDEBUG(6) .EQ. N ) THEN
    WRITE(IDEB,1000) (A(I), I=1,IMAX),
   1                 (B(I), I=1,IMAX),
   2                 (C(I), I=1,IMAX),
   3                  X, Y, Z
    ENDIF
```

Figure 7.3   Debug output control options.

debug output and compare these with the values printed at the end of the subroutine. If this cannot be conveniently done for a reasonable test problem in roughly 30 minutes to 1 hour, then the subroutine is too long and contains too many computations.

7.3.   DEBUGGING WITH SPECIAL COMPILER OPTIONS

Many FORTRAN compilers have so-called debugging aids as options that are set at compile time. With debugging taking as much as 75% of the software development time, all methods to ease this task should be utilized in the interest of development efficiency.

7.3.1.   FORTRAN Interpreters

One such debugging aid is the *FORTRAN interpreter.*[1] This processor is not really a true compiler. It interprets the source program statements as it "executes" them. No machine code is actually generated. This allows it to have complete control over the execution of a program and to pinpoint errors when they occur at execution time. It also provides extensive diagnostics during the compilation phase to tell the user when mistakes were made. This kind of processor is very convenient for moderate-size programs (such as those written in beginning programming classes); however, its interpretive nature makes it difficult to use with large, multimodule software such as we are discussing in this text.

7.3.2. Compiler Directives and Options

Most FORTRAN compilers have diagnostic features that are not part of the FORTRAN 77 standard but which are useful in program debugging. Non-FORTRAN statements are placed in the source program file as *directives* to the compiler. An option switch set when running the compiler instructs it to either interpret these special directives or to ignore them.

The IBM VS FORTRAN 77 Compiler[2] allows the insertion of *DEBUG statements* within the source program and a compiler option directs the activation or deactivation of these statements. The DEBUG statement has a number of options that allow the values of variables to be written to specified I/O unit numbers and that allow the execution of individual statements to be *traced*. This is demonstrated in Figure 7.4. At statement label 10 the trace option is turned on. Every time a statement with a statement label is executed, a message is written to unit 4 indicating the execution of that statement. This occurs until statement 25 is executed; then the trace option is turned off. The DISPLAY option prints the value of variable C to unit 4 every time statement 30 is executed. In this way the programmer sees how the value of C is accumulated in the DO loop.

```
      DEBUG TRACE, UNIT(4)
      AT 10
      TRACE ON
      AT 25
      TRACE OFF
      AT 30
      DISPLAY C
      END DEBUG
          .
          .
   10 A = 2.0
          .
          .
   25 DO 30 I = 1,5
          .
      C = C + FUNC(A,C)
          .
   30 CONTINUE
          .
      STOP
      END
```

Figure 7.4   IBM VS FORTRAN 77 compiler directives for debugging.

The DEC VAX/VMS FORTRAN compiler[3] conditionally compiles FOR-TRAN statements with a "D" as the first character in the line. When this option is turned off, all statements with a "D" are treated as comments, just as if the "D" were a "C." However, when the option is turned on these statements are compiled as though they were regular FORTRAN statements. This is demonstrated in Figure 7.5.

Each of these compiler directive debugging aids has the disadvantage that they introduce nonstandard FORTRAN statements into the source program. This makes the program less portable. As Figures 7.4 and 7.5 illustrate, different compilers have very different directives for accomplishing the same task.

This type of debugging is most suited to a batch style of computing. The programmer has no active control over the debugging until after the program

```
          SUBROUTINE BUBBLE( VECTOR, LENGTH )

C   THIS SUBROUTINE PERFORMS A BUBBLE SORT OF DATA INTO ASCENDING
C   ORDER
C   INPUT   — VECTOR – RAW DATA (REAL VECTOR)
C           — LENGTH – NUMBER OF ELEMENTS IN THE VECTOR OF RAW DATA
C   OUTPUT — VECTOR – SORTED DATA

          DIMENSION VECTOR(LENGTH)
          COMMON/IO/ NIN, NOUT
          LOGICAL DONE

D         WRITE(NOUT,*) ' ENTERING BUBBLE — VECTOR'
D         WRITE(NOUT,*) (VECTOR(I), I=1,LENGTH)

C   SET THE DONE SWITCH TO .TRUE. TO START
          DONE = .TRUE.

C   MAKE A PASS THROUGH THE DATA AND INTERCHANGE ELEMENTS THAT
C   ARE OUT OF ORDER
        5 DO 10 I = 1,LENGTH-1
            IF( VECTOR(I) .GT. VECTOR(I+1) ) THEN
              TEMP = VECTOR(I)
              VECTOR(I) = VECTOR(I+1)
              VECTOR(I+1) = TEMP
              DONE = .FALSE.
            END IF
       10 CONTINUE

C   CHECK TO SEE IF ANY CHANGES WERE MADE ON THIS PASS, IF NO
C   CHANGES WERE MADE THEN THE DATA IS SORTED
          IF( DONE ) THEN
D           WRITE(NOUT,*) ' EXITING BUBBLE — VECTOR'
D           WRITE(NOUT,*) (VECTOR(I), I=1,LENGTH)
            RETURN
          ENDIF

C   CHANGES WERE MADE, RESET THE SWITCH AND TRY AGAIN
          DONE = .TRUE.
          GOTO 5
          END


DEC VAX FORTRAN 11 compiler option to compile "D" lines

$  FORTRAN/D_LINES  BUBBLE.FOR
```

Figure 7.5 DEC VAX conditional debugging statements.

has run to completion. This method is quite out of date and is rarely used in today's interactive environment.

7.4. DEBUGGING WITH INTERACTIVE SYMBOLIC DEBUGGING TOOLS

Many operating systems have debugging aids that allow programs to be interactively debugged. There is no greater contributor to efficient software development than these debugging tools called *debuggers*. The program to be debugged can be executed one statement at a time with control returned to the programmer after each statement execution so that the values of variables can be viewed. These values can be referenced by their symbolic variable name rather than by their actual address in memory and the debugging software tool displays for the user the contents of this variable in the appropriate format. Statements within the program can be referenced by the number assigned to them by the compiler and printed in the compiler listing.

This is all made possible by saving the equivalent of the compiler variable map and the compiler listing statement numbers in the object module of the compiled subroutine. This is called a *symbol table*. This information for each object module is combined and saved in the executable program module by the linker as well. This is shown schematically in Figure 7.6. The compiled and linked FORTRAN program is then loaded into memory by an "executive" program (the debugger) that has complete control over the program execution and uses this symbol table to allow the programmer to reference variables and statements using familiar symbols rather than the more obscure machine addresses associated with them.

Debuggers on different computer systems of course have different command formats and features. We review the most important features of debuggers and use the VAX/VMS Symbolic Debugger[4] as our reference.

7.4.1. Creating Debugger Symbol Tables

Additional information in the form of symbol tables to allow symbolic debugging considerably increases the disk space required to hold the object and executable files for a FORTRAN program. For this reason, these symbol tables are not included unless appropriate compiler and linker options are specified. Once a program has been satisfactorily debugged, it is usually recompiled without the symbol tables. The commands to include the symbol tables on the VAX/VMS system are given in the following example:

```
$ FORTRAN/DEBUG/NOOPTIMIZE SOLVE.FOR
$ FORTRAN/DEBUG/NOOPTIMIZE RK4.FOR
$ FORTRAN/DEBUG/NOOPTIMIZE GETRHS.FOR
$ LINK/DEBUG SOLVE.OBJ+RK4.OBJ+GETRHS.OBJ
$ RUN/DEBUG SOLVE.EXE or $ RUN/NODEBUG SOLVE.EXE
```

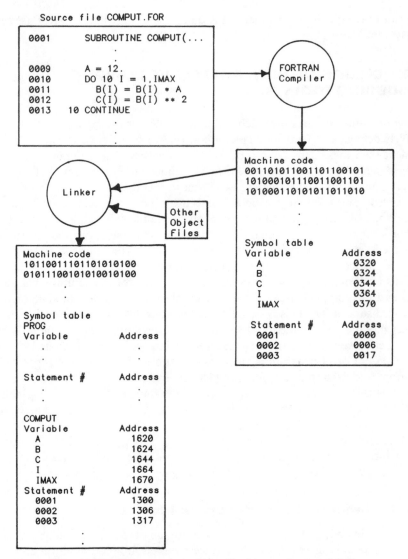

Source file COMPUT.FOR

```
0001        SUBROUTINE COMPUT(...
                .
                .
0009        A = 12.
0010        DO 10 I = 1, IMAX
0011           B(I) = B(I) * A
0012           C(I) = B(I) ** 2
0013    10 CONTINUE
                .
                .
```

FORTRAN Compiler

Machine code
001101011001101100101
101000101110011001101
101000110101011011010
    .
    .
    .

Symbol table Variable	Address
A	0320
B	0324
C	0344
I	0364
IMAX	0370

Statement #	Address
0001	0000
0002	0006
0003	0017

Linker

Other Object Files

Machine code
10110011101101010100
01011100101010010100
    .
    .

Symbol table
PROG

Variable	Address
.	.
.	.

Statement #	Address
.	.
.	.

COMPUT

Variable	Address
A	1620
B	1624
C	1644
I	1664
IMAX	1670

Statement #	Address
0001	1300
0002	1306
0003	1317
.	

Figure 7.6 Saving symbol tables with object and executable files.

A program to solve a first order differential equation along with two subprograms are compiled and linked. Compiler listings for these are given in Figure 7.7. The /NOOPTIMIZE option on the FORTRAN compilation disables optimization of the machine code. This ensures that the compiler generates machine code that directly corresponds to the statements in the source program and does not reorder statements or does not insert or remove statements in the process of optimization. This avoids ambiguity about the status of the calculation at any line number in the source program. Program execution is

```
0001           PROGRAM SOLVE
0002
0003     C   THIS DRIVER PROGRAM CALLS THE RK4 SUBROUTINE TO SOLVE A FIRST
0004     C   ORDER ODE, AND THEN PRINTS THE RESULT
0005
0006           PARAMETER( NOUT=6 )
0007           DIMENSION RESULT(1000), X(1000)
0008           EXTERNAL GETRHS
0009
0010           XBEGIN = 0.
0011           YBEGIN = 1.
0012           NEVALS = 10
0013           XFINAL = 5.
0014           NSTEP  = 10
0015
0016     C   GET THE INTERVAL BETWEEN EVALUATIONS OF THE SOLUTION
0017           XINT = (XFINAL - XBEGIN) / NEVALS
0018
0019     C   NOW WE ARE READY TO SOLVE THE EQUATION
0020
0021           XSTART = XBEGIN
0022           XEND = XBEGIN + XINT
0023           Y = YBEGIN
0024           DO 10 N = 1,NEVALS
0025             CALL RK4( XEND, NSTEP, GETRHS, XSTART, Y, IERR )
0026             IF( IERR .GT. 0 ) THEN
0027               WRITE(NOUT,*) ' ERROR CONDITION', IERR
0028               STOP
0029             ENDIF
0030             X(N) = XSTART
0031             RESULT(N) = Y
0032             XEND = XSTART + XINT
0033        10 CONTINUE
0034
0035     C   PRINT THE RESULTS
0036
0037           WRITE(NOUT,100) XBEGIN, XFINAL, NEVALS, XINT, XSTEP
0038           WRITE(NOUT,101) XBEGIN, YBEGIN,
0039          1                (X(N), RESULT(N), N=1,NEVALS)
0040           STOP
0041
0042       100 FORMAT(' BEGINNING POINT.................', 1P1E12.4/
0043          1        ' FINAL POINT....................', E12.4/
0044          2        ' NUMBER OF SOLUTION EVALUATIONS..', I12/
0045          3        ' INTERVAL BETWEEN EVALUATIONS....', E12.4/
0046          4        ' STEP SIZE FOR NUMERICAL SOLUTION', E12.4/' '/
0047          5        '        X           Y'/' ')
0048       101 FORMAT(1P2E12.4)
0049           END


0001
0002
0003           REAL FUNCTION GETRHS(X,Y)
0004
0005     C   THIS SUBROUTINE COMPUTES THE RIGHT HAND SIDE OF THE ODE
0006
0007           GETRHS = -Y
0008           RETURN
0009           END


0001
0002
0003           SUBROUTINE RK4(
0004          1 XEND, NSTEP, RHS,
0005          2 X, Y,
0006          3 IERR )
0007
0008     C   THIS SUBROUTINE USES A FOURTH ORDER RUNGE-KUTTA ALGORITHM
0009     C   TO SOLVE A FIRST ORDER DIFFERENTIAL EQUATION
0010     C   INPUT    XEND  - END POINT OF INDEPENDENT VARIABLE
0011     C            NSTEP - NUMBER OF STEPS
0012     C            RHS   - EXTERNAL FUNCTION TO PROVIDE THE RIGHT HAND
0013     C                    SIDE OF THE ODE
0014     C   UPDATED  X     - INITIAL POINT OF INDEPENDENT VARIABLE
0015     C                  - END POINT OF INDEPENDENT VARIABLE
0016     C            Y     - INITIAL POINT OF DEPENDENT VARIABLE
0017     C                  - END POINT OF DEPENDENT VARIABLE
0018     C   OUTPUT   IERR  - ERROR CONDITION =0 OKAY, =1 XEND<X
0019
0020           EXTERNAL RHS
0021           PARAMETER( SIXTH=1./6., HALF=1./2. )
```

Figure 7.7 Compiler listing of program to be debugged.

```
0022
0023      C   CHECK FOR SOME CONSISTENCY BEFORE STARTING
0024
0025              IF( XEND .LE. X ) THEN
0026                IERR = 1
0027                RETURN
0028              ENDIF
0029
0030      C   DEFINE LOCAL VARIABLES AND GET THE STEP SIZE
0031
0032              XLOCAL = X
0033              YLOCAL = Y
0034              XSTEP = (XEND - X) / NSTEP
0035              XSTEP2 = HALF * XSTEP
0036
0037      C   LOOP THROUGH THE NUMBER OF STEPS, SOLVING THE ODE
0038
0039              DO 100 N = 1,NSTEP
0040
0041      C   GET THE R-K TERMS BY EVALUATING THE RHS OF THE ODE
0042
0043              AK1 = XSTEP * RHS(XLOCAL, YLOCAL)
0044              AK2 = XSTEP * RHS(XLOCAL+XSTEP2, YLOCAL+HALF*AK1)
0045              AK3 = XSTEP * RHS(XLOCAL+XSTEP2, YLOCAL+HALF*AK2)
0046              AK4 = XSTEP * RHS(XLOCAL+XSTEP, YLOCAL+AK3)
0047
0048      C   UPDATE THE SOLUTION AND THE INDEPENDENT VARIABLE
0049
0050              YLOCAL = YLOCAL + SIXTH * (AK1 + 2.*AK2 + 2.*AK3 + AK4)
0051              XLOCAL = XLOCAL + XSTEP
0052
0053      100 CONTINUE
0054
0055              X = XEND
0056              Y = YLOCAL
0057              IERR = 0
0058
0059              RETURN
0060              END
```

Figure 7.7   (Continued)

either under control of the debugger or not, depending on the option used on the RUN command.

7.4.2.   Control of Program Execution

Program execution is controlled by debuggers through interactive commands issued by the programmer. The program is made to execute until an error condition or normal termination occurs, it executes until stopped at a user-specified *break point* or *watch point,* or it executes for a specified number of statements. Anytime that program execution is suspended by the debugger, commands are given to examine the values of variables, change the values of variables, set or cancel break points, and set or cancel other control mechanisms. A number of these commands are reviewed.

Break points are positions in the program where the execution is suspended by the debugger to allow examination of variables or other status of the calculation. The symbolic debugger allows the programmer to specify break points by reference to line numbers assigned to each statement in the compiler listing. To set a break point at line number 32 in the listing in Figure 7.7, we use

```
DBG> SET BREAK SOLVE\%LINE 32
```

The "DBG>" is the prompting symbol from the VAX/VMS debugger and does not play a role in our discussion. The symbol "SOLVE\%LINE 32" specifies line 32 in the compiler listing for subprogram SOLVE. Break points need not be activated every time they are encountered. One example is

```
DBG> SET BREAK/AFTER:5 SOLVE\%LINE 32
```

In this case the execution is suspended at line 32 of subprogram SOLVE after five executions of this line. In this way a loop is executed many times before execution is suspended. This is very useful for convergence loops, for instance, where problems come only after many passes through the loop. It would be inconvenient to suspend and restart execution 100 times before reaching the point where the problem is occurring. Break points are removed using a cancel command

```
DBG> CANCEL BREAK SOLVE\%LINE 32
```

Another powerful feature of symbolic debuggers is the watch point command. Watch points are variables that the debugger "watches" and suspends execution when the watch point value is changed. Watch points are valuable for detecting the unintended altering of a variable by a programming error. This can occur if a subscript is evaluated out of range causing the alteration of variables neighboring the vector with the erroneous subscript. Consider the following program:

```
      COMMON VECT(10), A, B
      A = 10.
      B = 20.
      DO 10 I = 1,11
        VECT(I) = I
   10 CONTINUE
      WRITE (6,100) A, B, (VECT(I), I=1,10)
  100 FORMAT(1P5E12.4)
      END
```

The value of A will be printed as 11. This is because the DO loop limit exceeds the dimension of VECT and A is the variable following this vector. In this simple example the error is obvious, but in a large program the unintended change of a global variable can be very difficult to find without the use of a watch point debugging command. The VAX/VMS form of this is

```
DBG> SET WATCH A
```

Program execution is initiated from the first statement of the program and execution continues until a break point, watch point, or termination condition (normal or abnormal) is reached. An alternative approach is to execute a specified number of statements before again suspending execution. These commands have the following forms:

```
DBG> GO
DBG> STEP 6
```

Once execution is suspended, either of these commands can be given again to continue execution until the next break point or for a specified number of statements.

7.4.3. Viewing and Altering Program Variables

When a program is suspended from execution, the values of variables can be observed and altered. To see the value of a variable, a command such as the following is given.

```
DBG> EXAMINE RK4\XLOCAL
```

Again the prefix of RK4\ tells the debugger that this local variable is in subprogram RK4. This distinguishes identical names of local variables in different subprograms.

The values of variables are altered using the debugger command

```
DBG> DEPOSIT SOLVE\NSTEP = 20
```

This is useful if an error is found and a correction of it involves changing the value of a variable. Normally, without a debugger, the change would be made to the source program. It must then be recompiled, relinked, and reexecuted. With a debugger, the value is changed in the executable code and the program is reexecuted. Of course the change must ultimately be made to the source program, but the immediate alteration of the executable program is much more effective during the debugging exercise.

7.4.4. Displaying the Source Program

The line numbers and variable names used by the symbolic debugger are the ones given in the compiler listing of the program. Thus, to use a symbolic debugger the availability of this listing is important. Another feature of many symbolic debuggers is a display of the source program on the programmer's terminal. This is often done in a window, with the output from the program and the debugger command lines in other windows. This is depicted in Figure 7.8. To allow this feature, the debugger must have access to the source program files as well as the symbol table that comes along with the executable program. In this way the need of a compiler listing with the statement numbers

```
- SRC: module SOLVE -scroll-source────────────────────────────
->   1:         PROGRAM SOLVE
     2:
     3: C  THIS DRIVER PROGRAM CALLS THE RK4 SUBROUTINE TO SOLVE A FIRST
     4: C  ORDER ODE, AND THEN PRINTS THE RESULT
     5:
     6:         PARAMETER( NOUT=6 )
     7:         DIMENSION RESULT(1000), X(1000)
     8:         EXTERNAL GETRHS
     9:
    10:         XBEGIN = 0.
    11:         YBEGIN = 1.
- OUT -output────────────────────────────────────────────────
```



```
-PROMPT -error-program-prompt────────────────────────────────

DBG>
```

Figure 7.8 Program listing, program output, and debugger commands in windows on CRT.

is reduced or eliminated depending on the programmer's zeal to remain "paperless."

The arrow in Figure 7.8 shows where execution has been suspended. In this case it is at the beginning of the program. The commands

```
DBG> SET BREAK %LINE 32
DBG> GO
```

followed by

```
DBG> EXAMINE X(1)
DBG> EXAMINE RESULT(1)
```

result in the display given in Figure 7.9. The arrow now points to statement 32. This feature is very valuable for debugging on personal computers or workstation computers where communication to the terminal is rapid. It also works for central computers where a high-speed network is used for communications. However, *scrolling* through the source program can be time consuming for terminals connected to slower speed communications. In this case, reference to a conventional compiler listing is more efficient.

7.4.5. Example Debugging Exercise

Suppose that the correct main program given in Figure 7.7 was initially written as shown in Figure 7.10. There are two errors in the program. These are the

```
- SRC: module SOLVE -scroll-source─────────────────────────────
     27:            WRITE(NOUT,*) ' ERROR CONDITION', IERR
     28:            STOP
     29:            ENDIF
     30:            X(N) = XSTART
     31:            RESULT(N) = Y
 -> 32:            XEND = XSTART + XINT
     33:       10 CONTINUE
     34:
     35: C  PRINT THE RESULTS
     36:
     37:            WRITE(NOUT,100) XBEGIN, XFINAL, NEVALS, XINT, XSTEP
- OUT -output──────────────────────────────────────────────────
break at SOLVE\%LINE 32
     32:            XEND = XSTART + XINT
SOLVE\X(1):     0.5000000
SOLVE\RESULT(1):       0.6065307



-PROMPT -error-program-prompt──────────────────────────────────
DBG> examine x(1)
DBG> examine result(1)
DBG>
```

Figure 7.9 Program listing, program output, and debugger commands on CRT following break point command and examine command.

```
0001            PROGRAM SOLVE
0002
0003     C  THIS DRIVER PROGRAM CALLS THE RK4 SUBROUTINE TO SOLVE A FIRST
0004     C  ORDER ODE, AND THEN PRINTS THE RESULT
0005
0006            PARAMETER( NOUT=6 )
0007            DIMENSION RESULT(1000), X(1000)
0008            EXTERNAL GETRHS
0009
0010            XBEGIN = 0.
0011            YBEGIN = 1.
0012            NEVALS = 10
0013            XFINAL = 5.
0014
0015     C  GET THE INTERVAL BETWEEN EVALUATIONS OF THE SOLUTION
0016            XINT = (XFINAL - XBEGIN) / NEVALS
0017
0018     C  NOW WE ARE READY TO SOLVE THE EQUATION
0019
0020            XSTART = XBEGIN
0021            Y = YBEGIN
0022            DO 10 N = 1,NEVALS
0023              CALL RK4( XEND, NSTEP, GETRHS, XSTART, Y, IERR )
0024              IF( IERR .GT. 0 ) THEN
0025                WRITE(NOUT,*) ' ERROR CONDITION', IERR
0026                STOP
0027              ENDIF
0028              X(N) = XSTART
0029              RESULT(N) = Y
0030              XEND = XSTART + XINT
0031         10 CONTINUE
0032
0033     C  PRINT THE RESULTS
0034
0035            WRITE(NOUT,100) XBEGIN, XFINAL, NEVALS, XINT, XSTEP
0036            WRITE(NOUT,101) XBEGIN, YBEGIN,
0037          1                (X(N), RESULT(N), N=1,NEVALS)
```

Figure 7.10 Program in Figure 7.7 with two errors included for debugging demonstration.

```
0038        STOP
0039
0040    100 FORMAT(' BEGINNING POINT..................', 1P1E12.4/
0041      1           ' FINAL POINT......................', E12.4/
0042      2           ' NUMBER OF SOLUTION EVALUATIONS...', I12/
0043      3           ' INTERVAL BETWEEN EVALUATIONS....', E12.4/
0044      4           ' STEP SIZE FOR NUMERICAL SOLUTION', E12.4/' '/
0045      5           '        X              Y'/' ')
0046    101 FORMAT(1P2E12.4)
0047        END


0001
0002
0003        REAL FUNCTION GETRHS(X,Y)
0004
0005  C  THIS SUBROUTINE COMPUTES THE RIGHT HAND SIDE OF THE ODE
0006
0007        GETRHS = -Y
0008        RETURN
0009        END


0001
0002
0003        SUBROUTINE RK4(
0004      1 XEND, NSTEP, RHS,
0005      2 X, Y,
0006      3 IERR )
0007
0008  C  THIS SUBROUTINE USES A FOURTH ORDER RUNGE-KUTTA ALGORITHM
0009  C  TO SOLVE A FIRST ORDER DIFFERENTIAL EQUATION
0010  C  INPUT    XEND  - END POINT OF INDEPENDENT VARIABLE
0011  C           NSTEP - NUMBER OF STEPS
0012  C           RHS   - EXTERNAL FUNCTION TO PROVIDE THE RIGHT HAND
0013  C                   SIDE OF THE ODE
0014  C  UPDATED  X     - INITIAL POINT OF INDEPENDENT VARIABLE
0015  C                 - END POINT OF INDEPENDENT VARIABLE
0016  C           Y     - INITIAL POINT OF DEPENDENT VARIABLE
0017  C                 - END POINT OF DEPENDENT VARIABLE
0018  C  OUTPUT   IERR  - ERROR CONDITION =0 OKAY, =1 XEND<X
0019
0020        EXTERNAL RHS
0021        PARAMETER( SIXTH=1./6., HALF=1./2. )
0022
0023  C  CHECK FOR SOME CONSISTENCY BEFORE STARTING
0024
0025        IF( XEND .LE. X ) THEN
0026          IERR = 1
0027          RETURN
0028        ENDIF
0029
0030  C  DEFINE LOCAL VARIABLES AND GET THE STEP SIZE
0031
0032        XLOCAL = X
0033        YLOCAL = Y
0034        XSTEP = (XEND - X) / NSTEP
0035        XSTEP2 = HALF * XSTEP
0036
0037  C  LOOP THROUGH THE NUMBER OF STEPS, SOLVING THE ODE
0038
0039        DO 100 N = 1,NSTEP
0040
0041  C  GET THE R-K TERMS BY EVALUATING THE RHS OF THE ODE
0042
0043        AK1 = XSTEP * RHS(XLOCAL, YLOCAL)
0044        AK2 = XSTEP * RHS(XLOCAL+XSTEP2, YLOCAL+HALF*AK1)
0045        AK3 = XSTEP * RHS(XLOCAL+XSTEP2, YLOCAL+HALF*AK2)
0046        AK4 = XSTEP * RHS(XLOCAL+XSTEP, YLOCAL+AK3)
0047
0048  C  UPDATE THE SOLUTION AND THE INDEPENDENT VARIABLE
0049
0050        YLOCAL = YLOCAL + SIXTH * (AK1 + 2.*AK2 + 2.*AK3 + AK4)
0051        XLOCAL = XLOCAL + XSTEP
0052
0053    100 CONTINUE
0054
0055        X = XEND
0056        Y = YLOCAL
0057        IERR = 0
0058
0059        RETURN
0060        END
```

Figure 7.10 (*Continued*)

omission of statements 14 and 22 from Figure 7.7. The user commands and debugger responses recorded in Figure 7.11 demonstrate how the debugger is used to find and remove the bugs from this program. Notice that all of these bugs come at execution time. We assume that the FORTRAN language syntax errors were found and removed before we reached this point.

After compiling and linking, the program is executed under the control of the debugger. The debugger is invoked and the program is executed with the GO command. The FORTRAN program returns with the output

ERROR CONDITION 1

which indicates an error in the subroutine RK4. A break point is set at line 25 of RK4 to allow the examination of variables. The program is reexecuted by restarting at the beginning of SOLVE with the command GO SOLVE. The break point in RK4 is reached and the debugger gives a message indicating this. The variables XEND and X are examined and both are zero. Looking back to SOLVE, we see that XEND is not initialized before the DO loop. We temporarily fix this by setting a break point at line 20 and DEPOSITing the correct value in XEND. The program execution is then restarted with a GO command. The break point at line 25 of RK4 again stops execution. This break point is no longer needed so it is canceled. Execution is again restarted and a floating point divide by zero error is returned. Looking at the listing, there are only two divisions, so both of the divisors are examined and we find that NSTEP is zero. Looking back at the listing we see that NSTEP is not initialized. We initialize it by DEPOSITing the value of 10 into it and restart execution at the beginning again by using the command GO SOLVE. The break point at line 20 is again reached and XEND is again set to its correct value. Execution is restarted from this point and the program prints its output and reaches a normal termination. Comparison of the printed values with the known solution to this simple ordinary differential equation indicates that the program has worked correctly on this problem.

This example demonstrates the general procedure for using a symbolic debugger. First, execute the program and wait for an error to occur. If the error is not obvious, set break points or watch points to gather additional information and restart the program at the beginning. Once the error is determined, try to temporarily correct it within the debugger and again restart the execution at the beginning and wait for the next error. Eventually all of the errors are found or the "modified" program becomes very messy. At this point the source program is changed to permanently make the error corrections. This is followed by recompilation, relinking, and more debugging if all of the errors are not found.

7.5. DEBUGGING HINTS

The process of debugging is one of diagnosis. Tests are made and their results hopefully lead to the cause of the symptoms. If not, then more inquiries must

```
run f7_10.exe

          VAX DEBUG Version V4.5-6

%DEBUG-I-INITIAL, language is FORTRAN, module set to 'SOLVE'
DBG> set module/all
DBG> go
 ERROR CONDITION                 1
FORTRAN STOP
%DEBUG-I-EXITSTATUS, is '%SYSTEM-S-NORMAL, normal successful completion'
DBG> set break rk4\%line 25
DBG> go solve
break at RK4\%LINE 25
    25:          IF( XEND .LE. X ) THEN
DBG> examine xend
RK4\XEND:       0.0000000
DBG> examine x
RK4\X:  0.0000000
DBG> set break solve\%line 20
DBG> go solve
break at SOLVE\%LINE 20
    20:          XSTART = XBEGIN
DBG> deposit xend=xint
DBG> examine xend
SOLVE\XEND:       0.5000000
DBG> go
break at RK4\%LINE 25
    25:          IF( XEND .LE. X ) THEN
DBG> cancel break rk4\%line 25
DBG> go
%SYSTEM-F-FLTDIV_F, arithmetic fault, floating divide by zero at PC=00002580, PS
L=03C00024
DBG> examine solve\nevals
SOLVE\NEVALS:    10
DBG> examine solve\nstep
SOLVE\NSTEP:      0
DBG> deposit solve\nstep=10
DBG> go solve
%DEBUG-I-CONFROMEXC, warning: you are continuing from a severe error
break at SOLVE\%LINE 20
    20:          XSTART = XBEGIN
DBG> deposit xend=xint
DBG> go
BEGINNING POINT................  0.0000E+00
FINAL POINT...................   5.0000E+00
NUMBER OF SOLUTION EVALUATIONS..      10
INTERVAL BETWEEN EVALUATIONS....  5.0000E-01
STEP SIZE FOR NUMERICAL SOLUTION  0.0000E+00


      X            Y

 0.0000E+00  1.0000E+00
 5.0000E-01  6.0653E-01
 1.0000E+00  3.6788E-01
 1.5000E+00  2.2313E-01
 2.0000E+00  1.3534E-01
 2.5000E+00  8.2085E-02
 3.0000E+00  4.9787E-02
 3.5000E+00  3.0197E-02
 4.0000E+00  1.8316E-02
 4.5000E+00  1.1109E-02
 5.0000E+00  6.7379E-03
FORTRAN STOP
%DEBUG-I-EXITSTATUS, is '%SYSTEM-S-NORMAL, normal successful completion'
DBG>
```

Figure 7.11 User commands and debugger responses to demonstrate the debugging of the program in Figure 7.10.

191

be made. There are no algorithms for debugging. Efficient debugging comes from using the best available debugging tools and, most importantly, from experience. Experience cannot be taught, but in this section we review some common causes of execution time errors.

Execution time errors come in two varieties: (1) those that cause the program to terminate abnormally and (2) those that simply produce the incorrect result upon normal termination. The first of these is the easiest to find and correct. The second requires in-depth monitoring of the program flow as it executes.

Abnormal terminations are often caused by attempted execution of inadmissible arithmetic expressions. The most common of these is *floating point overflow* which usually comes from division by zero. Perhaps 90% of the abnormal terminations encountered while debugging a new program are division by zero. This error is straightforward to find using interactive debuggers. The question is, why is the divisor equal to zero? There are several reasons for this and they are reviewed later. Other examples of inadmissible arithmetic expressions are logarithms and square roots of negative numbers and exponentials of arguments that are too large in magnitude. Such arguments produce results that are beyond the maximum magnitude representable in a floating point number. Inadmissible negative arguments are quite easy to correct since the numerical algorithm clearly did not call for them. Arguments that are out of the permissable magnitude range are more difficult to correct. They often mean that the algorithm must be modified to accommodate the finite precision, finite magnitude nature of digital computers.

Another type of common abnormal termination results from referencing addresses that are *out of the range* of addresses used by the program. This is sometimes called an *addressing exception*. This usually comes from incorrectly computing indexes to subscripted variables. The reference to the subscripted variable becomes a reference to a memory address that is out of range. This type of error is also easy to find with an interactive debugger. Its correction usually involves a programming mistake rather than a basic algorithmic error.

Errors in the results of an executing program are caused by inappropriate algorithms, incorrect algorithms, or nonfatal programming errors. This wide scope of possible reasons makes this the most difficult error to correct. Sometimes such errors are even difficult to detect. Inappropriate and incorrect algorithms are not discussed since they are beyond the scope of this text. Common programming errors and methods to reduce the occurrence of these errors are discussed.

Errors are often associated with variables that are assigned an unintended type by the FORTRAN compiler. This is particularly true if both double- and single-precision REAL variables are used. It can also occur if the FORTRAN default typing conventions are not used. The misassignment of correct type often occurs in subroutine linkages. Dummy arguments must correspond in number and type to the argument list in the CALL statement. In Figure 7.12a there is a mismatch in type between the arguments A and B and the dummy

(a)

```
      DIMENSION A(4), B(4), C(4)
      DO 10 I = 1,4
        A(I) = 1.
        B(I) = I
        C(I) = 2.
   10 CONTINUE
      CALL SUBR(A,B)
      WRITE(6,*) ' A=', A
      WRITE(6,*) ' B=', B
      WRITE(6,*) ' C=', C
      END
      SUBROUTINE SUBR(X,Y)
      DOUBLE PRECISION X(*), Y(*)
      DO 10 I = 1,4
        X(I) = 2.D0 * Y(I)
   10 CONTINUE
      RETURN
      END
```

A=	2.000000	2.000000	6.000000	4.000000
B=	4.000000	2.000000	4.000000	2.000000
C=	2.000000	2.000000	2.000000	2.000000
A=	2.000000	2.000000	6.000000	4.000000
B=	4.000000	2.000000	4.000000	2.000000
C=	2.000000	2.000000	2.000000	2.000000

(b)

```
      DIMENSION A(4), B(4), C(4)
      DO 10 I = 1,4
      A(I) = 1.
      B(I) = I
      C(I) = 2.
   10 CONTINUE
      CALL SUBR(A,B)
      WRITE(6,*) ' A=', A
      WRITE(6,*) ' B=', B
      WRITE(6,*) ' C=', C
      END
      SUBROUTINE SUBR(X,Y)
      DOUBLE PRECISION X(*), Y(*)
      DO 10 I = 1,4
      X(I) = 2.4 * Y(I)
   10 CONTINUE
      RETURN
      END
```

A=	2.400000	−3.6267776E+23	7.200000	−1.1920930E−07
B=	4.800000	−3.6267776E+23	4.800000	−3.6267776E+23
C=	2.000000	2.000000	2.000000	2.000000

(c)

```
      DIMENSION A(10), B(4), C(4)
      DO 10 I = 1,4
        A(I) = 1.
        B(I) = I
        C(I) = 0.
   10 CONTINUE
      CALL SUBR(A,B)
      WRITE(6,*) ' A=', A
      WRITE(6,*) ' B=', B
      WRITE(6,*) ' C=', C
      END
      SUBROUTINE SUBR(X,Y)
      DOUBLE PRECISION X(*), Y(*)
      DO 10 I = 1,4
        X(I) = 2. / Y(I)
   10 CONTINUE
      RETURN
      END
```

(d)

```
      DIMENSION A(4), B(4), C(4)
      DO 10 I = 1,4
      A(I) = 1.
      B(I) = I
      C(I) = 2.
   10 CONTINUE
      CALL SUBR(A,B)
```

Figure 7.12 Variable type mismatches in argument and dummy argument lists.

```
      WRITE(6,*) ' A=', A
      WRITE(6,*) ' B=', B
      WRITE(6,*) ' C=', C
      END
      SUBROUTINE SUBR(X,Y)
      DOUBLE PRECISION X(*), Y(*)
      DO 10 I = 1,4
      Y(I) = 2. * X(I)
   10 CONTINUE
      RETURN
      END
```

```
A=    1.000000        1.000000        1.000000        1.000000
B=    2.000000        1.000000        2.000000        1.000000
C=    4.000000        1.000000        4.000000        1.000000
```

(e)

```
      A0 = 12.
      BB = 10.
      C = BB * A0
      WRITE(6,*) ' A0=', A0
      WRITE(6,*) ' BB=', BB
      WRITE(6,*) ' C =', C
      STOP
      END
```

```
A0=   12.00000
BB=   10.00000
C =   0.0000000E+00
```

Figure 7.12   (*Continued*)

arguments X and Y. In this particular case no execution error results but the values of the variables following the subroutine call are those shown in the figure. The reason for these erroneous values is shown schematically in Figure 7.13 where the memory words assigned to A, B, and C are "reassigned" to the double-precision dummy arguments X and Y. Because the floating point numbers are all integer values, the high order bits of each double-precision dummy argument are zeros.

Had the result of the operations in SUBR yielded fractional values, A(2), A(4), B(2), and B(4) would have contained garbage. Such a program is given in Figure 7.12b along with the results from execution on a VAX computer. These results vary, depending on the kind of computer used to execute the program.

If the variable C had been initially set to zero as shown in Figure 7.12c, then a division by zero would have resulted. Without noticing the type mismatch between the subroutines, this would be a very difficult error to detect since the values of the divisor B remain correct in this case.

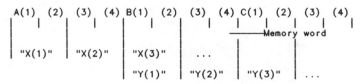

Figure 7.13   Memory assignments for mismatched dummy arguments.

If the X and Y variables are reversed in SUBR as shown in Figure 7.12d, then the values of C change even though this variable plays no part in this subroutine call. Subsequent use of C renders incorrect answers. In this simple example the error may be quite easy to find. However, if this error occurs in a large program where the variables A,B, and C are unrelated, then the incorrect results derived from using the C variable may be very difficult to relate back to the incorrect calculation of B. Whenever strange results are appearing where there seems to be no direct error committed, it is best to look at the subroutine linkages for a mismatch. These simple examples show how such a programming error can cause very strange symptoms.

Another common error is a misspelled variable name. The program in Figure 7.12e demonstrates this. With our move to interactive computing, there is little time spent in looking at the FORTRAN compiler output. A misspelled variable name is easily seen in the variable map that comes with the compiler output because it usually appears along with the correct name and is an obvious erroneous perturbation of it. As discussed in Chapter 6, if "strong typing" of variables is used, this error "sticks out" in the variable map because it is associated with a variable type that is not used by the program.

The declaration of a COMMON block must appear in every subprogram that accesses the global variables in that COMMON block. This repeated occurrence of COMMON statements leads to errors if each occurrence is not updated every time that a new variable is added to the COMMON block as part of the debugging exercise. Suppose that the situation displayed in Figure 7.14a existed as a result of incompletely updating the program source file when a new variable was added. A division by zero would likely result since the variable X does not appear in subroutine SUBR1 so the name X is assigned to a local variable that has not been defined with a value. Again, the variable map in the compiler listing would display this error, but these are rarely studied. Another approach to guard against this oversight is to use an *INCLUDE feature* in place of the repeated COMMON statements. This is not standard FORTRAN, and is not really part of the language, but the feature exists on most computer systems in some form. By replacing the COMMON statements with the INCLUDE statements as shown in Figure 7.14b, the same lines from the VARBLS.CMN file are used by the FORTRAN compiler in each place that the INCLUDE 'VARBLS.CMN' statement appears. In this way there is only one copy of the COMMON block to update and it is automatically updated in each place that it is used when the compilation is done.

A final updating error that often occurs is failure to recompile the source program after a file has been updated. This usually happens when there are many different files holding different subroutines. Several subroutines are updated, but neglecting to recompile one of them results in linking the version of the object program that corresponded to the previous version of that source file. If argument lists have been modified as shown in Figure 7.15, then failure to recompile both the calling and called subroutines creates linkage errors. Many computer systems have software development tools that keep a record

(a) Repeated COMMON statements

```
     COMMON A(10), B(10), C(10), IMAX, X
         .
         .
     IMAX = 10
     X = 10.
     DO 10 I = 1,IMAX
        A(I) = I
        B(I) = A(I) ** 2
  10 CONTINUE
     CALL SUBR1
         .
         .
         .
     SUBROUTINE SUBR1
     COMMON A(10), B(10), C(10), IMAX
     DO 10 I = 1, IMAX
        C(I) = B(I) / X
  10 CONTINUE
     RETURN
     END
```

(b) Use of INCLUDE file and statements

```
     INCLUDE 'VARBLS.CMN'
         .
         .
     IMAX = 10
     X = 10.
     DO 10 I = 1,IMAX
        A(I) = I
        B(I) = A(I) ** 2
  10 CONTINUE
     CALL SUBR1
         .
         .
         .
     SUBROUTINE SUBR1
     INCLUDE 'VARBLS.CMN'
     DO 10 I = 1, IMAX
        C(I) = B(I) / X
  10 CONTINUE
     RETURN
     END
```

In file VARBLS.CMN

```
     COMMON A(10), B(10), C(10), IMAX, X
```

Figure 7.14 INCLUDE feature for repeated COMMON statements.

of the current status of both source and object files and automatically recompile new source files before relinking. Use of these tools is advisable when developing large programs with many subroutines.

There is no FORTRAN standard for the initial value of a variable that has not been otherwise defined by a DATA statement. Generally the value is zero, but there is no guarantee that this will be the case on all computer systems. The program in Figure 7.16a might give different results on different systems. The program in Figure 7.16b is preferable. Failure to properly define variables often leads to subsequent errors such as division by zero.

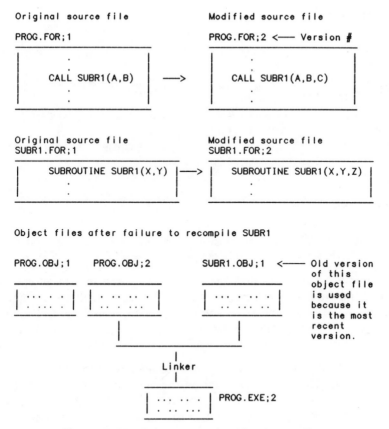

Figure 7.15 Failure to compile updated source file.

```
(a)
        DO 10 I = 1,100
        A = A + I
     10 CONTINUE
        WRITE(6,*) A
        END

(b)
        A = 0.
        DO 10 I = 1,100
        A = A + I
     10 CONTINUE
        WRITE(6,*) A
        END
```

Figure 7.16 Initial values of variables.

REFERENCES

1. FORGO 77 Reference Manual, Harris Corporation Publication Number 0866007-000.
2. VS FORTRAN Application Programming: Language Reference, Release 3.0, March 1983, IBM Corporation.
3. VAX-11 FORTRAN Language Reference Manual, Order No. AA-D034C-TE, April 1982, Digital Equipment Corporation.
4. VAX/VMS Symbolic Debugger Reference Manual, Order No. AA-Z411A-TE, September 1984, Digital Equipment Corporation.

EXERCISES

1. Discuss the debugging features available on your computer system (e.g., FORTRAN interpreter, symbolic debugger, compiler directives, etc.).

2. If you have a symbolic debugger, discuss the commands to set and cancel break points and watch points. Discuss the commands to examine variables, modify the value of variables, and step through the program. Discuss the compiler, linker, and execution commands necessary to invoke symbolic debugging.

3. Discuss the list of execution time error comments returned by your operating system. This is usually found in the operating system or FORTRAN documentation. Write 10 small FORTRAN programs that purposely have errors to force the operating system to give 10 different error comments.

4. Using a programming exercise from Chapter 4, insert debug output at the head and tail of the subroutines by including debug switches in a separate COMMON block. Execute the program with the debug output turned on and discuss the execution flow and values of variables from this output.

5. The following formulas give the voltage across the capacitor in a LRC circuit once a switch is closed. The functional form depends on whether the circuit is underdamped,

$$\overline{\alpha^2} > 0$$

$$V = \frac{V_o \exp\left(-\dfrac{Rt}{2L}\right) \cos\left(\alpha t - \tan^{-1}\left(\dfrac{R}{2L\alpha}\right)\right)}{\alpha \sqrt{LC}}$$

$$\overline{\alpha^2} = \frac{1}{LC} - \frac{R^2}{4L^2}$$

$$\alpha = \sqrt{|\overline{\alpha^2}|}$$

overdamped,

$$\overline{\alpha^2} < 0$$

$$V = V_o \exp\left(-\frac{Rt}{2L}\right)\left[\left(\frac{1}{2} + \frac{R}{4L\alpha}\right) \exp(\alpha t) + \left(\frac{1}{2} - \frac{R}{4L\alpha}\right) \exp(-\alpha t)\right]$$

or critically damped,

$$\bar{\alpha}^2 = 0$$

$$V = V_o \exp\left(-\frac{Rt}{2L}\right)\left(1 + \frac{Rt}{2L}\right)$$

Write a program that inputs L, R, C, and V_O and prints out the values of $V(t)$ along with an identification of the damped condition of the circuit.

Choose the time interval so that several cycles of the oscillatory solutions are resolved. For the asymptotic part of the solution, print only a few values once the solution is within 0.1% of the asymptote. Write and debug this program using all of the debugging aids available to you on your computer system. Record all of the bugs and mistakes that you made during the writing and debugging process and the time required to find and fix them. This should include compiler errors as well as execution errors.

━8

Portability

The portability of large-scale engineering software between different computers and computer systems is as important as the initial development of the software itself. Programs are likely to be developed on a single type of computer with a single operating system. However, the success of the program in the technical marketplace may depend on its distribution to other users with different computers. Portability must be built into the program during its development.

Portability of computational software has two aspects: (1) successful execution of the software on different computer systems and (2) consistency of computed results on different computer hardware. These are quite distinct. Successful execution requires that the program be properly modified to execute on the new system. Generation of identical results for the same input is much more difficult. Most engineering computations are done using floating point arithmetic. Different computers have different levels of precision and ranges of magnitudes for floating point numbers. These differences can produce different results for the same computation on different computers.

The basic rule leading to the production of portable software is adherence to a language standard like ANSI FORTRAN 77. Even with this rule there are still problems with machine-dependent features, such as word length and precision, that must be faced when moving a program from one machine to another. It is rare for a program written on one computer to execute on another computer of a different type without some change to the source program. However, the job of *porting* the program to the new system is made easier by understanding the features that make the program nonportable.

8.1. THE FORTRAN 77 ENVIRONMENT AND BEYOND

The features of the FORTRAN 77 language define the hardware environment in which the program must execute. This environment is shown in Figure 8.1. It consists of (1) input/output data sets defined by the disk file, magnetic tape, and other peripheral devices attached to the computer, (2) static executable program size defined by the word size and memory size, and (3) serial execution defined by the CPU characteristics of the computer. Other features of the computer system hardware and software extend beyond the boundary defined by the FORTRAN language and must be accessed through system-dependent subroutine calls. This is also shown in Figure 8.1. The environment defined by the FORTRAN language is generally a small subset of the features available on most modern computer systems.

One of the major problems with FORTRAN program portability comes from trying to make a FORTRAN program into something that it is not. In today's world of timesharing and distributed computing, supercomputers with parallel processing capabilities, and engineering workstations with virtual memory, programs are very often developed to extend beyond the bounds of the FORTRAN environment defined in Figure 8.1. Interactive input and output are built into the program and these make it difficult to port to other computers and computer systems. Special system calls to allow parallel computation and dynamic memory allocation to make full use of the computer's capabilities are common practices in FORTRAN programs. These also make the program less portable. These nonportable features are often important to the efficient implementation of the program on a specific type of computer.

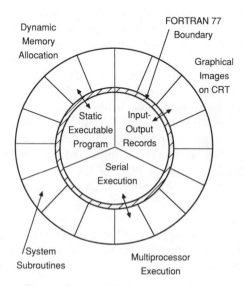

Figure 8.1   FORTRAN 77 environment.

Many of these features can be included in a program without totally sacrificing portability if the program is structured in the proper way. The subroutines containing calls to system-dependent subroutines should be clearly identified in the documentation. These calls should be limited to as few subroutines as possible, perhaps two or three.

8.1.1. Record-Oriented Input/Output

The FORTRAN 77 standard allows elaborate formatting in input and output in a record-oriented environment. It is designed to read card images (lines in a file) as input and to write formatted line printer output (lines in a file). It also allows the use of nonformatted or binary input and output. There is no facility to plot output or to read or write interactively from or to a CRT terminal in either the FORTRAN language or in the standard FORTRAN support library. The support library contains almost exclusively arithmetic functions as discussed in Chapter 4.

On today's timesharing systems and microprocessor-based scientific workstations, the user is likely to want to interpret the output of a large-scale computation in graphical format and to enter input in a "screen-oriented" fashion that allows the user to fill in the blanks in an input template rather than type line after line of input into a file. Each of these are implemented in a standard FORTRAN 77 program through proper structuring.

Input is generated through use of a separate input preprocessor as shown in Figure 8.2. This input preprocessor can take many different forms. The simplest is the use of a screen-oriented editor that is supplied with the computer system. A template file is set up to include comments that describe each line of input. This template file is copied to the working input file and a screen-oriented editor is used to fill in the blanks that have been left for the input quantities. This approach was discussed in Chapter 5. Comments appear after the input variable on each line to describe the contents of that line. A more elaborate scheme would still use the screen editor to enter input, but would use internal files to identify the number of entries on each line and would allow the input lines to appear in an arbitrary order. This was also discussed in Chapter 5. These methods require no development of the input preprocessor. All of the programming is in FORTRAN 77, but the software developer gives up the possibility of interactive interpretation of the input followed by interactive error correction.

Another approach is to write screen-oriented input preprocessor programs for each type of user interface that one expects to use with the large-scale program. This preprocessor might be written in BASIC or C or any other language that is suited to interface easily with the user's workstation or terminal. This smart preprocessor would then query the user for input and ask for each of the correct input quantities depending on the input previously supplied. The output of this preprocessor is a record-oriented file that the large-scale FORTRAN program reads with a simple format. Or it could produce a

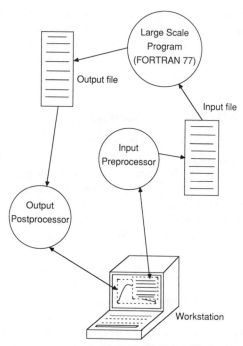

Figure 8.2 Input and output pre- and postprocessors to isolate the FORTRAN 77 program from system-dependent features.

file with the same structure as that discussed above. In any case, the use of some other language to interface with the user suggests that we have violated our axiom to remain within the bounds of the FORTRAN 77 environment. This is true. When this is done, one must make provisions that the program can still be used within the bounds. This is the case with the smart preprocessor. In the event that a user's hardware is not supported by the smart preprocessor, then a file editor is used to prepare an input file in the same format that the preprocessor would have written it. In this way, the only inconvenience comes from the use of a less sophisticated input generator. The documentation must include descriptions of each form of input generation.

The generation of output requires the same approach as input. A postprocessor retrieves output from a file and displays it on a CRT screen in graphical format or in character format suitable for screen-oriented workstations. The large-scale applications program writes its output to files in binary or in a condensed format without elaborate format statements. This information is then read by the postprocessor and formatted in the appropriate way. However, to be compatible with the strictest definition of the FORTRAN 77 environment, the program must have the option of generating line printer formatted output that can be sent directly to the printer.

Output is by far the weakest feature of the FORTRAN 77 environment.

Interactive use of large-scale software has been sacrificed in all of the discussion thus far. Even though we presume that the program is run from a terminal or workstation networked to a host mainframe, we also presume that it will not be interrupted before it has completed execution. Furthermore, no output will be viewed before execution is completed. This is quite unrealistic in today's world of interactive computation.

The previous discussion recommended auxiliary pre- and postprocessors to insulate the applications software within the FORTRAN 77 environment. Interactive use of a large-scale program necessarily requires stepping over the bounds of the FORTRAN 77 environment. This can be done in a way that is least susceptible to incompatibilities between computer systems.

Any program that is run interactively should have the option to be run in a noninteractive mode as described above. In addition to this batch mode of operation, the interactive portion of the program is isolated to a well-defined set of subroutines and data storage variables. If at all possible, the input is limited to the FORTRAN 77 set of characters and does not include special control characters for end of file, and so on. Additional control characters may be needed to tell the system that the keyboard is through transmitting, but these are tailored to each individual system by the user.

The logical unit numbers used for reads and writes in the FORTRAN program are variables or parameters to allow differences for preassignment to actual physical devices on different computer systems. These are again easily changed during the port of the software to a new system.

In conclusion, there is no good way to make large-scale programs written in FORTRAN 77 interactive while remaining within the FORTRAN 77 environment. The only approach is to limit the damage that is done to portability by restricting the assumptions made about interactive use to a well-defined set of subroutines.

8.1.2. Fixed Executable Program Size

FORTRAN 77 programs consist of subroutines that are separately compiled and linked before execution. FORTRAN 77 requires that all memory be fixed at link time. There are no provisions for dynamic memory allocation (i.e., memory allocation during program execution). This is alleviated within the bounds of FORTRAN 77 by the use of pseudodynamic memory allocation described in Section 4.3. This requires compiling the main program and relinking each time that the program is executed. This is extended beyond the bounds of FORTRAN 77 by allowing the main program to read the input and determine the size of the memory that is required for this particular execution. This is followed by calling a system-dependent routine to allocate this memory by adding it to the end of a COMMON block as shown in Figure 8.3. The linker must be instructed to position this COMMON block at the highest addresses in the executable program. The main program might look like that shown in Figure 8.4. Such a scheme for true dynamic memory allocation, im-

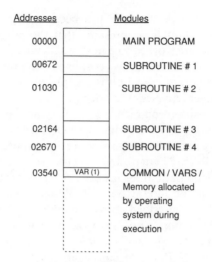

Addresses   Modules

00000   MAIN PROGRAM

00672   SUBROUTINE # 1

01030   SUBROUTINE # 2

02164   SUBROUTINE # 3

02670   SUBROUTINE # 4

03540   VAR (1)   COMMON / VARS /
Memory allocated
by operating
system during
execution

Figure 8.3 Extra memory dynamically added to the end of an executing program by the operating system.

```
      LOGICAL LDYN
      DATA LDYN/.TRUE./
      COMMON/VARS/ VAR(1)
          .
          .
          .

C
C DETERMINE WHETHER THIS IS A DYNAMIC MEMORY ALLOCATION VERSION OF
C THE PROGRAM.
      IF( LDYN ) THEN
C
C CALL A SUBROUTINE TO PREREAD THE INPUT DATA FROM UNIT 'IN'
C AND DETERMINE THE AMOUNT OF MEMORY THAT IS REQUIRED FOR THIS
C RUN.
         CALL PRREAD(
     1      IN,
     2
     3      LENGTH)
C
C GET THIS MUCH MEMORY ADDED TO THE VARS COMMON BLOCK BY CALLING
C A SYSTEM DEPENDENT ROUTINE — GETMEM
         CALL GETMEM(
     1      LENGTH,VAR(1)
     2
     3      )

      ENDIF
C
C REREAD THE INPUT AND SET UP THE POINTERS INTO VAR
      CALL REREAD( ...
          .
          .
          .
```

Figure 8.4 Program fragment to dynamically allocate memory.

plemented within a program that uses pseudodynamic memory allocation, can be activated and deactivated by using a logical switch depending on the attributes of the particular computer system.

This is a most useful feature for large-scale production programs that are used to solve problems of widely varying sizes. Again, the FORTRAN 77 environment must be violated to add this feature, but the damage is limited to a small segment of the program and is done in such a way that the conventional pseudodynamic allocation is used if the user's computer system does not have a truly dynamic memory allocation capability.

8.1.3. Serial Execution

The FORTRAN 77 language does not provide for multiple execution paths that are possible with multi-CPU computers. Parallel execution is a very system-dependent feature and is only beginning to emerge as a viable computational method. Because of its early stage of development, programs designed to execute on parallel architectures are considered as special purpose and are not expected to operate on other computer systems without significant modification.

8.2. PORTABILITY PROBLEMS WITHIN THE FORTRAN 77 STANDARD

Within the FORTRAN 77 standard the most serious problem in software portability is the computer word length. The word length determines the arithmetic precision. Single precision on computers such as the Cray is about equal to double precision on others like the VAX and IBM. The word length and precision of floating point arithmetic for various common computers are given in Table 2.1. Very often, programs written in single precision on Cray computers must be converted to double precision when executed on the other computers. The reverse is also true. Programs written in double precision on the others must be converted to single precision to run on Cray computers where the hardware does not support more than 64-bit floating point numbers. Maintaining the same level of precision is important for generation of consistent results on each computer. This problem is much more serious than one might suspect. Engineering calculations often involve the solution of many nonlinear partial differential equations using a large amount of physical data as input. Billions of floating point operations may go into producing the final results. Significant variations in the precision in each operation sometimes leads to significantly different results once billions of such operations are performed. To make software portable, it must be written so that this conversion is made as simply as possible.

Conversion of all default REAL variables to double precision is most easily accomplished by inserting

```
IMPLICIT DOUBLE PRECISION (A-H,O-Z)
```

as the first nonexecutable statement following the SUBROUTINE or FUNC-
TION statement. It is also necessary to declare all real functions as

```
DOUBLE PRECISION FUNCTION...
```

Even if a program has hundreds of subroutines, this procedure is not difficult
when using a file editor at a terminal. It is made easier if each subprogram has
an

```
IMPLICIT REAL (A-H,O-Z)
```

statement in it. Of course this is the default in FORTRAN anyway, but inclusion of this statement allows a "global replace" to be performed in the file
editor to switch to double precision. The same is true of function definitions.
Using

```
REAL FUNCTION FUNC(...
```

allows a global replacement to double precision.

There are other conversions that must be made that are much more troublesome. All explicit REAL declarations must be converted to DOUBLE PRECI-
SION, such as

```
REAL MATER ──► DOUBLE PRECISION MATER
```

Explicit REAL declarations of variables beginning with I-N are not affected
by the IMPLICIT DOUBLE PRECISION statement since explicit declarations
always override implicit ones. This points out the value of either strictly adhering to the default-type conventions for variable names or using strong typing.
Either of these makes conversion from double to single precision or vice versa
much easier.

Calls to FORTRAN library functions such as EXP, SQRT, and ABS are
automatically converted to double precision if they contain double-precision
arguments.

Format statements should be changed so that input and output formats are
converted.

```
E12.4 ──► D12.4
```

This is a costly process because the program must be scanned for all occurrences of floating point formats. This is made easier if *all* floating point variables are printed using the same format (e.g., E12.4). Then again, a global
replace in a file editor completes the conversion.

The most difficult conversion of precision is the constant conversion. It is
necessary to convert all real constants to their double-precision form to ensure

that complete double-precision arithmetic is done. Single-precision constants in an otherwise double-precision computation are not necessarily converted properly. For instance, the double-precision computation shown in Figure 8.5 is not done to the full precision because the fraction 4.0/3.0 and the value of pi are evaluated to only seven decimal digits. The compiler converts 4.0/3.0 and pi to double precision as

1.3333333000000000D0 and 3.1415930000000000D0

rather than their true double-precision values. The proper way to treat this conversion is also shown in Figure 8.5. In general the conversion of constants is very troublesome. The best way to simplify this for large-scale software development is to disallow the use of any constant expression in an arithmetic statement. A named COMMON block of constants or a block of PARAME-TER statements is created and used in each subroutine where constants are required. An example of this is shown in Figure 8.6. If an IMPLICIT DOU-BLE PRECISION statement appears in the subroutine, then each of the parameters is evaluated to its full precision by the compiler. If all parameters are REAL, then the double-precision evaluation is reduced to single precision by the compiler when defining the constant value. In this way, these constants are always evaluated to their full precision. Again, for these simple examples this seems like a lot of trouble, but for a 100,000-line program this uniformity of constant definition spells the difference between portability and nonporta-bility.

Another consequence of converting to double precision is the difference in the number of words associated with fixed and floating point variables. Typically integer and real variables have the same number of words and double-precision variables are twice as long. This difference in the number of words per variable shows up in two places. The first of these is in the EQUIVA-LENCEing of vectors as shown in Figure 8.7a. When the original program is converted to double precision, the one-to-one correspondence between the ele-

```
Incorrect conversion
      IMPLICIT DOUBLE PRECISION (A-H,O-Z)
          .
          .
      VOLUME = (4.0/3.0) * 3.14159265 * RADIUS ** 3
          .
          .
          .

  Correct conversion
      IMPLICIT DOUBLE PRECISION (A-H,O-Z)
      PARAMETER( PI=2.D0 * ASIN(1.D0) )
          .
          .
      VOLUME = (4.D0/3.D0) * PI * RADIUS ** 3
```

Figure 8.5 Conversion of constants from single to double precision.

```
PARAMETER( ZERO=0.D0, ONE=1.D0, TWO=2.D0, THREE=3.D0 )
PARAMETER( FOUR=4.D0, FIVE=5.D0, SIX=6.D0, SEVEN=7.D0 )
PARAMETER( EIGHT=8.D0, ANINE=9.D0, TEN=10.D0 )
PARAMETER( HALF=0.5D0, THIRD=1.D0/3.D0, FOURTH=1.D0/4.D0 )
PARAMETER( FIFTH=1.D0/5.D0, SIXTH=1.D0/6.D0 )
PARAMETER( SEVNTH=1.D0/7.D0, EIGHTH=1.D0/8.D0 )
PARAMETER( ANINTH=1.D0/9.D0, TENTH=1.D0/10.D0 )
PARAMETER( PI=2.D0*ASIN(1.D0) )
```

Figure 8.6   PARAMETERS used as constants.

ments of the floating point vector VAR and the integer vector IVAR is lost. This is a serious problem if the software developer meant for there to be this correspondence. There is no simple solution to this problem. One possible solution is to redefine IVAR(100) as IVAR(2,100); then we have the situation shown in Figure 8.7b. In this case we use only IVAR(1,J) but this has to be changed everywhere that IVAR appears in the program. This is of course very messy. The obvious solution to this is to never EQUIVALENCE the first element of real and integer vector variables and expect that they correspond element for element.

Computers that use two words to store a double-precision variable sometimes require that the variable be stored at a double-word address in memory. This is troublesome when defining COMMON blocks. This is shown schemati-

```
(a)
Original program:

      REAL VAR(100)
      INTEGER IVAR(100)
      EQUIVALENCE (VAR(1), IVAR(1))


VAR(1)  (2)     (3)     (4)     (5)     (6)     (7)     (8)     (9) ...
|-------|-------|-------|-------|-------|-------|-------|-------|-------|-
IVAR(1) (2)     (3)     (4)     (5)     (6)     (7)     (8)     (9) ...

Converted program:

      DOUBLE PRECISION VAR(100)
      INTEGER IVAR(100)
      EQUIVALENCE (VAR(1),IVAR(1))


VAR(1)          (2)             (3)             (4)             (5) ...
|-------|-------|-------|-------|-------|-------|-------|-------|-------|-
IVAR(1) (2)     (3)     (4)     (5)     (6)     (7)     (8)     (9) ...

(b)
      DOUBLE PRECISION VAR(100)
      INTEGER IVAR(2,100)
      EQUIVALENCE (VAR(1), IVAR(1,1))

and the variables would look like

VAR(1)          (2)             (3)             (4)             (5) ...
|-------|-------|-------|-------|-------|-------|-------|-------|-------|-
IVAR(1,1)       (1,2)           (1,3)           (1,4)           (1,5)...
        (2,1)           (2,2)           (2,3)           (2,4)
```

Figure 8.7   Equivalencing real and integer vectors.

cally in Figure 8.8a. In the past this would be flagged as an error by the compiler and not be allowed on IBM computers. On new computers it is allowed but may still generate a compiler warning. Hence it is a situation to be avoided if possible. It can always be avoided by separating the integer and real variables in a COMMON block as shown in Figure 8.8b.

Another place that the length of variables becomes a problem is in the definition of character data. In FORTRAN 77 one can define character variables to hold characters and this is an extremely useful feature. However, this feature was not available in FORTRAN 66. Characters were often placed in integer or real variables using DATA statements. The number of characters that can be stored in a variable depends on the number of bytes to which the variable corresponds. Hence, any output or input that uses real and integer variables to hold characters will likely have to be changed when moving a program from one machine to another. Again, there is no simple and easy way to fix this. If such a problem is encountered one must simply rewrite the program so that it works. This is not very comforting when the program is very long.

8.3. EXTENDED FORTRAN LANGUAGE FEATURES

Just as each manufacturer's computer is quite different, so is the FORTRAN compiler that they supply to translate user source programs into machine code.

```
(a)
Original program:

      COMMON/DATA/ IN(3), V(5), IV, T(4)

IN(1) (2)   (3)   V(1)  (2)   (3)   (4)   (5)   IV    T(1)  (2)..
|-----|-----|-----|-----|-----|-----|-----|-----|-----|-----|
      Double word addresses - all even addresses for instance.

Converted program:

      IMPLICIT DOUBLE PRECISION (A-H,O-Z)
      COMMON/DATA/ IN(3), V(5), IV, T(4)

IN(1) (2)   (3)   V(1)        (2)         (3)         (4)    ...
|-----|-----|-----|-----|-----|-----|-----|-----|-----|-----|
                  |___ double precision variable does not start
                       on a double word address.
(b)
      COMMON/DATA/ VAR(5), TEMP(5), ...
  1   .
  2   .
  3   .     <------ always add new real variables here
  4 INT(3), IV, ...
            <------ always add new integer variables here.
```

Figure 8.8 Double-word addresses for double-precision variables.

However, it is relatively safe to say that each computer vendor now supplies a compiler that accepts the FORTRAN 77 language as specified in the official guidelines. Unfortunately, to the standard FORTRAN language each vendor has added its own "special features." These special features are not the same for each manufacturer and use of them causes great heartache when trying to move programs from one computer to another. Once again the basic rule of portability is: Do not use special features. Use only the accepted FORTRAN 77 standard. The problem here is of course becoming familiar with FORTRAN 77 so that one identifies the so-called special features as foreign to the acceptable language.

8.3.1. Compiler Option to Accept Only FORTRAN 77

Most compilers allow the extended language features in the source program as the default condition when compiling. However, all of these compilers have an option to force the compiler to accept only the FORTRAN 77 standard. When developing software with a goal of portability, this option should always be chosen. The VAX/VMS command for the compilation of a FORTRAN program with the restriction of the FORTRAN 77 language standard is

```
$ FORTRAN/STANDARD PROG.FOR
```

Using this option is also a good check of a programmer's understanding of the FORTRAN 77 standard, even when the standard is not being maintained. In the following sections we list the most common incompatibilities between various FORTRAN languages and the standard FORTRAN 77.

8.3.2. Digital Equipment Corp. VAX

The extensions to standard FORTRAN 77 are given in blue in the VAX FORTRAN Manual.[1] We give here a brief recount of the most important differences.

- Comments can be denoted by an ! in column 1.
- Lower case letters and special symbols "_!: < > % & are part of the acceptable characters.
- Debugging statements can be included in the source code by using a D in column 1. These statements are included in the compilation when the / D_LINES compiler command qualifier is specified and they are treated as comments when this command qualifier is not specified.
- An INCLUDE statement can be used to include text from another file within the source code of a FORTRAN program. This is handy for specifying COMMON blocks.
- An OPTIONS statement can be used in the source code to specify compiler options just the same as a compiler command qualifier.

- Symbolic names can be up to 31 characters in length, including the _ character. The $ symbol should not be used in a symbolic name because this is reserved for DEC-supplied software.
- The additional data types REAL*4, REAL*8, REAL*16, COMPLEX*8, and COMPLEX*16 are allowed. REAL*4 corresponds to single precision on the VAX computer. REAL*8 corresponds to double precision and REAL*16 corresponds to even more precision. COMPLEX*8 corresponds to a pair of single-precision variables specifying the real and imaginary parts of a complex number and COMPLEX*16 is the same except that each part of the complex number is now double precision. The notation here designates the number of bytes used by the variable. Other types include INTEGER*2, LOGICAL*1, and LOGICAL*2.
- The D_floating option allows REAL*8 variables and constants to vary from 0.29D-38 to 1.7D38 while the G_floating option allows these variables and constants to vary over the extended range from 0.56D-308 to 0.9D308.
- Array element indices can be other than integer and are converted to integer as they are used.
- The DO WHILE statement can be used along with END DO.
- DO loops may have an extended range whereby you can jump out of and back into them without losing the DO loop indices.
- Use of a single subscript for an array designation in an EQUIVALENCE statement when the array is multiply dimensioned.
- Use of %VAL, %REF, %LOC, and %DESCR built-in functions to call nonstandard routines from FORTRAN programs.
- NAMELIST input/output.
- Indexed READ and WRITE, REWRITE and ACCEPT statements.
- Octal and hexadecimal FORMATs.
- DELETE and UNLOCK statements and various other auxiliary input/output statements.
- ENCODE and DECODE statements.

8.3.3. IBM 360, 370, 30xx, and 43xx Series

The IBM VS FORTRAN Application Programming: Language Reference manual[2] calls out the extensions to standard FORTRAN 77 by the notation

```
                    _____IBM Extension_____
  ┌─────────────────────────────·────────────────────────┐
  │                              ·                         │
  │                              ·                         │
  └─────────────────End of IBM Extension──────────────────┘
```

Important extensions are included in Appendix C of the manual and these are

- NAMELIST statement.
- Double-precision complex.
- Z and Q format descriptors.
- G format for integer and logical.
- The functions ALGAMA, ARCOS, ARSIN, CCOS, CDAMS, CDCOS, CDEXP, CDLOG, CDSIN, CDSQRT, COTAN, CQABS, CQCOS, CQEXP, CQLOG, CQSIN, CQSQRT, DARCOS, DARSIN, DBLEQ, DCMPLX, DCONJG, DCOTAN, DERFC, DERF, DFLOAT, DGAMMA, DIMAG, DLGAMA, DREAL, ERF, ERFC, GAMMA, HFIX, IMAG, IQINT, LGAMMA, QABS, QARCOS, QARSIN, QATAN, QATAN2, QCMPLX, QCONJG, QCOSH, QCOS, QCOTAN, QDIM, QERFC, QERF, QEXP, QEXTD, QEXT, QFLOAT, QIMAG, QINT, QLOG, QLOG10, QMAX1, QMOD, QREAL, QSIGN, QSINH, QSIN, QSQRT, QTANH, QTAN, SINGLQ.
- CALL DVCHK, CALL DUMP/PDUMP, CALL EXIT, CALL OVERFL.
- Asynchronous READ, WRITE, and WAIT.
- Extended precision for REAL and COMPLEX.
- Extended debug facility.
- Hexadecimal constants and Z format.
- Free-form source statements.
- The dollar sign ($) as an alphabetic character.
- Data initialization in type specification statements.
- Optional length specification in specification statements (INTEGER, REAL, COMPLEX, LOGICAL) and in FUNCTION statements.
- Mixed mode expressions involving complex and double precision.
- FORMAT identifier in noncharacter array.
- Continuation line may have anything in columns 1–5 other than a C in column 1.
- RETURN statement is the same as STOP in a main program.
- Partitioned data sets.
- Closing of data set on ABEND.
- STOPn where n is a return code.
- Initialization with hexadecimal constants.
- EQUIVALENCE statement allows equivalencing of character and non-character data types.
- COMMON statement allows character and noncharacter data types in the same COMMON block.

8.3.4. Cray Research XMP Series

Cray Research supercomputers use the CFT[3] or the CFT77[4] FORTRAN compilers. These optimizing compilers accept standard FORTRAN source programs and generate vectorized machine code without the need for special function calls. However, there are a number of *compiler directives* that aid the compilers in optimization. These directives have the characters

CDIR$

as the first five characters in columns 1–5. The compiler distinguishes these statements from normal comment statements by this unique combination of characters. Extensions of the FORTRAN 77 standard are distinguished in the CFT and CFT77 manuals with the notation

---

The ANSI FORTRAN standard does not provide ...

The following are a list of extensions to the CFT and CFT77 FORTRAN compilers.

- Lower case letters and " and ! are allowed characters.
- Nonstandard characters are included in the lexical collating sequence.
- A line can contain 96 columns.
- Comments can appear on a line to the right of !.
- Compiler directives follow the characters CDIR$ in columns 1–5.
- An argument list is allowed on the PROGRAM statement to make CFT compatible with other vendors' compilers, particularly Control Data Corporation.
- A subprogram can call itself recursively, if the stack option is specified at compilation.
- Both static and stack-based variable storage options are available.
- Multiple unnamed BLOCK DATA subprograms are allowed.
- The name of a BLOCK DATA subprogram may be the same as a COMMON block name.
- BOOLEAN and POINTER variable types are allowed.
- The IMPLICIT NONE statement disables all default variable typing, thus requiring all variables to be declared (and hence implementing strong variable typing as in Pascal).
- The .T. and .F. forms of logical constants are allowed.
- Quotation marks may be used to delimit character strings.
- Pointee arrays are allowed as a form of dynamic variable dimensioning.
- Function references, array elements, and noninteger variables are allowed in array dimensions.
- Fewer subscript expressions than initial declarators are allowed to reference arrays.
- DATA statements can be intermixed with specification statements.

- Variables in blank COMMON can be initialized in DATA statements.
- COMMON block names may be the same as constants, intrinsic functions, or external procedures.
- Named COMMON blocks may be referenced with variable sizes in different subprograms.
- TASK COMMON blocks are allowed for multitasking programs.
- Eight characters are allowed for variable, subprogram, etc., names.
- Complex and double-precision data types may be mixed.
- The abbreviations .N., .A., .O., .X. may be used for the logical operators .NOT., .AND., .OR., and .XOR.
- The .XOR. operator is allowed.
- Masking expressions may be used by using a logical operator on an integer, real, or boolean operand.
- The expression in a computed GOTO statement need not be integer.
- No more than 15 DO loops may terminate on the same statement label.
- End-of-data records are allowed.
- Unformatted and buffered I/O statements can read and write formatted data records.
- Formatted and unformatted data records can be mixed in a file.
- Multiple file data sets can be used.
- Unit specifiers 5 and 6 are preconnected.
- File identifiers are allowed.
- The WRITE f, [iolist] statement format is allowed.
- Reading or writing nonexistent files automatically creates them.
- Files are not automatically closed at program termination.
- The NAMELIST form of I/O is allowed.
- The BUFFER IN and BUFFER OUT statements are allowed.
- Commas are optional as delimiters between most items in format statements.
- A repeat specifier may be used with the / in format statements.
- The $ can be used as a format descriptor in interactive I/O to leave the terminal print position at the end of the text so a typed response follows on the same line.
- Octal format O and hexadecimal format Z are allowed.

REFERENCES

1. VAX-11 FORTRAN Language Reference Manual, Order No. AA-DO34C-TE, April 1982, Digital Equipment Corporation.

2. VS FORTRAN Application Programming: Language Reference, Release 3.0, March 1983, IBM Corporation.

3. CFT Reference Manual, Cray Research Inc. Publication Number SR-0009, 1986.

4. CFT77 Reference Manual, Cray Research Inc. Publication Number SR-0018, 1986.

EXERCISES

1. Discuss the extended FORTRAN language features available on the compiler you are using. Do you often use any of these features?

2. What are the default input and output unit specifiers on your computer system? To what physical devices do they correspond?

3. Using a programming exercise from Chapter 4, convert the program from single to double precision, including all constants, formats, and so on. Rewrite the program using the style suggestions from Chapter 6 with the goal that it be easy to convert from single to double precision and back. Discuss the specific style features that make this conversion easier.

4. Using the program from problem 3, port it to a computer from a different vendor than the one it was written on. Discuss all of the problems associated with the port, including how it was moved (network, magnetic tape, cards, etc.), learning the new operating system commands, compiler inconsistencies, execution inconsistencies, and so on.

5. Using a programming text or perhaps a compiler manual as a reference, discuss the major differences between FORTRAN 66 and FORTRAN 77.

6. If you have access to the information, discuss the differences between FORTRAN 77 and the proposed FORTRAN 8x.

━9

Software Design Concepts

An understanding of time-proven software design concepts[1-9] is important to the engineer faced with the task of developing a large-scale software product. Large-scale engineering software is complex, expensive to produce, and expensive to maintain. Application of software design principles offers the best chance of successfully completing the development project on time and within budget. In a production environment, cost overruns in the creation of engineering software jeopardizes its chances of completion and eventual use. In a research environment, late delivery of software antagonizes the users and leads them to seek alternatives. On the other hand, improvement in the efficiency of software production expands the set of problems that are economically solved using the software.

9.1. SOFTWARE DEVELOPMENT LIFE CYCLE

Large-scale engineering applications software has a *life cycle* of six phases. The six phases are as follows:

1. Objectives
2. Problem specification
3. Software specification
4. Software generation
5. Testing, and
6. Maintenance

These phases require differing amounts of resources in the form of time and money, but each is important to a succcessful software product. The typical percentage of total cost devoted to each is shown in Figure 9.1.

Each of these six steps represents a distinct function in software development. However, the steps are usually not executed in a sequential fashion with one completed before the next is initiated. Instead, software development is an *iterative process* with frequent backtracking and changes in direction. Oversights in the software design, discovered at the program generation stage, force the developer to return to an earlier design specification stage to correct the problem. Errors uncovered in testing may require a part of the program to be rewritten, thus a return to the generation step. For large projects, different parts of the program may be in different stages at one time. Thus all of the steps must be designed to adapt on a dynamic basis. This dynamic nature of software development is one of its most challenging aspects. Accommodation of dynamic change is built into the design concepts and is their most important property.

9.1.1. Objectives

The objectives of the software development task are a short and concise statement of the reason for undertaking this development. Such a simple statement may seem inconsistent with the complexity of the whole problem but nevertheless is important to understand before starting any of the detailed work. It is surprising to find that many large software development efforts have been underway for years without a firm understanding of the specific goal of the work. Each proposed change to the development is weighed against this objective to ensure that it is essential to meeting the objective. A clear understanding

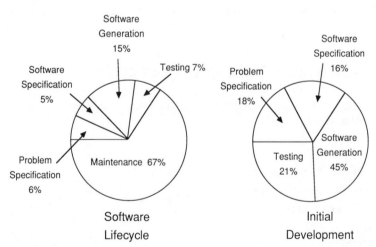

Figure 9.1   Typical fractions of effort in each stage of the software life cycle.

of the objective helps to define when the development is complete. The creation of an objectives statement requires very little time and does not appear in Figure 9.1.

Objectives are often defined by upper management, where decisions are made without regard to specific details as to how the objectives are to be satisfied. Unrealistic objectives must be reported back after the problem specification step has shown them to be such. The following are examples of objectives statements.

- Determine the amount of styrene produced in a chemical plant as a function of the feedstock and other relevant parameters so that new plants can be designed optimally.
- Determine the power distribution in a fission reactor core as a function of position and time so that reload fuel cycles can be designed.
- Determine the lift of an airfoil for different airfoil designs.

9.1.2. Problem Specification

The problem specification is a detailed accounting of the components that make up the problem to be solved. These include the physical models, the levels of engineering approximation, the solution methods to be used, and the data required. In an ideal world the problem specification makes no reference to software or computers, leaving this for the software specification. However, in almost all practical circumstances, the computer to be used, the people required for the development, and the project schedule are specified at this step.

A great deal of care must be taken to develop a *complete* problem specification. The problem specification provides a blueprint to follow to meet the objectives. On the other hand, if the objectives are ambiguous or overly ambitious for the amount of resources available, the problem specification determines this and a reassessment of the project should be made before continuing.

The key to successful problem specification is *realism* and *conservatism*. If the ending date of the project and the manpower to be devoted to it have been determined before this step, as is often the case, then a problem specification that meets these constraints must be developed. If this specification falls far short of original objectives, then an assessment of the predetermined resources is made. Under any circumstances, the next step is not taken until this step is completed and the resources required to complete the project have been dedicated.

The problem specification step is often ignored or incompletely executed, while Figure 9.1 shows that this step represents only a small fraction of the overall development cost. Why should such an inexpensive step be slighted? Failure to complete this step happens because it comes first in the development plan and there is immediately a fear that too much time is being "wasted" and that actual coding must begin as soon as possible since this part of the development consumes the most time. This fear stems from bad past experiences with unsuccessful software development projects or from an unfamiliarity with software design principles. In fact, the execution of the first three phases of the development life cycle have profound effects on the more costly phases that follow. In analogy to building a house, a complete design and blueprint gives the construction crew the best chance of completing the project on time and within budget. It does not guarantee it. On the other hand, an incomplete design and blueprint gives the construction people little chance of doing their job efficiently. Every day spent in improving the problem specification saves many days later on in the development.

9.1.3. Software Specification

Software specification closely parallels the problem specification. As we discuss later, well-designed software is structured to resemble the problem specification. Software specification includes the definition of all modules, data structures, and major variables. Argument lists that couple modules are defined. Conventions to use in coding the modules and naming of files and procedures to use in compiling and updating the program are also specified at this step.

Structured design methods are used at this step to divide the problem into manageable sized pieces where each piece corresponds to a module in the program. Evaluation of modules is made to determine their degree of cohesion and coupling. These are measures of the independence of modules with respect to one another. Several iterations may be required before a final acceptable software specification is completed.

The problem and software specification steps are usually performed by the same team of engineers. For this reason, they are often combined with little distinction between the two steps. This is unavoidable. The best approach is to begin with only the problem specification and smoothly make a transition into the software specification only after the problem specification seems to be complete.

The centerpiece of the software development project is the software specification step. The software specification determines the character of the final product and even plays a role in determining the problem specification. The software specification must take into account not only the problem to be solved, but also the structure of the team that works on the software. The software specification is different for a team of experienced professionals that have worked together on other projects than it is for a team of novices with only one experienced person heading the team.

9.1.4. Software Generation

The software generation step involves writing the program according to the software specification. This phase also includes debugging the program. If the software specification has been prepared correctly, then the software generation can be performed by a larger group of people than the previous steps. This large group can include earlier participants or may be an entirely different group with only the management of the first group remaining to direct this step of the project. Figure 9.1 shows that this is the most costly step in the initial development (i.e., excluding maintenance). The inclusion of more people therefore reduces the time to completion but not the cost.

While the software specification step treats the software at the module level, software generation is the step where structured programming and good programming practices are exercised to create the bodies of the modules. Debugging represents the most critical element of this step. The time consumed in debugging a project often overshadows all other previous steps. Hence, the emphasis at this step is the use of state-of-the-art debugging tools and techniques by all members of the team. Frequent evaluations of the software are made by peer groups. This is described in Chapter 11.

9.1.5. Testing

The testing step refers to functional testing of the final version of the software. This is often done by people who were not involved in the software development but who are knowledgeable about the software. They may be potential users of the software. Here, for the first time, the software is subjected to actual use in the environment for which it was intended. The team that specified and wrote the software continues to work closely with the users so that errors can be corrected and suggestions implemented quickly.

Version 0 of the program might be that which is initially released for testing. Future releases of the program might be numbered 0.1, 0.2, and so on as changes are made. As the program reaches a stage where it is used successfully to solve the problems that it was intended to solve, then version 1 is released with full documentation.

Early releases of the program are often given to so-called *beta test sites*. These are groups of users who are knowledgeable about the problem to be solved and the software itself. They independently test the program and report any errors found. This serves as a final check for errors before the program is released to the general user community.

9.1.6. Maintenance

Once a software product has been released, the development team usually breaks up and members turn their attention to other projects. However, the program still requires attention in the form of maintenance. As additional errors or inconsistencies are found, they must be corrected for future releases of the program. If the program is successful, then users often request additional features or extensions to the existing program. These may be full-scale software development tasks in themselves. These activities may be performed by the original group or may be delegated to another group. The continuing success of the program depends in large part on the responsiveness of the maintenance team.

Figure 9.1 shows maintenance to be the dominant cost in the software life cycle. This would seem to be the place to emphasize improved efficiency. In fact, the efficiency of the software maintenance is most affected by improvements in the software design. A well-designed program is easy to understand, modify, and debug, and these are the time-consuming aspects of maintenance. The goal here is to design software so that a minimum number of lines of code and a minimum number of modules are modified when a change is made. This in turn minimizes the chance of introducing additional errors.

9.1.7. Documentation

No discussion of software development is complete without the subject of documentation. Documentation serves three distinct purposes. Clearly written and complete documentation is important to the eventual success of a large-scale software product because it facilitates both the use and modification of the program once it has been delivered to the end user. Documentation must also be written as the program is developed to give continuity to the product as design team members come and go.

User documentation is usually written once the program has reached its final stages of development. It consists of three parts. In the first part, the *principles* embodied in the program are thoroughly discussed. This might consist of the physical problems that can be solved by the program, the mathematical description that underlies the computation, and the numerical methods used to solve the equations. The specific implementation in the coding is not included. The second part of the user documentation is a *manual* that describes the input and output. This is useful to the experienced user as a reference. The third part of the documentation is a *tutorial* that leads the novice user through the process of preparing input for the program, executing it, and interpreting the output. Good user documentation must include all three of these elements.

Programmer documentation concentrates on the specific details of the software product and is distinct from the user documentation. This documentation is written as the program is developed. The structure chart that displays the module hierarchy is continually updated as the software is written. This is a dynamic tool that undergoes constant changes and additions. A dictionary of all variables and their definitions is continually updated. Individual modules contain internal documentation in the form of comments as discussed in Chapter 6. Large-scale software projects involve many people and span years of work. Over this time, it is expected that people will move on to other positions and be replaced. Continuous documentation allows the replacement person to move ahead with the work with a minimum of backtracking.

9.1.8. Management of Software Development

A definition of each life cycle step does not give a complete picture of how software is developed. We must also review how this development is managed by people. Many of the principles and strategies introduced in this chapter were first developed for the production of business applications software. It is therefore instructive to first view the management of business software development.

In this situation a user or possibly upper management comes to the data-processing group with a problem. This could also be representatives of a company coming to a software vendor. First a *systems analyst* defines the problem and its solution by gathering information from the user. In the case of business applications, the software is likely to be an entire system including hardware and software (e.g., an airline reservation system or banking transaction system). The end users of the system as well as the people requesting the system are unlikely to be familiar with the technical concepts needed to accomplish the task. The systems analyst is the interface between the technical people who create the software and the management requesting it and the user who executes it. The systems analyst defines the problem using *structured analysis* methods and tools. These tools are graphical in nature and can be understood in concept at least by the people requesting the software. In this way the systems analyst creates a common language between the technicians producing the software and the users. The systems analyst must be a person with experience in both the technical and business aspects of the software application. This person is generally a senior level member of the software development team.

Next, the *systems designer* uses the definition of the problem and its solution to define the software system to implement the solution. This person uses *structured design* concepts to accomplish this. In contrast to the structured analysis tools, the structured design tools are more closely related to the actual software that will be produced. The systems designer does not talk with the end user but goes through the systems analyst. The structured design of the software is a blueprint for the programmers who will write and debug it. The systems designer interfaces closely with the programming team.

Finally, a team of programmers works with the systems designer to create the software to solve the problem according to the structured design definition of the software. This programming team has an internal structure of its own. There is usually a chief programmer and a documentarian as well as the individual programmers. The chief programmer leads the team and makes any choices among different options. The documentarian ensures that all coding is completely documented as it is written.

The situation in the world of engineering can be quite different. An example demonstrates this. Upper management decides processing costs are too large for a certain product—chemical, mechanical, and so on. Lower management responds by authorizing the development of a computer model to simulate the processing required to produce the product to allow an optimization study to be done. A team of engineers is given the task of reviewing the old methods and developing a new model to better assess the situation. They write a large-scale computer program to do this.

In this example the team of engineers is likely to play the role of systems analyst, systems designer, and possibly programmer as well. From this example we see how the division of labor between problem definition at the systems analysis level and structured design and software definition are not as well defined in the engineering application as they are in the business application. This situation necessitates that the engineer be familiar with all aspects of software development, from solution definition to programming.

The overriding reason for the use of structured methods is the improvement of software development efficiency and the reduction of cost. Experience has shown that the software development cost is cut by a factor of 2 through use of these methods. The subsequent maintenance costs are cut by factors of 2–10 for programs that are produced using these structured methods. The factor of 2 reduction comes largely from reduced debugging costs, since the modules are easier to write correctly the first time and their independence makes the integrated system tests more likely to proceed without major problems. The large improvement in the maintenance cost is related to the ease of modification. Changes to the program are isolated to a few modules in a well-structured program.

Such factors of improved efficiency are clearly important to organizations that rely on large-scale software development for their product development or their research goals. But these factors of improvement are also important to graduate students writing a computer program as part of their thesis research. Since the research usually is not the program itself, it is important to get the program working as quickly as possible so that the results can be forthcoming. These techniques are valid for 1000 line programs as well as for 100,000 line programs.

9.2. PROBLEM SPECIFICATION—STRUCTURED ANALYSIS

The definition of an engineering solution requires several different skills. A background in the engineering discipline itself is required for a thorough understanding of the problem. A background in mathematics and numerical analysis is required to pose the problem in the form of mathematical equations and to choose an appropriate numerical solution to these equations. A background in *structured analysis* is required to put the solution method into a form that is suitable for the following structured design step. Neither the specific engineering discipline nor numerical analysis is the subject of this text. It is expected that the reader is already equipped with the necessary background in these two areas.

The objective of structured analysis is to depict the solution to an engineering problem in a form that a designer can use for the software definition step. In an ideal world, this functional specification of the solution is all that the designer would need to design the software. In most engineering situations the solution definition and the software definition are coupled together. For the purposes of our discussion we assume that they are not coupled and treat each separately.

The rule of structured analysis is to decompose the solution into an ever-increasing level of detail. This is done through use of a graphical representation of the solution that is concise, top-down partitioned, and logical and not physical. By this last attribute we mean that the functional specification represents the essence of the solution and not the particular implementation of the solution. Ideally, a functional specification should not be language- or machine-specific. This decision should come at the design stage. However, this is rarely the case. Generally, the team of engineers working on a project already know the target computer and the language that they will use. The tools of the structured analyst are the data flow diagram, data dictionary, and process specification via pseudocode, structured English, or decision tables or trees.

9.2.1. The Data Flow Diagram

The primary tool of structured analysis is the *data flow diagram* or DFD. It is through the DFD that the solution is partitioned and completely and concisely specified. The DFD is a network representation of the solution and consists of four graphical elements: the data flow, processes, source/sinks, and data stores. These are shown in Figure 9.2. The data flow is represented as arrows between the different processes with a concise definition of the data that is flowing. One can picture a factory with conveyor belts moving data between stations where it is processed. A process transforms data in two ways: it changes the structure of the data by reformatting it, or it changes the content of the data or creates new data. A data store is a time-delayed repository of data, generally a disk file. Sources and sinks are simply sources of data and sinks of data. They are generally disk files again, with the difference from a

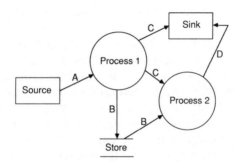

Figure 9.2 Data flow diagram.

data store being that the data that they hold is used only once and not retrieved. In historic terms, they could be considered card readers and line printers. The data flow diagram is often referred to as a *bubble diagram* because the processes are represented by circular "bubbles."

The DFD represents the flow of data and not the flow of control or the sequential execution of statements that the more familiar flow chart expresses. The DFD represents the steady-state flow of data and does not emphasize initialization or termination functions. Data may flow in several different directions upon the results of a test or comparison, yet these different paths are given equal weight in the DFD and no comparison is shown. The DFD represents the essence of the solution and includes only those data that are intimately part of the solution. It excludes flags, error sentinels, and the like.

9.2.2. Leveling the Data Flow Diagram

The complete specification of an engineering solution may consist of thousands of processes and data elements. The paper needed to hold all of these little circles and arrows would cover the walls of a large room. There is therefore a need to partition the data flow diagram. This could be done by taking the large piece of paper holding all of the information and cutting it into 8-1/2 × 11 inch pieces and putting these into a notebook. This is analogous to starting with a huge map of the United States with all of the streets, down to the smallest court and lane shown, and cutting the map into 8-1/2 × 11 inch pieces and putting them into a notebook. A better approach is to layer the DFD in a top-down way. At the top or zeroth level there is a single circle (or bubble) called the *context layer* that shows how this particular solution fits into the overall picture. It can also serve as the objective of the problem to be solved. Following this are levels with ever-increasing amounts of detail. Each level is simply an elaboration of the next level up. This is done until the lowest level contains bubbles that are functionally defined in terms of the detailed solution. An example is shown in Figure 9.3. Process 2 has one input B and two outputs C and D. Upon examination of the partitioning we see that process 2 consists of three subprocesses 2.1, 2.2, and 2.3. At this more detailed level we still see the single input B and the two outputs C and D. Only now there is more information about how C and D are created from B by the three subprocesses.

The numbering system for the bubbles should be obvious. The first level is numbered 1, 2, 3, ... The next level of detail for each of these bubbles is numbered 1.1, 1.2, . . . , and so on. This top-down partitioning of the data flow diagram has the following property. Given a complete DFD, the lower levels can be removed without removing the substance of the solution, only some of the details. This can be done all the way up to the top level, where the statement of the solution is a single bubble. This is equivalent to making a map of the United States showing only the outline of the states and the major interstate highways, then making maps of each state showing the interstate

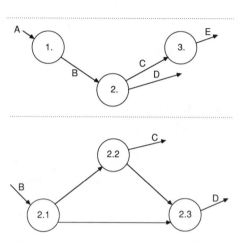

Figure 9.3 Leveling a data flow diagram.

highways and state highways, and then making maps of each county in each state showing all of the above highways and each county road and city street. With each new level there is ever-increasing detail. In the end, there is the same collection of small areas represented, but in addition to these there are larger areas with less detail. Depending on the use of the map book, each of these levels is very useful. Traveling from New York City to Los Angeles begins by finding ones way to the interstate highway using a detailed map of NYC. From here, the large map of the United States is much more useful than following the route through each of the smallest pieces. After arriving in Los Angeles, a more detailed map is again more useful.

The leveling of the data flow diagram is a convenient way of segmenting the specification of the solution. However, it should be remembered that only the processes in the lowest level of the DFD are real processes. All levels above this are simply convenient ways to group the real processes together into more manageable bundles. Later on in the structured design, these bubbles will roughly correspond to modules.

9.2.3. The Data Dictionary

The *data dictionary* or DD is simply a data base of all of the data referenced in the DFD. The specific data item is included along with a definition of it. In business applications, data items would likely correspond to records with several different subfields, although it should be remembered that for the DFD the use of variable names is not required. We are only interested in the essence of the solution method and not the computer implementation of it. These subfields are related to the larger data grouping through the use of the notation shown in Figure 9.4. The contents of files are also defined in the data dictionary. Data structures for the files are defined in the data dictionary. The important point is that all data flows of the DFD are defined in the DD and all subordinate data items are defined. An incomplete data dictionary (or DFD)

```
=       means IS EQUIVALENT TO

[]      means EITHER OR, select one of the options enclosed in
        the brackets

{}      means REPETITION OF THE COMPONENT ENCLOSED

()      means the enclosed component is OPTIONAL

+       means logical AND

|       means logical OR

*  ..  *   means that this is a description of the data

Example:

    hydrodynamic dependent = density + velocity + [energy |
    quantities                                    temperature]

    density = { mesh cell density }
            = * density in units of grams/cubic centimeter for
              all mesh cells *

    velocity = { mesh point velocity }
             = * velocity in units of centimeters/second for all
               mesh points *

    energy = { mesh cell energy }
           = * specific internal energy in units of ergs/gram
             for all mesh cells *

    mesh cell density = * density of a single mesh cell *

    mesh point velocity = * velocity of a single mesh point *

    mesh cell energy = * specific internal energy of a single
                       mesh cell *

    equation of state = pressure + [temperature | energy]

    pressure = { mesh cell pressure }
             = * pressure in units of dynes/square centimeter
               for all mesh cells *

    temperature = { mesh cell temperature }
                = * temperature in units of kelvin for all
                  mesh cells *
                  .
                  .
                  .
```

Figure 9.4 Data dictionary notation.

indicates an insufficient understanding of the problem solution. This should be remedied at this stage before the software definition is started.

9.2.4. Process Definition

The DFD and DD are used to partition the engineering solution and define the interfaces between processes. The solution specification is completed with the definition of the bottom level bubbles or the *functional primitives* of the DFD. Recall that only the bottom bubbles are really functions or processes. All overlying bubbles are simply groupings of the bottom ones. The specification of these processes is accomplished through a number of different mechanisms. In all cases, the specification must be limited to a single goal: to define the transformation of input to the bubble into output from the bubble.

9.2.4.1. *Structured English.*   The process specification can be accomplished using so-called *structured English*. Here the process is described using English or any other spoken language. However, the grammar is changed to look more like structured programming. An example is shown in Figure 9.5.

This method of specification is particularly useful when the solution specification must be understood by people without any background in computing. It gives them an appreciation of the logical constructs of programming but avoids technical details.

9.2.4.2. *Decision Tables or Trees.*   The same process described above is described using a decision tree as shown in Figure 9.6. Such trees are usually more convenient for programmers and others with an understanding of programming and systems analysis.

9.2.4.3. *Mathematical or Engineering Specification.*   In a situation where all persons involved in the software development project are familiar with engineering and mathematics, the process is concisely defined by using the appropriate mathematical formulas. The simple algorithm in Figure 9.7

```
Solve for the roots of the quadratic equation
            2
        a x  + b x + c = 0

      2
IF b  — 4ac is less than zero

THEN compute two imaginary roots of the equation
            2
ELSE IF b  — 4ac is equal to zero

THEN compute a single real root

ELSE compute two real roots.
```

Figure 9.5   Structured English for process specification.

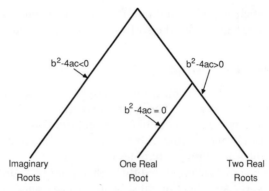

Figure 9.6   Decision tree for process specification.

Suppose we are to advance the solution of a first order ODE using the Adams-Moulton predictor-corrector method. The specification could be given as

For the differential equation

$$y' = f(x,y)$$

and with h fixed and $x_n = x_0 + nh$
and with (y_0,f_0), (y_1,f_1), (y_2,f_2), (y_3,f_3) given
for each fixed n = 3,4,...

1. Compute $y_{n+1}^{(0)}$, using the formula

$$y_{n+1}^{(0)} = y_n + h/24 \ (55f_n - 59f_{n-1} + 37f_{n-2} + 9f_{n-3})$$

2. Compute $f_{n+1}^{(0)} = f(x_{n+1},y_{n+1}^{(0)})$

3. Compute

$$y_{n+1}^{(k)} = y_n + h/24[9f(x_{n+1},y_{n+1}^{(k-1)}) + 19f_n - 5f_{n-1} + f_{n-2}]$$
$$k = 1,2,...$$

4. Iterate on k until

$$\frac{|y_{n+1}^{(k)} - y_{n+1}^{(k-1)}|}{|y_{n+1}^{(k)}|} < \epsilon$$

Figure 9.7   Mathematical or engineering specification of a process.

gives all of the information that is needed by the software designer. The rule in process specification is to be concise and brief. Whatever method of specification best meets this requirement is the best one to use.

9.3. SOFTWARE SPECIFICATION—STRUCTURED DESIGN

Software specification is the process whereby the solution to an engineering problem is translated into a blueprint for the software. The systematic translation of an engineering solution into a computer program blueprint is accomplished using a process called *structured design*. Structured design allows the engineer to specify not only a program to solve a problem but also provides the definition of an *optimum programming solution*. Structured design is concerned with the architecture of the program and not the actual lines of code in the program itself.

The two fundamental principles of structured design are *divide and conquer* and *form follows function*. A large engineering problem has a multifaceted solution including many different equations to solve and a large amount of data to manipulate. The software solution to this problem consequently has many parts. This software solution must be broken up into *modules* to correspond to each of these parts. But how many modules? Which modules? How do we know if we have made a good choice? How do we know if we have made a bad choice? How should information be exchanged between modules? Structured design is the art of designing the components of a system and the interrelationship between those components in the *best possible way*.

As with any design process, structured design has tools and methodologies for accomplishing its goals. In the following sections we introduce the concepts of structured design. In Chapter 10 we describe the qualities and measures of a good design. In Chapter 11 we look at the design methodologies that are followed to translate an engineering solution into an optimum software specification.

9.3.1. Definition of Software Design Goals

The objective of structured design is to produce a good computer program while minimizing the time and effort involved. This is done by systematizing the design procedure. To understand this design procedure we must first define what is meant by a "good" computer program.

There are seven different characteristics that are used to define an optimum computer program. These are efficiency, reliability, maintainability, modifiability, flexibility, generality, and utility. Depending on the application, each of these is given a different weight in determining the particular optimum of interest.

9.3.1.1. Efficiency. By efficiency we mean the minimization of scarce resources such as processor time, memory, disk storage, input/output peripherals, user time, and engineer/programmer time. Different applications have different priorities for these resources. In a typical example of engineering design software, such as a finite element program for stress analysis, the priority might be user friendliness to minimize the user's time in executing the program. In today's world, computer hardware is inexpensive compared to software. A typical cost breakdown for a large-scale software development effort is

20% Hardware

80% Software

This clearly indicates the unimportance of spending weeks of programmer time to squeeze out the last microsecond in execution time. This time would be better spent on improving user friendliness in the user interface. For many applications execution speed and memory use have a lower priority than in past years due to the reduction in the cost of these resources. There are exceptions to this. Real time applications put a high priority on execution speed. Solutions to problems that tax the capabilities of today's fastest supercomputers also require attention to execution speed and memory. Thus, the definition of "efficiency" depends on the specific application.

9.3.1.2. Reliability. Reliability answers the question, does the program work for all cases of interest? In business systems this is easy to define in terms of mean time between failures (MTBF). In engineering software it is more difficult to track down the failure mechanism. Sources of failure include programming bugs, code design errors, inadequate numerical treatments, and inadequate physical models. Error detection at execution time for inadequate numerical treatments and physical models is possible. Diagnosis of problems of applying the physical model to a particular input specification or using the numerical scheme for a problem where its error is too large should be made by the program and appropriate output issued to alert the user to these problems.

9.3.1.3. Maintainability. Maintainability is closely related to reliability. Once a problem has been found in the program, how easy is it to fix (i.e., how long does it take to fix)? This is extremely important in engineering applications. Programming bugs and code design errors are the same as in business systems software. However, inadequate numerics and models are more relevant to modeling physical systems. Program structure is decisive in determining the time necessary to fix such problems. Figure 9.1 shows the average breakdown of software costs throughout the program's lifetime. The overwhelming majority of the cost is in maintenance. This is therefore a most important aspect of program optimization.

9.3.1.4. Modifiability. Modifications are not motivated by failures but by recognition that requirements are changing and the software must change to meet new goals. Sometimes the program must be explicitly written to optimize its modifiability. A program with good maintainability also has the properties to give it good modifiability.

9.3.1.5. Flexibility. Flexible programs are able to handle many variations on the same theme. This is a more fundamental property than modifiability. It often means that the input is designed in such a way that the user can specify all of the fundamental quantities in the model and that none of these quantities are "hard-wired" into the coding. In this way a clever user can use the program for situations that were not even considered by the program designers.

9.3.1.6. Generality. Generality defines the scope of the themes or problems that the program handles without modification. Care must be taken to avoid developing a program that is too general. Such programs are often said to have "everything but the kitchen sink" in them. A program that is too general, one that solves many different unrelated problems, is difficult to develop and maintain because it is so large and diverse. For programs with a long and seasoned history, the maintainer is often faced with the question of modifying the program one more time to add another feature or to start with a new program. The answer to this question must be made within the context of the organization in which the program is developed. In a university setting, where graduate students come and go on 4- and 5-year intervals and documentation is not extensive, it is best to keep the program small so that the next student quickly understands the entire program. In a research laboratory with a permanent staff of program developers, a program is allowed to grow to a larger size.

9.3.1.7. Utility. Utility is a measure of the ease of use of the program. It is the human interface. Input should look like the problem to be solved and not some strange "computer talk." Output should give the numbers requested, not obscure intermediate results. User friendliness is most closely related to utility, while the actual computation done by the program is secondary to utility.

Hence the overall objective of structured design is efficiency, maintainability, modifiability, generality, flexibility, and utility. We want a program that is cheap to develop, cheap to operate, cheap to maintain, and cheap to modify. Usually, absolute minima are not obtained for each of these so one is faced with *trade-offs*.

9.3.2. Achievement of Software Design Goals

We stated earlier that the two basic rules of structured design are (1) divide and conquer and (2) form follows function. These rules are actually implemented in software design by following a set of guidelines.

Developing a large program is least costly when the parts of the problem are *manageably small* and *solvable separately*. What is manageably small? Maybe a better question is: what is unmanageably large? These questions have no absolute answers, but practicality dictates that to design, write, and test a module in a day is probably an indication that the module is too limited in scope, whereas to do the same in a year is clearly a tip-off that the module is too large. Probably a week to a month is about the average time required to design, write, and test a module, with most of the time spent in testing.

Implementation, maintenance, and modification costs are minimized when each piece of the program corresponds to exactly one small, well-defined piece of the engineering solution, and each relationship between program pieces corresponds only to a relationship between pieces of the solution. This demands that the software design not introduce artificial interrelationships between modules. This is the most common fault of poorly designed software. Structured design leads to the best solutions by partitioning and organizing pieces of the program. Highly interrelated parts of the solution should be in the same piece of program. Unrelated parts of the solution should be in unrelated pieces of the program.

These rather trivial statements form the heart of structured design. The best solution is one that is partitioned and organized in such a way that it most closely mimics the problem that it is designed to solve. This should be true in the way that each piece of the program is defined and the interrelationships between the pieces. We next look at ways to represent the pieces of the program.

9.3.3. The Black Box

We start the discussion of structured design tools with the familiar engineering concept of a black box. A true black box is a system, subsystem, or function that is fully exploited without knowledge of what is inside it. This is shown conceptually in Figure 9.8. Prespecified inputs always yield well-defined outputs using a well-defined procedure. The way that this procedure is implemented is unimportant to the user of the black box.

To most people automobiles, television sets, and stereos are nearly black boxes. They know that they must keep the car filled with gasoline for it to run. They know that they must turn the ignition key to start up the car. They

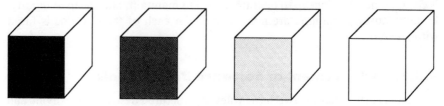

Figure 9.8 Black box concept for engineering design.

are trained to drive the car in most normal situations. Yet they know little about internal combustion engines, the combustion of gases, automatic transmissions, kinematics of gears, and the like.

Another more technical example of a black box might be a Runge-Kutta subroutine that solves first order differential equations. The user specifies the functional form of the right-hand side of the equation, an initial value, and the end point where the solution is desired, and the subroutine solves the differential equation under most circumstances. The user is not required to remember the specific details of the Runge-Kutta algorithm to use the subroutine in an applications program.

The opposite of a black box is a white box. Here understanding the details of the inner workings is important to the eventual outcome. A white box might be a college course or a jig-saw puzzle. In reality, most parts of large programs are gray boxes. They are somewhere in between the ideal black box and the undesirable white box.

Black boxes are used to great advantage in structured design. Once a certain process is defined, along with inputs and outputs, it is put into the design as a black box without regard to its detailed implementation. This of course has to eventually be determined when the program is written.

9.3.4. Structure of Computer Software

To partition a computer program into pieces it is important to understand how statements in the actual coding relate to one another. Here we define general relationships with particular applications to FORTRAN 77.

A computer program is a precise, ordered sequence of statements and aggregates of statements which in total define, describe, and characterize some task and direct the computer to perform this task. The program structure is this ordered sequence of statements. This is the classic *algorithmic* view of programs. By virtue of this characterization, programming took on this algorithmic approach. This line of thought is embodied in the so-called *flow chart* that charts the path of the program execution. (More on this later.)

These statements—lines of code in FORTRAN—are defined as having several types of structure associated with them. The definitions of these structures are useful in interpreting the program coding.

Conceptual structure refers to all statements of the same kind, such as FORMAT statements.

```
10 FORMAT(' THE DATA IS AS FOLLOWS')
11 FORMAT(10E12.4)
```

Referential structure refers to explicit references in one part of the program to things in other parts of the program. References to variables in COMMON blocks or through argument lists are examples of referential structure.

```
COMMON/VARBLS/ A(100), B(100), C(100)
           .
           .

   DO 10 I = 1,100
      A(I) = B(I) + C(I)
10 CONTINUE
           .
           .
```

Communication structure refers to the flow of data between different statements and pieces of the program.

```
DISTAN = VELOC * TIME
FORCE = XMASS * ACCEL
        .
        .
WORK = FORCE * DISTAN
```

Control structure refers to the flow of control between different statements or different pieces of the program.

```
   IF( VAR1 .GT. 0. ) GOTO 500
        .
        .
500 IF( VAR2 .LT. 78. ) GOTO 600
        .
        .
600 VAR2 = 10. * VAR1
        .
        .
```

Lexical structure is simply the order of statements as they appear in the source program.

In FORTRAN some statements serve to aggregate other statements into a *block*. Such statements define the boundaries of the aggregate or block.

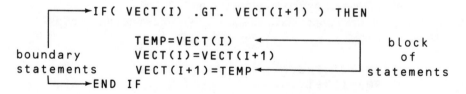

A block of statements is referenced as a group by using an aggregate or *block identifier*. This defines a programming module. *A module is a lexically contiguous sequence of program statements, bounded by boundary statements, having an aggregate identifier.* A bounded aggregate not having an aggregate identifier is a *segment*. Examples of modules and segments are given in Figure 9.9.

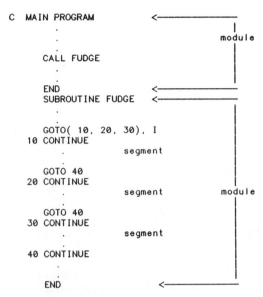

Figure 9.9 Modules and segments.

9.3.5. The Module

The module is the building block of structured design. In FORTRAN 77 a module is a SUBROUTINE or a FUNCTION. More specific than the definition above, a module is defined as a collection of program statements with four basic attributes: input and output, function, mechanics, and internal data. Input and output are obviously the information that the module receives and the information that the module returns upon completion of its task. In FORTRAN this is usually accomplished through argument lists. The function of a module is the transformation that it performs to generate its outputs from its inputs. These two features of a module are the view taken by the outside observer. The best module is a classic black box as defined earlier. The mechanics and internal data of a module are the inside view of the module. The mechanics are the specific procedure and logic used to perform the function of the module. Internal data is data kept by the module in its own workspace and used only by it. These are local variables in FORTRAN. In structured design we are interested only in the outside view of modules. The inside view is the concern of structured programming.

Structured design uses a graphical representation of modules and their relation to one another. These graphical representations are displayed in Figure 9.10. Modules are represented by a rectangular box with the name of the module (its aggregate identifier) inside the box. Predefined modules—subroutines in system libraries, for instance—are represented by rectangles with two vertical lines. Connections between modules in the form of CALL statements are shown with arrows. A single module can of course call several other modules and many modules can call a single module. Communications between mod-

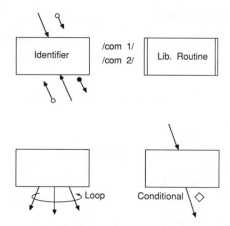

Figure 9.10   Graphical notation for structure chart.

ules is through argument lists. These are shown graphically with small arrows. The direction that the arrow points indicates the direction of information exchange. Actual data is shown with an open tail on the arrow and logical data or a "flag" is shown with a closed tail on the arrow. It is best to refer to the data by its name rather than by the FORTRAN variable name associated with it.

Another way for modules to communicate data is through global data areas. In FORTRAN this is called a COMMON block. This is represented by listing the named global data areas along the side of the module. There are no arrows used here to represent data flow. Furthermore, the name of the global data area is used to indicate that not only the data of interest is available, but also any other data in this area.

9.3.6. The Structure Chart

The most important tool of structured design is the *structure chart*. The structure chart shows the hierarchy of module interrelations. The flow chart shows the path of program flow. The difference here is between *procedure* and *structure*. This is demonstrated in Figure 9.11. The structure chart does not show program flow. It only shows interconnections between modules and the data passed between them. A good analogy can be drawn between structure charts and corporate structure, as shown in Figure 9.12. Organization theory tells us that each manager in an organization should only have 7 ± 2 people directly reporting to them. Many fewer than this indicates there are unneeded people in the so-called line organization. This is shown in Figure 9.13. Many more than this indicates that too much information flows through a single person. A single individual cannot assimilate this much information. This is called "pancaking" in the organization. The structure chart is flat as shown in Figure 9.14.

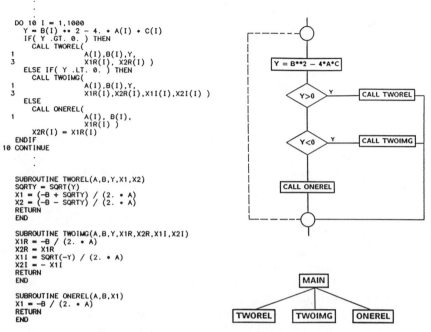

```
      .
      .
      .
   DO 10 I = 1,1000
      Y = B(I) ** 2 - 4. * A(I) * C(I)
      IF( Y .GT. 0. ) THEN
         CALL TWOREL(
   1                  A(I),B(I),Y,
   3                  X1R(I), X2R(I) )
      ELSE IF( Y .LT. 0. ) THEN
         CALL TWOIMG(
   1                  A(I),B(I),Y,
   3                  X1R(I),X2R(I),X1I(I),X2I(I) )
      ELSE
         CALL ONEREL(
   1                  A(I), B(I),
                      X1R(I) )
         X2R(I) = X1R(I)
      ENDIF
10 CONTINUE
      .
      .

   SUBROUTINE TWOREL(A,B,Y,X1,X2)
   SQRTY = SQRT(Y)
   X1 = (-B + SQRTY) / (2. * A)
   X2 = (-B - SQRTY) / (2. * A)
   RETURN
   END

   SUBROUTINE TWOIMG(A,B,Y,X1R,X2R,X1I,X2I)
   X1R = -B / (2. * A)
   X2R = X1R
   X1I = SQRT(-Y) / (2. * A)
   X2I = - X1I
   RETURN
   END

   SUBROUTINE ONEREL(A,B,X1)
   X1 = -B / (2. * A)
   RETURN
   END
```

Figure 9.11   Structure chart and flow chart.

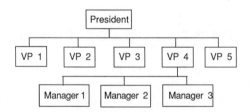

Figure 9.12   Analogy of software structure chart to corporate organization chart.

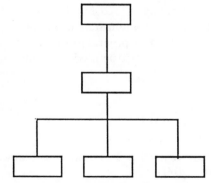

Figure 9.13   Unneeded modules in structure chart.

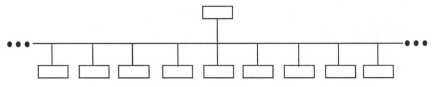

Figure 9.14   Pancaked structure chart.

Likewise, computer program structure follows the same rules. Too many or too few modules called by a single module indicates weakness in the organization of the program. Structure charts are most useful for describing intermodular relations. Flow charts are most useful for describing algorithms within a module.

Some procedural information is often useful to include in the structure chart. Modules called only once are distinguished from modules called from within a loop or modules called on a conditional basis by the notation shown in Figure 9.10. These procedural embellishments of the structure chart are regarded as annotations rather than central to the program design. They serve to document the program.

The structure chart is used by the software designer to develop, optimize, and ultimately define the software design. It embodies the information that determines the quality of the software design.

9.4.   SOFTWARE GENERATION—STRUCTURED PROGRAMMING

Little will be said about structured programming because this is emphasized in all beginning programming courses and such background is prerequisite for this text. Structured programming is mainly concerned with the use of three constructs to form the logic for all program structures. These are sequential statements, loops, and IF-THEN-ELSE blocks. Within the context of this discussion, structured programming is used for the inside view of modules and is important to the creation of program statements for each module. Because each module is about the size of a program in a beginning FORTRAN programming course, the concepts of structured programming carry over completely.

REFERENCES

1. W. P. Stevens, G. J. Meyers, and L. L. Constantine, "Structured Design," *IBM Systems Journal 2*, 115 (1974).
2. *IEEE Transactions of Software Engineering*, **SE-3**(1), January 1977.

3. T. DeMarco, *Structured Analysis and System Specification*, Yourdon Press, New York, 1978.

4. E. Yourdon and L. Constantine, *Structured Design*, Yourdon Press, New York, 1978.

5. E. Yourdon, Ed., *Classics in Software Engineering*, Yourdon Press, New York, 1979.

6. M. Page-Jones, *The Practical Guide to Structured Systems Design*, Yourdon Press, New York, 1980.

7. G. Myers, *Composite/Structured Design* Van Nostrand Reinhold, New York, 1978.

8. B. Dickinson, *Developing Structured Systems*, Yourdon Press, New York, 1980.

9. S. Pfleeger, *Software Engineering: The Production of Quality Software*, Macmillan, New York, 1987.

EXERCISES

1. Compare the breakdown of costs (time) for commercial software in Figure 9.1 with a similar breakdown for the production of software for a college class such as this one. Where are the large differences in these two situations?

2. Write objectives statements for (a) your participation in this class, (b) your college career, (c) your social life.

3. Draw a problem specification for each of the objectives in problem 2 using a data flow diagram.

4. Using a process or procedure from your field of engineering, draw a problem specification for it using a data flow diagram, data dictionary, and process definitions. Also draw a flow chart of the process and discuss the differences between the flow chart and the data flow design.

5. Discuss the concept of a black box using the four fundamental attributes: input/output, function, mechanics, and internal data. Give examples of black boxes, white boxes, and gray boxes found in the world around you.

6. Using a large-scale program from your field of engineering, draw the structure chart for the program.

━━10

Qualities of Optimum Software Design

The qualities of a software design are the basis for determining when it is optimum. We learned in the last chapter about the underlying principles of structured design and the tools that are used to apply these principles to computer software. In this chapter we explore the detailed features that modules must have, both internally and in relation to other modules, to be considered elements of an optimum design. We use the structure chart to evaluate these features.

10.1. MODULE COUPLING

The independence of modules is the keystone of structured design. A well-partitioned program consists of a hierarchy of modules, each with its own specific task to perform. No module requires understanding of other modules to perform its own task. It simply needs inputs, and from these it produces well-defined outputs. It is therefore useful to have a measure of the degree of independence of modules. This is called *coupling*. Two modules are entirely independent if each can function without the presence of the other one. In this case they are *decoupled*. In general, modules are coupled and we must determine whether they are "strongly" coupled or "weakly" coupled. Hence coupling is an *intermodular* property. It is desirable for modules to be as weakly coupled as possible for this means that they can be developed, debugged, and maintained independently of the other modules in the design. This independence translates into lower development costs.

The key question is, how much of one module must we know in order to understand another module? The more we must know about other modules

245

to understand a given module, the more they are coupled (and the less they are the ideal black box). Factors that influence coupling are type of connection between modules, complexity of the interface, and binding time of the connections.

10.1.1. Type of Connection Between Modules

Minimally connected modules in FORTRAN are simple subroutines with a single entry point and an unconditional return. (This is the normal situation in FORTRAN subroutines.) This represents the least coupling. Figure 10.1 gives an example of minimally connected modules, our familiar bubble sort subroutine.

Normally connected modules are subroutines with multiple ENTRY points, each of which is minimally connected or where control returns to other than the next sequential statement in the calling program. This has more coupling.

```
C   A PROGRAM TO SORT DATA INTO ASCENDING ORDER
          .
          .
        CALL  BUBBLE ( VECT,25 )
          .
          .
        END

        SUBROUTINE BUBBLE( VECTOR,LENGTH )
C   THIS SUBROUTINE PERFORMS A BUBBLE SORT OF DATA INTO ASCENDING
C   ORDER
C   INPUT   — VECTOR – RAW DATA (REAL VECTOR)
C           — LENGTH – NUMBER OF ELEMENTS IN THE VECTOR OF REAL DATA
C   OUTPUT  — VECTOR – SORTED DATA
C
        DIMENSION VECTOR(LENGTH)
        LOGICAL DONE

C   SET THE DONE SWITCH TO .TRUE. TO START
        DONE = .TRUE.

C   MAKE A PASS THROUGH THE DATA AND INTERCHANGE ELEMENTS THAT
C   ARE OUT OF ORDER
      5 DO 10 I = 1,LENGTH—1
          IF( VECTOR(I) .GT. VECTOR(I+1) ) THEN
            TEMP = VECTOR(I)
            VECTOR(I) = VECTOR(I+1)
            VECTOR(I+1) = TEMP
            DONE = .FALSE.
          END IF
     10 CONTINUE

C   CHECK TO SEE IF ANY CHANGES WERE MADE ON THIS PASS, IF NO
C   CHANGES WERE MADE THEN THE DATA IS SORTED
        IF( DONE ) RETURN

C   CHANGES WERE MADE, RESET THE SWITCH AND TRY AGAIN
        DONE = .TRUE.
        GOTO 5
        END
```

Figure 10.1 Minimally connected modules.

The table look-up subroutine and entry point are given in Figure 10.2 as an example.

Pathologically connected modules are where one module transfers control to a statement internal to another module (the statement is not a module identifier). This cannot occur in FORTRAN programs.

10.1.2. Complexity of the Interface

By complexity we mean complexity in human terms. The number of arguments, special punctuation, and the like needed to make the subroutine call is a measure of the complexity. Complex interfaces lead to more coupling between subroutines. The subroutine calls in Figures 10.1 and 10.2 demonstrate this. The subroutine with fewer arguments is less complex than the one with more arguments.

10.1.3. Information Passed Through the Interface

There are two types of information that are shared through the interface between two modules: data and control information. Communication of data between modules is directly related to the engineering solution that the program design is to accomplish. In principle, this is all that is necessary for a functioning software solution. *Data coupling* is sometimes called input/output coupling because all that is needed to use a module is a knowledge of the input and the expected output. This is demonstrated in Figure 10.1 with the bubble sort.

Control coupling covers all forms of connection that communicate elements of control. This may involve the actual transfer of control or it may involve the passing of data that change, regulate, or synchronize the called module or the calling module. This is demonstrated in Figure 10.3. Control coupling is stronger than data coupling and is an indication that the solution has not been partitioned properly. In Figure 10.3 the flag returned by the DECIDE subroutine determines the computation to be performed by the main program. In essence, the subordinate module is telling its superior what it should do. Following the corporate analogy, this shows a poor chain of command.

10.1.4. Binding Time of Intermodular Connections

Binding time refers to when (on the time line) a program element value is fixed.

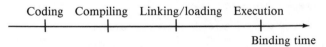

Late binding time is desirable because it indicates weaker coupling. Modules are more flexible when they have a late binding time. The last of the subrou-

```
C   THIS PROGRAM CALLS TABLE TO INTERPOLATE.  IT WILL EXTRAPOLATE
C   BELOW THE TABLE LOWER BOUNDARY BUT WILL NOT EXTRAPOLATE ABOVE
C   THE TABLE UPPER BOUNDARY.  IT USES ALTERNATE RETURNS TO DECIDE
                  .
                  .
        CALL TABLE(YTAB,XTAB,X,Y,NINT,&10,&20)
                  .
                  .
    10 CALL INTERP(YTAB,XTAB,X,Y,NINT)
                  .
                  .
    20 CONTINUE
                  .
                  .
        END

        SUBROUTINE TABLE( YTAB, XTAB, NTAB, X, Y, NINT, *, *)

C   THIS SUBROUTINE FINDS THE INDEX IN A VECTOR OF TABULATED
C   X-VALUES THAT FALLS JUST BELOW THE INTERPOLANT X AND THEN
C   INTERPOLATES TO OBTAIN THE VALUE Y.  SHOULD X FALL OUTSIDE
C   THE BOUNDS OF THE TABLE, CONTROL IS RETURNED TO THE CALLER.
C   SHOULD THE CALLER WISH TO EXTRAPOLATE THEN A CALL TO THE
C   ENTRY POINT INTERP WILL DO THIS.
C   INPUT    YTAB   - VECTOR OF DEPENDENT TABULATED VALUES
C            XTAB   - VECTOR OF INDEPENDENT TABULATED VALUES
C            NTAB   - DIMENSION OF THE TABLE VECTORS
C            X      - INDEPENDENT VARIABLE TO INTERPOLATE
C   OUTPUT   Y      - DEPENDENT INTERPOLATED VALUE
C            NINT   - INDEX IN TABLE BELOW INTERPOLANT X

        REAL XTAB(*), YTAB(*)

C   FIND THE INDEX
        DO 10 N = 2,NTAB
          IF( X .LT. XTAB(N) ) THEN
            NINT = N - 1
            GOTO 20
          ENDIF
    10 CONTINUE

C   IF WE REACH HERE, X IS GREATER THAN THE MAX TABLE VALUE
C   XTAB(NTAB).  RETURN TO SECOND ALTERNATE RETURN POINT
        RETURN 2

C   CHECK FOR X BELOW LOWEST TABLE VALUE.  IF BELOW, RETURN TO
C   FIRST ALTERNATE RETURN POINT
    20 CONTINUE
        IF( X .LT. XTAB(1) ) RETURN 1

C ALL IS WELL, GO ON TO INTERPOLATE
        GOTO 100

        ENTRY INTERP( YTAB, XTAB, NTAB, X, Y, NINT )

C   THIS ENTRY INTERPOLATES IN A TABLE, GIVEN THE INDEX CLOSEST
C   TO THE INDEPENDENT VARIABLE - NINT

   100 CONTINUE

C   USE A SIMPLE LINEAR INTERPOLATION
        SLOPE = (YTAB(NINT+1) - YTAB(NINT)) /
       1        (XTAB(NINT+1) - XTAB(NINT))
        Y = YTAB(NINT) + SLOPE * (X - XTAB(NINT))

        RETURN
        END
```

Figure 10.2 Normally connected modules.

```
C  MAIN PROGRAM
          .
   CALL DECIDE(X,Y,Z,IFLAG)
   GOTO (100,200,300), IFLAG
          .
          .
   END
          .
   SUBROUTINE DECIDE(A,B,C,IFLAG)
          .
   IF( B**2 - 4. * A * C .EQ. 0. ) THEN
      IFLAG = 1
      RETURN
   ELSE IF( B**2 - 4. * A * C .LT. 0. ) THEN
      IFLAG = 2
      RETURN
   ELSE
      IFLAG = 3
      RETURN
   END IF
   END
```

Figure 10.3 Control coupling between modules.

tines in Figure 10.4 is the most desirable and has the weakest coupling to its calling subroutine because the dimensions of the matrices are determined at execution time. The calling subroutine need know little about the internals of the INVERT subroutine because all information is passed into it under the control of the caller. In the first two cases the calling routine must know that the matrices must be dimensioned 50×50 in order for the INVERT subroutine to operate upon them. If the argument matrices do not have this dimension, then the INVERT subroutine produces garbage.

10.1.5. Common Environment Coupling

A somewhat different form of coupling called *common environment coupling* is extremely important to FORTRAN programs. In this form of coupling, several modules are implicitly coupled by their common access to global variables in COMMON blocks. The use of COMMON blocks in large FORTRAN programs has been accepted as a good programming practice. The number of errors that come with accessing data are thought to be reduced. However, in the structured design approach to software design, common environment coupling is considered the strongest of the coupling mechanisms and is therefore discouraged. But because there are no absolutes in the structured design approach, named COMMON blocks can be used to advantage when properly defined. The complexity of the interface is a coupling mechanism that grows with the number of variables in the argument list. Therefore, a named COMMON block with these variables in it may be more desirable than an argument list with many elements.

```
SUBROUTINE INVERT(AMATRX,BMATRX)
                    .                        coding time
                    .
DIMENSION AMATRX(50,50), BMATRX(50,50)
                    .
END
```

```
SUBROUTINE INVERT(AMATRX,BMATRX)
                    .                        compile time
                    .
PARAMETER (MDIM=50, NDIM=50)
                    .
DIMENSION AMATRX(MDIM,NDIM), BMATRX(MDIM,NDIM)
                    .
END
```

```
SUBROUTINE INVERT(AMATRX,BMATRX,MDIM,NDIM)
                    .                        execution time
                    .
DIMENSION AMATRX(MDIM,NDIM), BMATRX(MDIM,NDIM)
                    .
END
```

Figure 10.4 Binding time of coupling.

10.1.6. Summary

The coupling of modules plays a key role in determining the optimum design of software. Two different forms of coupling through the module interface and the special case of common environment coupling are identified with the following degrees of strength.

> Data coupling   Weakest
> Control coupling   ↓
> Common coupling   Strongest

There are no totally inflexible rules in structured design but only guidelines. Therefore, each individual circumstance is resolved on its own merits. In general, these guidelines identify the strength and weakness of the partitioning of the program and pinpoint the weakest modules.

10.2. MODULE COHESION

In the last section we looked at the relations between modules and defined module coupling. We asked the question, how easy is it to use this module? Another way of measuring the quality of a structured design is by the internal relatedness of the modules. *Modules should be defined in such a way that they each perform one well-defined function.* This function can be quite global, such as "read all input," or it might be very limited in scope, such as "read next record." In either case the function of the module is quite clear and the module can be considered a black box. This internal functional relatedness of modules is called *cohesion*. Hence cohesion is an *intramodular* property as compared to coupling which is intermodular. Cohesion and coupling are obviously related. Coupling compares the external properties of a module against the ideal black box while cohesion compares the internal properties of a module against the ideal black box. The greater the cohesion, the smaller is the coupling between modules. Maximizing cohesion is nearly equivalent to minimizing coupling.

In actual practice it is easier to first deal with cohesion and then use the coupling guidelines as a check when building a structured design. To measure cohesion we must introduce associative principles. Elements in a module are grouped together because they are somehow related to one another or associated with one another. Seven levels of association are identified:

1. Coincidental association   Least cohesive
2. Logical association
3. Temporal association
4. Procedural association
5. Communicational association
6. Sequential association
7. Functional association   Most cohesive

Levels 1–3 are very low, and generally unacceptable, levels of cohesion. Levels 4–7 are generally acceptable levels of cohesion. Once again, it is important to emphasize that structured design guidelines are not absolutely rigid. That is the reason we use the word "generally" so frequently in this discussion. We now describe each of these levels of association and give an example of each.

10.2.1. Coincidental Cohesion

Modules with coincidental cohesion have little or no constructive relationship between their elements. If the particular test and subsequent arithmetic operation shown in Figure 10.5 were found in many unrelated places throughout a program, the tendency might be to create a subroutine like that shown in Figure 10.5. This comes from a desire to "break up" the program into modular form, mistakenly called structured design. This reasoning is incorrect. Structured design molds the program into the structure of the problem. It could be argued that the subroutine in Figure 10.5 saves memory. This is again erroneous reasoning. Most large programs are 90% variable storage and 10% machine code. A few repeated lines of program have little effect on the total memory that is used. This approach to modularization is historic—when computers had small, expensive memories every few words saved were important.

```
            .
            .
      DO 10 I = 1,N
      IF( C(I) .GT. D(I) ) THEN
         A(I) = B(I) * C(I) + D(I) / E(I)
      END IF
   10 CONTINUE
            .
            .
      DO 30 J 1,LAST
      IF( G(I) .GT. H(I) ) THEN
         G(I) = C(I) * G(I) + H(I) / D(I)
      END IF
   30 CONTINUE
            .
            .
            .
      SUBROUTINE ARITH(NMAX,V,W,X,Y,Z)
      DIMENSION V(1), W(1), X(1), Y(1), Z(1)
      DO 10 I = 1,NMAX
      IF( X(I) .GT. Y(I) ) THEN
         V(I) = W(I) * X(I) + Y(I) / Z(I)
      END IF
   10 CONTINUE
      RETURN
      END
```

Figure 10.5   Coincidental cohesion.

Memory is no longer expensive and processors are parallel and pipelined today. Random jumping from module to module is disastrous to efficiency.

In contrast to the program segment in Figure 10.5, the subroutine segment in Figure 10.6 is not coincidental, but we must be careful in our interpretation. All tables must have the same dimensions or these must be passed. All tables must have the same internal structure, and so on. Identification of coincidental association depends on the motivation for grouping elements. If it is part of

```
            .
            .
      DO 10 J = 1,JMAX
            .
            .
   C  GET ENTHALPY
      CALL INTERP(ETHTAB,TEMPER(J),PRESS(J),ENTHAL(J),IFLAG)
            .
            .
   C  GET ENTROPY
      CALL INTERP(ETRTAB,TEMPER(J),PRESS(J),ENTROP(J),IFLAG)
            .
            .
   10 CONTINUE
            .
            .
      SUBROUTINE INTERP(TABLE,TEMPER,PRESS,VALUE,IFLAG)
      DIMENSION TABLE(50,100)
            .
            .
            .
```

Figure 10.6   Functional cohesion.

the problem structure (either physical, looking up data in steam tables, or numerical, inverting matrices that all are similar), then this is okay. But if groups of statements are combined into modules simply for "convenience," this is bad structure. This point is quite subtle, but should be consciously evaluated when defining modules. Such coincidentally associative modules are often called "utility routines." This is a sure tip-off that they really hold no place of their own in the structured design; they can't even be given a decent name to describe them. Good structured design does not contain utility routines.

10.2.2. Logical Cohesion

The elements of a module are logically associated if they fall into the same logical class of related functions. In Figure 10.7 all error statements are printed by subroutine ERROR; thus the statements in ERROR are logically associated. This is stronger cohesion than coincidental cohesion but is still quite weak.

```
            .
            .
      IF( X .GT. Y ) CALL ERROR(6)
            .
            .

      IF( G .LT. H .AND. X .GT. Z ) CALL ERROR(4)
            .
            .

      SUBROUTINE ERROR(INDEX)
C  .
C  THIS SUBROUTINE OUTPUTS ERROR MESSAGES
      PARAMETER( IOUT = 6 )
      IF( INDEX .GT. 10 ) THEN
         WRITE(IOUT,5) INDEX
         WRITE(IOUT,6)
    5    FORMAT(' ERROR CODE=',I3)
    6    FORMAT(' ERROR CODE IS TOO LARGE')
         RETURN
      ELSE
         WRITE(IOUT,5) INDEX
         GOTO( 10,20,30,40,50,60,70,80,90,100 ), INDEX
C
   10    WRITE(IOUT,11)
   11    FORMAT('  INCONSISTENT VARIABLE MAGNITUDES')
         GOTO 200
C
   20    WRITE(IOUT,21)
   21    FORMAT('  CALCULATED INDEX OUT OF BOUNDS')
         GOTO 200
            .
            .
            .
  200    CONTINUE
      END IF
      RETURN
      END
```

Figure 10.7 Logical cohesion.

10.2.3. Temporal Cohesion

It is common to place all initialization functions in a large program into a module. These include mounting and rewinding tapes, setting variables to default values, and so on. All of these functions come at one time and hence are called temporally associated. This time relatedness makes temporal cohesion stronger than logical cohesion. Temporally cohesive modules are likely to be logically cohesive also, but the converse is not always true. The subroutine segment in Figure 10.8 is taken from a magnetohydrodynamics simulation program. It is the first subroutine called in the program and in turn it calls a number of subroutines to initialize variables, read input, print a summary of the input, and the like.

10.2.4. Procedural Cohesion

Procedurally associated elements are combined into the same module because they are all part of some procedural unit. Procedural units include an iteration loop, decision process, or linear sequence of statements where *control* flows from one element in the sequence to the next. Modules with procedural cohesion are often found when modularization of a program comes from a flow chart rather than a structure chart. Procedural cohesion is in the middle so far as its strength is concerned. The main program in Figure 10.9 is from the same magnetohydrodynamics program. It is clearly procedural since it consists of a simple loop of subroutine calls that advance the solution to the magnetohydrodynamics equations in time and space.

10.2.5. Communicational Cohesion

Communicational cohesion is the lowest level where we find elements of a module tied together by the structure of the particular problem to be solved. Communicationally associated elements all work on the same input data and/ or produce the same output data. The subroutine segment in Figure 10.10 computes the volume of finite difference zones for three different types of coordinate systems. Each element of the subroutine computes the same quantities, but for different geometric options. Thus they all use the same input quantities to produce the same output quantities.

10.2.6. Sequential Cohesion

Sequential association comes when the output of one element serves as input to the next. As with lower cohesive levels, sequential cohesion often comes from flow chart thinking. One or more contiguous steps in a flow chart are combined into a module that serves as a subroutine for the process as a whole. The subroutine in Figure 10.11 computes ion and electron densities in a plasma given the specific volume of the plasma V2A, the atomic weight of the ions

```
      SUBROUTINE INITIA
C
C  INITIA IS THE INPUT AND STORAGE INITIALIZATION ROUTINE
C
      IMPLICIT REAL (A-H,O-Z)
      LOGICAL TIMING
C
C  ALL INPUT IS VIA NAMELIST
      NAMELIST /INPUT/
     +    ATW2B,          CON,            DN2B,           DR2B,
     +    DTB,            DTMAX,          DTMIN,          IDELTA,
     +    ISW,            JMAX,           TA,             NMAX,
     +    NO,             NI,             RI,             TBC,
     +    TSCI,           TSCDI,          CHLEN,          RCDIST
C
C***********************************************************************
C
C  THIS IS WHERE IT ALL BEGINS
C
C  SET ALL VARIABLES TO ZERO
      CALL CLEAR
C
C  SET DEFAULT VALUES
      CALL INIT1
C
C  NOW READ THE NAMELIST INPUT FROM UNIT 5
      READ (5,INPUT)
C
C  TEST FOR A RESTART
      IF (IRS.EQ.0) GO TO 1
C  ELSE   THIS IS A RESTART, READ IN THE COMMON BLOCKS
      CALL UNREAD
C
C  READ INPUT CHANGES
      READ (5,INPUT)
C
C  COMPLETE THE PREVIOUS TIME CYCLE
      IF (TIMING(DUMMY)) CALL QUIT
      CALL SHIFTT
      GO TO 2
C
C  THIS IS NOT A RESTART, JUST A NORMAL ZPINCH RUN
C
    1 CONTINUE
C
C
C  SET UP VARIABLES
      CALL INIT2
C
C  SET UP MORE VARIABLES
      CALL INIT4
C
C  SET UP MORE VARIABLES
      CALL INIT3
C
C  OUTPUT THE INITIAL INPUT
    2 CALL INIT5
C
      CALL OUT1
      RETURN
C
      END
```

Figure 10.8 Temporal cohesion.

```
      PROGRAM ZPINCH
      LOGICAL TIMING
C
C  THIS MAIN ROUTINE IS ONLY A SERIES OF SUBROUTINE CALLS
C  INITIA - SETS UP DEFAULT VARIABLES AND READS INPUT FROM UNIT 5
C
C  HYDRO  - SOLVES THE MOMENTUM CONSERVATION EQUATION FOR THE FLUID
C             VELOCITY
C
C  ENERGY - SOLVES THE ENERGY CONSERVATION EQUATIONS FOR RADIATION
C             AND ION TEMPERATURES
C
C  EOS    - OBTAINS RADIATION AND PLASMA PRESSURES FROM THE PLASMA
C             DENSITY AND TEMPERATURES
C
C  MAGCUR - SOLVES THE MAGNETIC DIFFUSION EQUATION AND THE CURRENT
C             EQUATION
C
C  ECHECK - DOES A TOTAL ENERGY CONSERVATION CHECK ON THE PLASMA FLUID
C             AND PERFORMS THE CURRENT AND FLUX CONSERVATION CHECKS
C
C  OUT    - OUTPUTS A SUMMARY OF THE RESULTS OF THE COMPLETED TIME CYCLE
C
C  TIMING - DETERMINES THE NEXT HYDRO TIME STEP AND ALSO DETERMINES
C             WHETHER THE MAXIMUM TIME OR TIME CYCLE LIMITS HAVE BEEN MET
C
C  QUIT   - WRAPS UP THE  CALCULATION
C
C  SHIFTT - SHIFTS VARIABLES BACK FROM TIME LEVEL (N+1) TO (N) IN
C             PREPARATION FOR THE NEXT TIME CYCLE
C
      CALL INITIA
    1 CALL HYDRO
      CALL ENERGY
      CALL EOS
      CALL MAGCUR
      CALL ECHECK
      CALL OUT
      IF( TIMING(DUMMY) ) CALL QUIT
      CALL SHIFTT
      GOTO 1
      END
```

Figure 10.9 Procedural cohesion.

ATW2B, and the charge state Z2B. Each statement uses the results of the previous statements. This of course is the common approach to programming. The problem here is defining modules (i.e., group functional elements) in such a way that they are most weakly coupled and most strongly cohesive. Given a flow diagram there are many alternative ways to group the functional steps into modules.

10.2.7. Functional Cohesion

Functional cohesion is whatever is not sequential, communicational, procedural, temporal, logical, or coincidental. A module which is truely functional has no extraneous elements related by weaker associative principles. It is the ideal black box. The square root function or any intrinsic function in FORTRAN is considered to have functional cohesion. Any coding within the

```
      SUBROUTINE VOLUME

         .  (COMMON block definitions)
         .
         .
C
C  DECIDE WHICH GEOMETRY WE ARE USING AND CALCULATE SPECIFIC VOLUME
      GO TO (30,40,50), IDELTA
C
C  PLANAR GEOMETRY
      30 DO 35 J = 2,JMAX
         RS1A(J) = 1.E0
         RS1B(J) = 1.E0
         VOL2C = VOL2A(J)
         VOL2A(J) = DR2A(J)
         VOL2B(J) = .5E0 * (VOL2C + VOL2A(J))
         V2A(J) = VOL2A(J) / DMASS2(J)
      35 CONTINUE
         GO TO 60
C
C  CYLINDRICAL GEOMETRY
      40 DO 45 J = 2,JMAX
         RS1A(J) = R1A(J)
         RS1B(J) = .5E0 * (RS1C(J) + RS1A(J))
         VOL2C = VOL2A(J)
         VOL2A(J) = .5E0 * GEOFAC * DR2A(J) * (R1A(J)+R1A(J-1))
         VOL2B(J) = .5E0 * (VOL2C + VOL2A(J))
         V2A(J) = VOL2A(J) / (GEOFAC * DMASS2(J))
      45 CONTINUE
         GO TO 60
C
C  SPHERICAL GEOMETRY
      50 DO 55 J = 2,JMAX
         RS1A(J) = R1A(J)**2
         RS1B(J) = .5E0 * (RS1C(J) + RS1A(J))
         VOL2C = VOL2A(J)
         VOL2A(J) = DR2A(J) * GEOFAC * (R1A(J) * R1A(J-1) +
     1           .33333333333333E0 * DR2A(J) * DR2A(J))
         VOL2B(J) = .5E0 * (VOL2C + VOL2A(J))
         V2A(J) = VOL2A(J) / (GEOFAC * DMASS2(J))
      55 CONTINUE
      60 CONTINUE
         RETURN
         END
```

Figure 10.10   Communicational cohesion.

```
      SUBROUTINE NUMDEN
C
C  NUMDEN CALCULATES ION AND ELECTRON NUMBER DENSITY AT N+1/2 AND N+1

      COMMON/DENSTY/ DN2A(259), DE2A(259), DN2B(259), DE2B(259),
     1               V2A(259), ATW2B(259), Z2B(259), JMAX

      DO 100 J = 2,JMAX
         DN2C = DN2A(J)
         DE2C = DE2A(J)
         DN2A(J) = .6023E24 / (V2A(J) * ATW2B(J))
         DE2A(J) = DN2A(J) * Z2B(J)
         DN2B(J) = .5E0 * (DN2C + DN2A(J))
         DE2B(J) = .5E0 * (DE2C + DE2A(J))
     100 CONTINUE
C
         RETURN
         END
```

Figure 10.11   Sequential cohesion.

SQRT function is there for only one purpose—the accurate calculation of the square root.

Identification of functional cohesion usually comes through the process of elimination used for its definition. A module is tested against each of the lower forms of cohesion and if it fails all of the tests then it is said to be functionally cohesive.

10.2.8. Identifying the Level of Cohesion

The following guidelines are used to identify less than functional modules:

1. The operation of a functional module is fully described in an imperative sentence of simple structure, usually with a single transitive verb and specific nonplural object.

2. If the only reasonable way of describing the module's operation is a compound sentence, or a sentence containing a comma, or a sentence containing more than one verb, then the module is probably less than functional. It may be sequential, communicational, or logical.

3. If the descriptive sentence contains such time-oriented words as *first, next, after, then, start, step, when, until,* or *for all,* then the module probably has temporal or procedural cohesion.

4. If the predicate of the descriptive sentence does not contain a simple specific object following the verb, the module is probably logically cohesive.

With these guidelines, we see that it is useful to have a single concise statement in the form of a sentence in the comments at the head of a subroutine. This not only documents the subroutine but allows a determination of its cohesion level. An even better approach is to include a note in the comments along with the sentence to identify the level of cohesion.

The cohesion of a module is approximately the highest level of cohesion which is applicable to all elements of processing in the module. The total cohesive nature of a program is determined by assigning a numerical value to each level of cohesion. One proposed scale is the following:

0 = Coincidental
1 = Logical
2 = Temporal
5 = Procedural
7 = Communicational
9 = Sequential
10 = Functional

We have looked at two measures of good structured design, *coupling* and *cohesion.* Program structure should mirror problem structure. Program modules should be independent, self-contained functional units (i.e., no coupling, maximum cohesion) to most easily write, debug, and maintain the software.

10.3. PROGRAM MORPHOLOGY

The functionality of each module and its relation to the modules interacting with it are the measures of the quality of a structured design. There are other elements in the creation of good software that do not fall into either of these two categories. These are related to the overall picture or *morphology* of the structure chart. They are discussed next.

10.3.1. Factoring

The structure chart was compared earlier to the executive organization of a corporation. This is shown again in Figure 10.12. To this end, those modules near the top are

1. Concerned with global features, not details, and
2. Do no detailed work but only make decisions or control the activities of those below.

As one moves down the structure chart, this situation becomes less and less the case until the "atomic" modules at the bottom

1. Perform detailed functions, and
2. Make no decisions.

Factoring is the process of separating the structure chart into levels. The number of vertical levels is called *depth* and the number of horizontal modules at

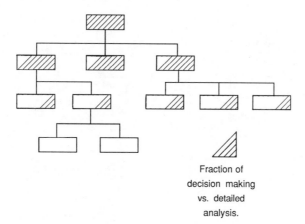

Fraction of
decision making
vs. detailed
analysis.

Figure 10.12 Decision making in the structure chart.

each level is called *width*. *Fan-out* is the number of lower modules called by a given module. This is also called the span of the module. Organizational theory tells us that it is best to have between three and nine modules in a fan-out. A greater number of modules indicates that the calling subprogram is probably responsible for too much and is likely to be weakly cohesive. *Fan-in* is the number of modules that call a single module. Greater fan-in is desirable if it is not at the sacrifice of cohesion of the module. A module that is called by many other modules either serves a specific function in great demand or it is filled with many different functions and it must be called whenever any of these functions is required. Such a utility routine is not indicative of good structured design.

10.3.2. Scope of Effect / Scope of Control

Every decision (i.e., IF statement) in a program has some consequences. Something happens or doesn't happen as a result of this decision. The scope of effect of a decision is the collection of all modules containing any processing that is conditional on that decision. The scope of control of a module is the module itself and all of its subordinates. Scope of control is purely a structural term. *For any decision, the scope of effect should be a subset of the scope of control of the decision-making module.* It is best that decisions are made no higher in the hierarchy than is necessary to include the scope of effect in the scope of control as shown in Figure 10.13. Again, the analogy to the corporate structure is apparent. The president of a large corporation should not make the decision about which detergent to use for cleaning the floors. This decision should be made by the janitor's immediate superior or possibly by the manager for maintenance. It is the president's job to decide whether more or less floor space is needed to better run the company and maximize profits for the shareholders.

Such decision-making rules are most often violated by the use of "flags."

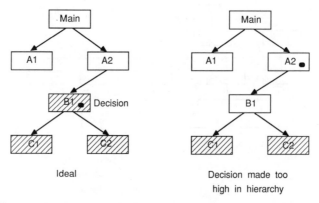

Ideal

Decision made too high in hierarchy

Figure 10.13 Scope of effect should be subset of scope of control.

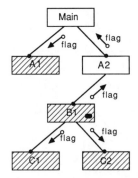

Figure 10.14 Use of flags usually violates scope of effect and scope of control relationship.

These are usually integer or logical variables that carry information about a decision to all other parts of the program that might want to know about it. The use of flags like that shown in Figure 10.14 is a tip-off that the scope of effect is not a subset of the scope of control.

10.3.3. Data Flow

Modules are categorized into four types depending on how they operate on data. These are as follows:

1. Afferent or pass-up
2. Efferent or pass-down
3. Transform, and
4. Coordinate flow

These categories relate to the direction in which information flows through the module and are shown in Figure 10.15 using the notation of the structure chart. In an afferent or pass-up situation the module receives data from below it in the structure chart and passes the data up to its superordinate either unchanged or after transforming it. In an efferent or pass-down situation the module receives data from above it in the structure chart and passes the data to a subordinate module. In a transform situation, the module receives data from above, transforms it, and sends it back up. In coordinate flow the module receives information from below and sends it back down to another module. Such categories can be mixed. To its superordinate module A in Figure 10.15 looks like a pass-up module. However, to A itself it looks like a coordinate flow module.

The general flow of data through the structure chart is observed by defining the nature of each module. Again, it is a good idea to include such an identification in the comment section at the beginning of each subroutine. These def-

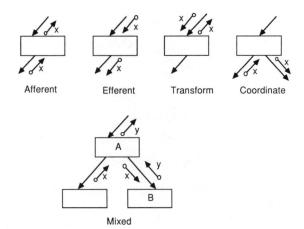

Figure 10.15 Four types of data flow to and from a module.

initions identify logjams of data or superfluous modules that do nothing but pass data without operating on it.

REFERENCES

1. M. Page-Jones, *The Practical Guide to Structured Systems Design*, Yourdon Press, New York, 1980.
2. E. Yourdon and L. Constantine, *Structured Design*, Yourdon Press, New York, 1978.

EXERCISES

1. Using a large-scale program from your field of engineering, identify the level of cohesion of 10 subroutines. Comment on the degree of coupling between these subroutines and those that call them.

2. Discuss the relative merits of using argument lists and COMMON blocks to pass values to subroutines. Give circumstances where each is preferable.

3. Give examples of four different binding times in the argument lists that couple modules. Discuss why late binding time is preferable.

4. For the structure chart drawn in problem 6 of Chapter 9, discuss the morphology of the program. Is it good or bad, and why do you come to this conclusion?

5. Using the program from problem 6 of Chapter 9, identify the data flow through 10 different modules as afferent, efferent, transform, or coordinate flow.

━11

Software Design Strategies

The creation of large-scale engineering applications software is an engineering design exercise in itself. No precise recipe exists for starting from scratch and producing a final working product. The engineering design exercise is filled with trials and errors and restarts until an optimum design begins to take shape. The experience and intuition of the designer detects this emergence of an optimum design, with the help of the measures discussed in Chapter 10. How one "does a design" is therefore difficult to describe. Nevertheless we attempt in this chapter to outline some procedures that are recommended to move a project from a dead start to a final product. This discussion follows the six steps of the software life cycle.

A specific example is used throughout the chapter. It is a simple yet powerful two-dimensional fluid dynamics algorithm called SALE[1] that allows the simulation of fluid flow at all speeds (i.e., it models both compressible and incompressible flows). The description of this *s*imple *a*rbitrary *L*agrangian-*E*ulerian algorithm is given in Appendix A. This description is used to develop a data flow diagram and structure chart.

11.1. OBJECTIVE

The objectives statement is a concise description of the goal of the software project. It does not elaborate on the methods to be used.

The objective of our demonstration exercise is to develop a general-purpose computer program that solves the Navier-Stokes equations in two dimensions, either Cartesian or cylindrical, for fluid flows at all speeds.

11.2. PROBLEM SPECIFICATION

The problem specification step combines engineering creativity, mathematical expertise, and systems design techniques to create a concise and complete specification of the solution to the engineering problem. Unfortunately, there is often such a strong desire to "get on with the software development" that this step is not completed. The misconception that a software development project is making no progress unless it is generating source code is generally the reason for this. While excessive amounts of time should not be devoted to this or any other step, it must be emphasized that an error at this stage is very costly to correct later in the development. It is therefore important that the problem specification receive enough attention to ensure the soundness of the solution.

11.2.1. Mathematical Modeling and Solution Methods

Most engineering systems must be described through the use of mathematics to allow the computer to analyze or simulate them. A clear partitioning of the engineering modeling of the system and the mathematical solution technique that is used to solve it is desirable. An intermixing of these two parts of the solution definition results in a difficult program to modify and debug. Many subroutine libraries are available today to solve sets of algebraic equations and ordinary differential equations. Use of these libraries cuts development time considerably and is encouraged. Should the original choice of numerical technique be inadequate to solve the equations due to instabilities or accuracy problems then the partitioning of the numerical method from the physical model allows the replacement of the method with another without disturbing the model. This distinction between the model itself and the mathematical solution of it is important to keep in mind when developing the data flow diagram.

The mathematical description for the SALE algorithm that we have chosen to solve the Navier-Stokes equations is given in Appendix A. We work from an existing method rather than developing one from scratch. This allows the emphasis to be placed on software development rather than on mathematical methods. This is a finite difference method that has three phases (explicit Lagrangian, implicit Lagrangian, and Eulerian) that are executed in one of four sequences to produce the same fluid quantities. These different options are given in Table 11.1. The independent variables are time t and two spatial coordinates, either x and y for Cartesian or r and y for cylindrical. The dependent variables are the fluid density, two components of the fluid velocity, and the specific internal energy. This last quantity is related to the temperature. The pressure is determined as a function of density and specific internal energy from an equation of state to close the set of equations.

11.2.2. Structured Analysis

The designer not only specifies the engineering model of the system under study and the numerical solution of it, but also poses these in a form that is

TABLE 11.1 Different Options for SALE Algorithm Execution

Option 1	Explicit Lagrangian		
Option 2	Explicit Lagrangian ⟶	Implicit Lagrangian	
Option 3	Explicit Lagrangian ⟶	Eulerian	
Option 4	Explicit Lagrangian ⟶	Implicit Lagrangian ⟶	Eulerian

suitable for further translation into a computer program design. This step is most often left out of engineering software development. The engineer usually just takes the numerical solution to the problem (like the one in Appendix A) and "puts together" some subroutines to solve the problem. For small problems, like those encountered in college courses, this works out most of the time. For large-scale software development, it leads to disaster or at best to a costly, unmaintainable product. The proper development of a data flow diagram helps to avoid these problems.[2]

11.2.2.1. Drawing a Data Flow Diagram. The data flow diagram, DFD, is a graphical representation of the data flow between processes in the solution algorithm. It is not meant to determine logic decisions or the order of processing of the data. In this way it is quite distinct from the flow chart. There is no fixed recipe for drawing a data flow diagram, but the following steps are a good approach:

1. Identify all net input and output data flows to and from the solution algorithm.
2. Work from the inputs to the outputs or vice versa, filling in the processes in between.
3. Label all of the interface data flows between processes.
4. Label the bubbles in terms of their inputs and outputs.
5. Ignore initialization and termination. Assume the algorithm is operating in its steady-state mode.
6. Omit details of trivial error paths.
7. Do not show flow of control or control information.
8. Be prepared to start over.

These steps need not be done in this order but each plays a role in developing a complete DFD. At the beginning one concentrates on the big picture and not on the details. The details come in the DFD leveling process. The point here is to strip away all extraneous considerations and to capture the essence of the solution algorithm. For this reason, no consideration is given to initialization or termination. These are not the major features of the solution and are not given the same status as the "guts" of the algorithm. The same is true for control information. "Flags" that determine the particular choice of algorithm or that determine whether conditional sections of code are executed are not considered data in the context of the DFD. Data flows to conditional processes are shown with no distinction between them.

The context layer of the DFD for the SALE algorithm is shown in Figure 11.1. Inputs to the algorithm are the initial and boundary conditions and any body forces on the fluid. These are the classical conditions that must be specified to solve the fluid equations. Additional input such as the solution option and the coordinates of the mesh points are not shown. This is a detail at this point. Outputs of the algorithm are the fluid density, velocity components, temperature, and pressure as functions of time and spatial coordinates. Again, these are the basic quantities of interest in fluid dynamics. Other quantities such as viscosity, Courant numbers, and so on are not shown. The context layer is a graphical description of the objectives statement.

11.2.2.2.   *Leveling a Data Flow Diagram.*

For large-scale software it is impossible to draw the DFD on a single page of paper. It may in fact require hundreds of pages. For this practical reason, the DFD is drawn in a top-down fashion. Much has been written about top-down programming and top-down analysis and design. Applied here, we mean that the DFD is drawn in ever increasing levels of detail with each lower level an elaboration of its predecessor. In this way the top level is a very general description of the solution algorithm and its data flows. Once all of the major process categories and data flows are present, then one of the processes is picked and the next lower level is drawn. It should be obvious at this point that these levels have some correspondence to the factoring of the structure chart that is derived from the DFD. However, the DFD does not show hierarchy in its levels. This is only a convenient way to think about complex algorithms and data flow without having to consider the entire problem at once.

The most important levels are the top and bottom ones. The middle levels naturally lead to the bottom ones if the design is good. The top level includes

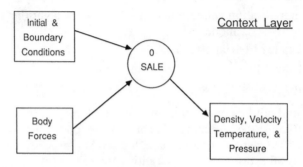

Figure 11.1   Context layer of the DFD for the SALE algorithm.

the major features of the solution. No hard rules dictate the number of processes to include at each level but a maximum of about seven is advisable. If the top level has many more than seven processes, then it is best to rethink the grouping of the major elements in the solution and try to regroup them into fewer major processes. This rule was discussed earlier in the section on organizational theory. The top level ultimately determines the organization of the structure chart and hence the computer program. It is here that the "form follows function" rule is put into play.

The first layer of the DFD in our example should display the major processes in the SALE algorithm. A possibility is shown in Figure 11.2. The density, pressure, explicit and implicit Lagrangian velocity updates, and energy calculation are shown along with the Eulerian update step. Although this DFD is a valid description of the SALE algorithm, it is quite awkward. The cyclic nature of the solution is responsible for this. Data does not have a directional flow through the processes from a source to a sink as it does in many other applications. Results from a time step serve as initial values for the next time step. Because procedural information is not shown on DFDs, this cyclic behavior is not evident and the DFD is confusing. Notice that no distinction is made for the order in which the processes are executed or which processes are executed. This is the characteristic of the DFD.

It is interesting to draw the classic flow chart using the same process definitions used in Figure 11.2. This flow chart, shown in Figure 11.3, gives the flow of control of this algorithm. The flow of control appears straightforward and well behaved. The question then is, which of these two descriptions of the solution should be used to guide the program design? For this choice of first level processes, the flow chart shows a simple path of execution while the DFD indicates a complex flow of data. According to structured analysis and design

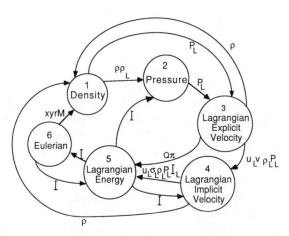

Figure 11.2 Possible first layer of bubbles in the DFD for the SALE algorithm.

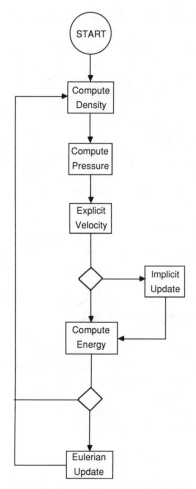

Figure 11.3 Flow chart for the SALE algorithm.

methods, the data flow is the one to be trusted. Clearly, the data flow for this combination of processes is unacceptably messy and must be improved.

A better choice for first layer process definition is shown in Figure 11.4. Here there are only two processes, Lagrangian and Eulerian. This breakdown is easily justified from the algorithm description since the SALE algorithm is a mating of the implicit continuous-fluid Eulerian (ICE) and arbitrary Lagrangian-Eulerian (ALE) methods. The cyclic nature is now evident from the data flows between the two processes. This layer shows source data coming into the cyclic algorithm and sink data leaving it, while the dependent variables in the solution are reused. This DFD layer is much more intuitive than the one shown in Figure 11.2 and for this reason it is superior. Of course the details

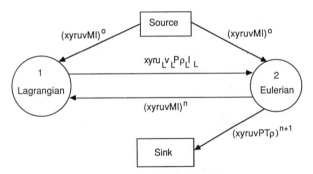

Figure 11.4 A better process definition for the first layer in the DFD for the SALE algorithm.

have been hidden and must be displayed in lower layers. A data dictionary for the quantities used in this layer is given in Figure 11.5.

The Lagrangian solution of the fluid equations (process 1) is further decomposed into explicit and implicit updates and the energy calculation as shown in Figure 11.6. No details of the actual solution are evident yet at this layer. The decision to use only an explicit or both an explicit and implicit update is indicated by the multiple data paths between the three processes but is not displayed in any procedural way.

Process 1.1 is now decomposed into the separate processes that make up the actual explicit update. These are given in Figure 11.7. The input and output data flows to this layer correspond to those shown for process 1.1 in the overlying layer, only now more detail is given about which subprocesses receive the data.

Moving down to the next layer, the explicit velocity calculation (process 1.1.4) is elaborated in Figure 11.8. The contributions to the change in velocity due to artificial viscosity, stress deviator, and pressure gradients are computed. Finally the velocity components are updated. The three processes (1.1.4.1, 1.1.4.2, and 1.1.4.3) are shown in parallel because they all use the same input data.

The implicit update calculation (1.2) is the iterative process shown in Figure 11.9. The iteration loop is displayed with the inputs and outputs to each subprocess moving in a ring. There is no distinction made about where the loop is exited on the DFD. This again is control information.

Once a bottom layer process is defined in the DFD, a functional specification is written for it. For this particular application, these specifications are conveniently written in mathematical formulas. The pressure acceleration calculation process (1.1.4.3) is shown in Figure 11.10.

Defining the processes to implement the SALE algorithm makes quite clear the fact that the structured analysis approach to algorithm implementation using data flow diagrams is very different from the way that engineers have

```
x       = { x(i,j) }
        = • x coordinate positions of all mesh points •

y       = { y(i,j) }
        = • y coordinate positions of all mesh points •

r       = { r(i,j) }
        = • r coordinate positions of all mesh points •

u       = { u(i,j) }
        = • x or r component of velocity of all mesh points •

v       = { v(i,j }
        = • y component of velocity of all mesh points •

M       = { M(i,j) }
        = • mass of all mesh cells •

V       = { V(i,j) }
        = • volume of all mesh cells •

I       = { I(i,j) }
        = • specific internal energy of all mesh cells •

P       = { P(i,j) }
        = • pressure of all mesh cells •

ρ       = { (i,j) }
        = • density of all mesh cells •

T       = { T(i,j) }
        = • temperature of all mesh cells •
```

x(i,j) = • x coordinate position of mesh point (i,j) •

y(i,j) = • y coordinate position of mesh point (i,j) •

r(i,j) = • r coordinate position of mesh point (i,j) •

u(i,j) = • x or r component of velocity of mesh point (i,j) •

v(i,j) = • y component of velocity of mesh point (i,j) •

M(i,j) = • mass of mesh cell (i,j) •

V(i,j) = • volume of mesh cell (i,j) •

I(i,j) = • specific internal energy of mesh cell (i,j) •

P(i,j) = • pressure of mesh cell (i,j) •

ρ(i,j) = • density of mesh cell (i,j) •

T(i,j) = • temperature of mesh cell (i,j) •

```
u       = { u (i,j) }
        = • x or r component of velocity of all mesh points in
            lagrangian update •

v       = { v (i,j }
        = • y component of velocity of all mesh points in
            lagrangian update •

I       = { I (i,j) }
        = • specific internal energy of all mesh cells in
            lagrangian update •

P       = { P (i,j) }
        = • pressure of all mesh cells in lagrangian update •

ρ       = { (i,j) }
        = • density of all mesh cells in lagrangian update •
```

u (i,j) = • x or r component of velocity of mesh point (i,j) in
            lagrangian update •

v (i,j) = • y component of velocity of mesh point (i,j) in
            lagrangian update •

I (i,j) = • specific internal energy of mesh cell (i,j) in
            lagrangian update •

P (i,j) = • pressure of mesh cell (i,j) in lagrangian update •

ρ (i,j) = • density of mesh cell (i,j) in lagrangian update •

Figure 11.5 Data dictionary for SALE algorithm.

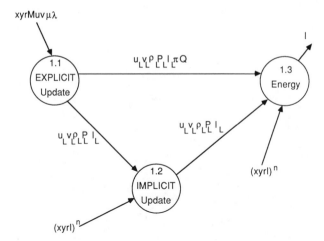

Figure 11.6 Subprocesses in the Lagrangian solution process in the SALE algorithm.

normally written such software using the conventional flow chart. The DFD leads to a different program organization from the algorithmic approach. The organization is based on data flow rather than flow of execution.

The elements of the structured analysis of an engineering solution are given in Figure 11.11. The mathematical algorithm or engineering description of the problem and solution are the starting point for the structured analysis. The data flow diagram is a top-down description of the data flows that will ultimately determine the structure of the software. The data dictionary defines

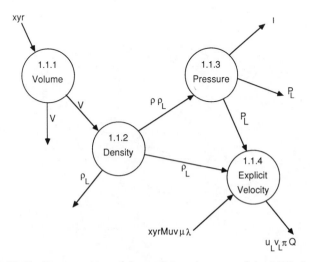

Figure 11.7 Decomposition of the explicit update part of the SALE algorithm.

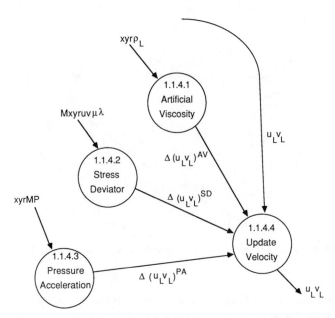

Figure 11.8 Decomposition of the explicit velocity update part of the SALE algorithm.

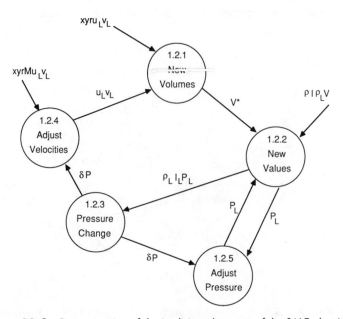

Figure 11.9 Decomposition of the implicit update part of the SALE algorithm.

Pressure Acceleration

for i = 1 ... imax
for j = 1 ... jmax

$$\Delta u_{L1} = \frac{\delta t}{2m_1} P_{ij}\, r_1\, (y_2 - y_4) \qquad \Delta v_{L1} = -\frac{\delta t}{4m_1} P_{ij}(r_2 + r_4)(x_2 - x_4)$$

$$\Delta u_{L2} = \frac{\delta t}{2m_2} P_{ij}\, r_2\, (y_3 - y_1) \qquad \Delta v_{L2} = -\frac{\delta t}{4m_2} P_{ij}(r_1 + r_3)(x_3 - x_1)$$

$$\Delta u_{L3} = -\frac{\delta t}{2m_3} P_{ij}\, r_3\, (y_2 - y_4) \qquad \Delta v_{L3} = \frac{\delta t}{4m_3} P_{ij}(r_2 + r_4)(x_2 - x_4)$$

$$\Delta u_{L4} = -\frac{\delta t}{2m_4} P_{ij}\, r_4\, (y_3 - y_1) \qquad \Delta v_{L4} = \frac{\delta t}{4m_4} P_{ij}(r_1 + r_3)(x_3 - x_1)$$

endloop j
endloop i

Figure 11.10 Functional specification of pressure acceleration calculation in the SALE algorithm.

each of the data elements and the functional definitions of each process allow the modules to be described in the following software design step.

We will not complete the DFD for the SALE algorithm. The remaining data flows and process definitions are left as an exercise for the reader. Instead, we turn to development of the structure chart.

11.3. SOFTWARE SPECIFICATION

The software specification determines the modules (i.e., subroutines) in the program and their hierarchical relationship to one another through the graphical representation of the structure chart. The structure chart is drawn according to the specification of the engineering problem's solution. This specification is made in the form of a DFD as described in Section 11.2. With a DFD in hand, one uses established methods to derive the structure chart from it.

11.3.1. Transform and Transaction Analysis

Transform analysis is a method of identifying the central transform or process in a data flow diagram and using this as the centerpiece of the structure chart.

```
Solution algorithm for the engineering problem

Data flow diagram representing the solution algorithm

Data dictionary defining all data in the data flow diagram

Definitions for all processes in the data flow diagram
```

Figure 11.11   Elements of the problem specification.

This is a direct application of the "form follows function" rule. Using the example DFD in Figure 11.12, one traces the input data from the edge of the diagram toward the center until the input has been entirely processed from its raw form and is ready to be used for the purposes of problem solution. Likewise, one traces the output data back toward the center until its source is identified. This process or set of processes that utilize the pure input data and are the source of the output are the *central transform*. This central transform then becomes the centerpiece of the structure chart. This seemingly trivial application of common sense is very often completely missed when designing software. The DFD allows one to identify the central transform and to build the structure chart around it.

A variation of this idea is called *transaction analysis*. When the DFD looks like that shown in Figure 11.13, a number of different independent data paths are taken. In this case the corresponding structure chart is built around these different *transaction centers*.

Under most circumstances the DFD is a mixture of both transaction and transform centers at different levels of the DFD. The application of these two methods to produce the structure chart is used as appropriate. We turn now to the SALE algorithm to demonstrate these methods.

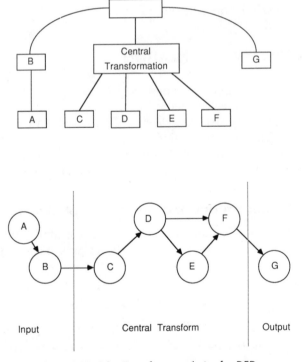

Figure 11.12 Transform analysis of a DFD.

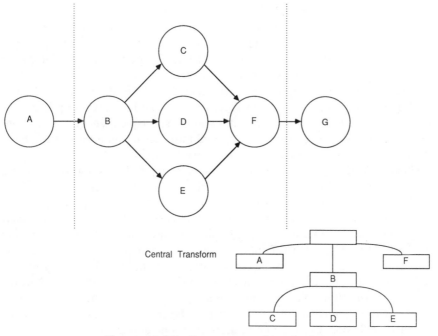

Figure 11.13   Transaction analysis of a DFD.

Examination of the first layer of the DFD in Figure 11.2 clearly indicates that processes 1 and 2 are equal partners in the solution algorithm and form the transform center of the DFD. Initial data flows into these processes and results flow out. Thus the first two levels of the structure chart are drawn as shown in Figure 11.14. Input and output modules are added to this level along with the central transform. Since input is done only at the beginning of such a computation, it is convenient to have it at this level. An alternative is to test for the first time step in the LAGRAN module and retrieve the input as the

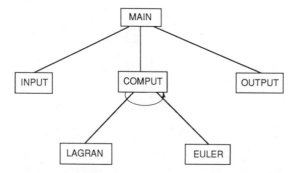

Figure 11.14   First two levels of the structure chart for the SALE algorithm.

initial values for this special case. This is inefficient because this test is done on each succeeding time step and fails for all but the first time step, needlessly adding extra execution time. The output is put here to balance the input. The notation indicates that the LAGRAN and EULER modules are called in a loop executed in the COMPUT subroutine, the central transform.

The next level in the structure chart under the LAGRAN module is derived from Figure 11.6 and is shown in Figure 11.15. The Lagrangian update is divided into explicit and implicit updates and the subsequent energy calculation. The explicit update is further decomposed into the computations of the basic fluid dynamic quantities as shown in Figure 11.16.

Further factoring of the explicit velocity computation is shown in Figure 11.17. A transaction center type of structure is evident in Figure 11.8 so EXPVEL is made a transaction center and updates the velocity after calling the modules that deliver the different contributions to the change in velocity.

Figure 11.18 is a factoring of the implicit update calculation using the DFD in Figure 11.9. The IMPLCT module controls the iteration process while the four modules that it calls do the computation. Again, the rule is that superordinate modules make decisions while subordinate ones do the actual work. Notice that the VOLUME module is used again to compute new updated volumes for the iterative solution. By proper choice of modules we are able to use this highly cohesive module in more than one application.

Transform and transaction analysis are used to give the structure chart its initial shape. The partial structure chart developed for the SALE algorithm thus far is given in Figure 11.19. Once this initial shape is determined, there is still a considerable amount of refinement to be done to ensure a minimum coupling and maximum cohesion.

11.3.2. Refining the Structure Chart

Using the DFD and transform and/or transaction analysis to define the general shape of the structure chart ensures that the shape is determined by the flow of data and not the flow of control. Recall that the DFD shows no control

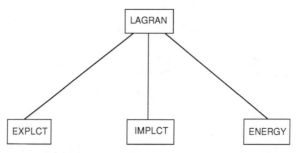

Figure 11.15 First level of the structure chart for the Lagrangian update part of the SALE algorithm (see Figure 11.6).

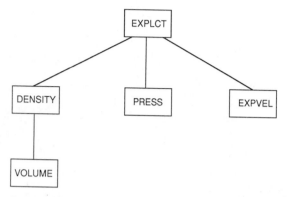

Figure 11.16 Structure chart for the explicit update part of the SALE algorithm (see Figure 11.7)

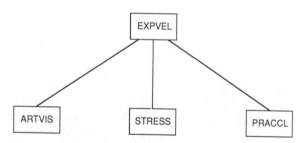

Figure 11.17 Factoring of the explicit velocity computation in the SALE algorithm.

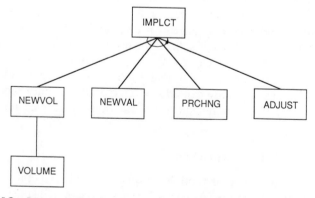

Figure 11.18 Factoring of the implicit update computation of the SALE algorithm (see Figure 11.9).

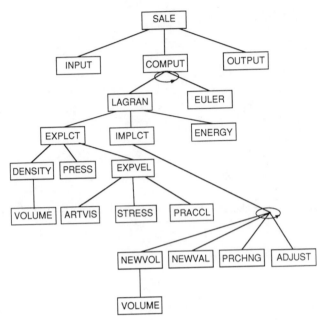

Figure 11.19 Partial structure chart for the part of the SALE algorithm completed thus far.

functions. Leveling the DFD ensures that the bubbles at the bottom of the structure chart are primitive functions. Those near the top contain only decision-making or control functions that must be added during this structured design stage. Although this procedure seems quite arbitrary, experience has proven that software produced in this manner is more likely to be completed on time and is easier to maintain. It is partitioned into independent modules and the structure of the software mirrors the true structure of the solution without extraneous factors influencing the design.

Just as there are no hard rules about drawing a DFD, there are also no hard rules about the structure chart. Once the initial shape is determined, redefinition of modules and even rearrangement of modules may be required to improve cohesion. For instance, if subroutine libraries are available to solve certain equations, the structure chart may have to be modified to include these. Each module is defined concisely and is rated according to its cohesion. Weakly cohesive modules are candidates for redefinition into more cohesive units. But before this is done, more information about each module is required.

11.3.3. Module Definitions

Along with the hierarchy of modules displayed in the structure chart, each module is completely defined as part of the software design stage. Functional definition statements for the modules defined thus far in Figure 11.19 are given in Figure 11.20. These are single statements that describe the function of the

COMPUT — Perform the SALE algorithm to solve the fluid dynamics equations.

INPUT — Read input quantities.

OUTPUT — Write output quantities.

LAGRAN — Perform the lagrangian update of the fluid dynamics dependent quantities (density, pressure, velocity components and energy).

EULER — Perform the eulerian update of the fluid dynamics dependent quantities (density, pressure, velocity components, and energy).

EXPLCT — Perform the explicit lagrangian update of the fluid dynamic quantities (density, pressure, and velocity components).

IMPLCT — Perform the implicit lagrangian update of the fluid dynamic quantities (density, pressure, and velocity components).

ENERGY — Perform the lagrangian energy update.

DENSTY — Compute the density of fluid in each finite difference cell in the explicit lagrangian part of the SALE solution.

PRESS — Compute the pressure of fluid in each finite difference cell.

ENERGY — Compute the energy of the fluid in each finite difference cell in the lagrangian part of the SALE solution.

VOLUME — Compute the volume of each finite difference cell.

EXPVEL — Compute the explicit update of the fluid velocity in the lagrangian part of the SALE solution.

ARTVIS — Compute the artificial viscosity contribution to the velocity change of the cell vertices.

STRESS — Compute the stress deviator contribution to the velocity change of the cell vertices.

PRACCL — Compute the pressure gradient contribution to the velocity change of the cell vertices.

NEWVOL — Update the vertex coordinates and compute new cell volumes for the implicit velocity update.

NEWVAL — Update the values of the fluid dynamic quantities (density, pressure, specific internal energy) as a result of the volume change for the implicit velocity update.

PRCHNG — Compute pressure relaxation in the implicit lagrangian solution.

ADJUST — Adjust the pressure and velocities as a result of the pressure relaxation.

Figure 11.20 Functional definition of modules in SALE algorithm.

module and help to determine the cohesion of the module. They appear in the comment statements at the head of the subroutine corresponding to each module.

Interfaces between modules are defined and evaluated for complexity. The dummy argument lists for each module are defined at this point in the design.

This documents the input and output from a module while also starting the software generation. The head of subroutine DENSTY is shown in Figure 11.21 as an example. If COMMON blocks are used, variables are grouped together into separate named COMMON blocks. The data flows on the DFD and the data dictionary help to group variables that "travel together."

The process definition of a module is determined by the information in the DFD. Many times a module in the structure chart corresponds to a process "bubble" in the DFD. In this case the module process definition is only a transfer of information. In other cases the module must be defined using a combination of information from the structured analysis stage. The process definition of a module is specified using the same techniques described for structured analysis: structured English, decision tables and trees, and mathematical formulas. A popular alternative for process definition in the software design stage is *pseudocode*. When using pseudocode the logic and formulas in the process are described using a programming language rather than a natural language or mathematical formulas. This programming language is usually the

```
                    SUBROUTINE DENSTY

          1                 (X, Y, R, XMASS,
          2
          3                 VOL, DENS)

   C   COMPUTE THE DENSITY OF FLUID IN EACH FINITE DIFFERENCE CELL
   C   IN THE EXPLICIT LAGRANGIAN PART OF THE SALE ALGORITHM

   C   INPUT:   X      — X COORDINATES OF ALL VERTICES
   C            Y      — Y COORDINATES OF ALL VERTICES
   C            R      — R COORDINATES OF ALL VERTICES
   C            XMASS  — MASSES OF ALL CELLS
   C   OUTPUT:  VOL    — VOLUMES OF ALL CELLS
   C            DENS   — DENSITY OF ALL CELLS

   C   PROCESS:  THE DENSITY IS COMPUTED BY FIRST CALLING VOLUME TO
   C   COMPUTE THE VOLUMES OF ALL MESH CELLS.  THE DENSITIES OF ALL
   C   MESH CELLS ARE COMPUTED BY DIVIDING THE MASS BY THE VOLUME.

   C   DESIGNED BY: GREGORY A. MOSES        DATE: 10/8/87
   C   PROGRAMMED BY: GREGORY A. MOSES      DATE:  12/2/87

   C                   ********************

         REAL X(IMAXV,JMAXV), Y(IMAXV,JMAXV), R(IMAXV,JMAXV)
         REAL XMASS(IMAXC,JMAXC), VOL(IMAXC,JMAXC)
         REAL DENS(IMAXC,JMAXC)

         COMMON/STATIC/ IMAXV, JMAXV, IMAXC, JMAXC, CYL, ....
         COMMON/CONST/ CON(100)

   C***************** END HEADER — BEGIN BODY ******************



   C******************** END BODY ***************************
                        RETURN
                        END
```

Figure 11.21 Head of subroutine DENSTY.

same as the one used to write the software, but this is not necessary. The pseudocode can be written in Pascal while the actual programming is in FORTRAN, for instance. The language is called "pseudocode" because it is not complete enough to allow compilation. Many details, such as nonexecutable declaration statements, are left out of the pseudocode definition of a module. The "coding" may be annotated with comments to clarify the procedure in any way that the designer feels is appropriate. Actual variable names may or may not be used. Since FORTRAN limits the length of variables to six characters, it is often appropriate to use complete names for the variables in the pseudocode rather than true variable names. When using Pascal this restriction is removed and actual variable names are appropriate. A pseudocode definition of the density calculation process from the SALE algorithm is shown in Figure 11.22.

The use of pseudocode is allowed for module definition because this information is shared between only the designer and the programmers who must generate the actual coding. Thus it is a natural language for their communication. The users never see the software design, thus no care must be taken to make it understandable to them. Recall that those people requesting the software work through the system analyst.

Elements of the software design are listed in Figure 11.23. The final product consists of well-defined modules related by a structure chart and well-defined interfaces between modules. The modules have names and the interfaces have variable names established. The complete definition of a module is one that allows a programmer to apply the module process to the input interface variables and produce the results in the output interface variables with no ambiguity.

```
Structured english:

    Get the volumes of all mesh cells

    for all mesh cells

        density = mass / volume

    end loop


More explicit FORTRAN:

    CALL VOLUME(... VOL)

    DO 10 J = 1,JMAXC
    DO 10 I = 1,IMAXC

        DENSITY(I,J) = MASS(I,J) / VOL(I,J)

 10 CONTINUE
```

Figure 11.22 Pseudocode definition of the density calculation.

```
Structure chart to give hierarchy of modules

Module interface definitions

Module process definitions

Variable names and definitions

COMMON block names and definitions
```

Figure 11.23 Elements of software specification.

11.4. SOFTWARE GENERATION

With all that has been done thus far, not a single line of FORTRAN code has been written. With the modules and variables all defined, the programming begins. When the design is done carefully, the code generation goes smoothly. This is very important since most of the time spent in software development is spent in software generation and debugging. Although programming bugs will always be with us, these are much easier to correct than a more fundamental structural error that comes from inadequate attention to the software design. Modules are written and tested independently by different people, thus reducing the elapsed time to completion.

The question now comes, is there any preferred order in which to write the software? Which modules should be written first? The tendency of the engineer is to write the primitive functions first, since this is where all of the real work is done. This, however, is not the preferred order. Modules are written and debugged in a top-down order, with those at the top of the structure chart completed first. But since these modules call subordinate modules below, how can they be developed when their subordinates do not exist? This is accomplished by using *stub modules* as shown in Figure 11.24 for the DENSTY and VOLUME subroutines. The DENSTY subroutine is written and debugged before the subordinate VOLUME subroutine is completed. The headings of all modules, including the VOLUME subroutine, are completed at the software design stage to define their interfaces. However, there is no functional coding in the body of the subroutines. At the software generation stage, while the body of the DENSTY subroutine is written and debugged, the body of the VOLUME subroutine takes the form of simple assignment statements to define volumes for the mesh cells in the test calculation used for debugging the DENSTY subroutine. This form of the VOLUME subroutine is called a stub. The functional coding is replaced with simple assignment of the output variables so that the calling module receives information when it calls the subordinate. This assignment of values to the interface variables is done so that the DENSTY subroutine is debugged using realistic input from the stub without danger that the subordinate subroutine is supplying erroneous data. Once the DENSTY subroutine is written and debugged, the VOLUME subroutine is treated in the same fashion. This process continues for all modules until the bottom of the structure chart is reached.

The exact order of module software generation of course depends on additional factors such as the number of programmers assigned to the task and the expertise of each person. Suppose that the team has two research engineers and four programmers and the research engineers are to leave the project before its completion. It might be wise to alter the order to allow them to write and test the critical modules that contain the most difficult modeling aspects of the project before they leave. So long as the design of the software is sound, deviations from these general rules are not a problem.

The top-down approach has other advantages. It allows the large-scale program to produce "results" long before the software generation is complete.

```
              SUBROUTINE DENSTY
      1                   (X, Y, R, XMASS,
      2
      3                   VOL, DENS)

C  COMPUTE THE DENSITY OF FLUID IN EACH FINITE DIFFERENCE CELL
C  IN THE EXPLICIT LAGRANGIAN PART OF THE SALE ALGORITHM

C  INPUT:   X      — X COORDINATES OF ALL VERTICES
C           Y      — Y COORDINATES OF ALL VERTICES
C           R      — R COORDINATES OF ALL VERTICES
C        XMASS  — MASSES OF ALL CELLS
C  OUTPUT: VOL    — VOLUMES OF ALL CELLS
C           DENS   — DENSITY OF ALL CELLS

C  PROCESS:   THE DENSITY IS COMPUTED BY FIRST CALLING VOLUME TO
C  COMPUTE THE VOLUMES OF ALL MESH CELLS.  THE DENSITIES OF ALL
C  MESH CELLS ARE COMPUTED BY DIVIDING THE MASS BY THE VOLUME.

C  DESIGNED BY: GREGORY A. MOSES        DATE: 10/8/87
C  PROGRAMMED BY: GREGORY A. MOSES      DATE:  12/2/87

C                      *********************
      REAL X(IMAXV,JMAXV), Y(IMAXV,JMAXV), R(IMAXV,JMAXV)
      REAL XMASS(IMAXC,JMAXC), VOL(IMAXC,JMAXC)
      REAL DENS(IMAXC,JMAXC)

      COMMON/STATIC/ IMAXV, JMAXV, IMAXC, JMAXC, CYL, ....
      COMMON/CONST/ CON(100)

C****************** END HEADER — BEGIN BODY ******************
      CALL VOLUME
      1 (X, Y, R,
      2
      3  VOL)

C  COMPUTE THE DENSITIES

      DO 100 J = 1,JMAXC
      DO 100 I = 1,IMAXC
        DENS(I,J) = XMASS(I,J) / VOL(I,J)
  100 CONTINUE

C********************** END BODY **************************
                       RETURN
                       END
```

Figure 11.24 Stub modules used for debugging.

```
                              SUBROUTINE  VOLUME
             1                (X,  Y,  R,
             2
             3                    VOL)

      C   COMPUTE THE VOLUME OF ALL MESH CELLS

      C   INPUT:   X    — X COORDINATE OF ALL MESH VERTICES
      C            Y    — Y COORDINATE OF ALL MESH VERTICES
      C            R    — R COORDINATE OF ALL MESH VERTICES
      C   OUTPUT: VOL   — VOLUME OF ALL MESH CELLS

      C   PROCESS:  THE VOLUME OF ALL MESH CELLS IS COMPUTED FOR
      C   EITHER CARTESIAN OR CYLINDRICAL GEOMETRY BY A SINGLE FORMULA
      C   THAT INVOLVES X, Y, AND R, WITH X=R FOR CYLINDRICAL AND
      C   X=1. FOR CARTESIAN GEOMETRY.

      C   DESIGNED BY:   xxxx
      C   PROGRAMMED BY:    xxxx

      C                       ********************
              REAL X(IMAXV,JMAXV), Y(IMAXV,JMAXV), R(IMAXV,JMAXV)
              REAL VOL(IMAXC,JMAXC)

              COMMON/STATIC/ IMAXV, JMAXV, IMAXC, JMAXC, CYL, ....
              COMMON/CONST/ CON(100)

      C***************** END HEADER — BEGIN BODY ******************

              VOL(1,1) = 10.
              VOL(2,1) = 10.
              VOL(3,1) = 10.
              VOL(1,2) = 5.
              VOL(2,2) = 5.
              VOL(3,2) = 5.
              VOL(1,3) = 20.
              VOL(2,3) = 20.
              VOL(3,3) = 20.

      C*********************** END BODY ***************************
                                RETURN
                                END
```

Figure 11.24   (Continued)

This has great psychological impact for projects that take years to complete. Sponsors of the project are most often anxious to see results, and years of waiting makes them intolerant to requests for additional time and money. However, if results of ever increasing realism are forthcoming throughout the project, then they feel a sense of progress and are more receptive to the developer's requests. Of course, this is not the justification for structured methods, but is a pleasant by-product of them.

11.5. QUALITY CONTROL

Debugging and testing of software is estimated to consume 50% of the time and cost of its initial development. Subsequent maintenance of the software is estimated to consume two-thirds of the total life cycle cost. Hence, over

75% of the total life cycle cost of software is devoted to finding and fixing bugs in the program. This leads to the obvious question, why can't the program be written correctly the first time? This dismal situation is improved considerably with the use of the proper methods.

Several factors have led to the poor quality of software in the past. The absence of any rigorous techniques for the development of large-scale software led to ad hoc and very individualized methods of software production that were mostly hit-and-miss. There were a few programming "gurus" who could miraculously produce working programs in record time, but the majority of programmers simply would grind out their product with great investment of man-hours and no uniformity from one person to the next. This problem has been largely eliminated with the structured concepts that are reviewed in this text. Yet software developers continue to make mistakes and, more importantly, these mistakes take man-years to uncover and fix.

Accepting the fact that human beings will always make mistakes, efforts must then be concentrated on methods that uncover the mistakes soon after they are made. Uncovering these mistakes relies on the fact that people cannot see their own errors. This is pure and simple psychology. Two people looking at the same subroutine, one who wrote it and one who did not, see the coding differently. The most obvious errors may go undetected by the writer while they "leap out" at the other person. Therefore the answer to finding errors quickly is to have them pointed out by someone else. It is also a fact of life that people do not like to have their shortcomings pointed out to them. Thus software generation problems are replaced with human relations problems. After all, programmers must work in a harmonious atmosphere to be most productive. So how does one proceed?

The best answer to this dilemma to date is to treat the software development project as an industrial process and apply quality control principles to it. In an industrial process, such as making paper for instance, there are many steps from the pulp feedstock to the end product, paper wound on a roll. Each of these steps has an input stream and an output stream. At various places along the process the stream is inspected to see that it meets the specifications set for it, such as water content in the paper pulp or thickness of the paper. If it does not fall within the range that is acceptable, then actions are taken. There is feedback to the preceding process to alter it so that the process stream comes into the range of specification at the next inspection point. There is feed-forward to momentarily alter downstream processes to correct the immediate material that is "out of spec." Finally, a log of all actions is kept to record the history of the inspections to detect any long-term trouble spot. For instance, a certain process step does not remain stable and must be repeatedly adjusted to bring it back into the proper settings.

Quality control of software is based on the same procedure. The development steps are treated as an industrial process with *software inspections*[3,4] distributed between and within them as shown in Figure 11.25. Each inspection comes at a point in the development sequence where entrance and exit require-

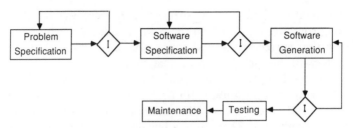

Figure 11.25 Software inspections come at several key points in the software development process.

ments for the product are specifically identified. In this way it is clear when the individual's work is ready to be inspected—once a clean compilation of a subroutine is achieved, for instance. The work does not proceed to the next step until it has passed the inspection and therefore meets the exit requirements. As shown in Figure 11.25, inspections are done throughout the development process. This is done to find errors as soon as possible after they are made. Software design errors are 10–100 times costlier to correct when left undetected until the second half of the development process when code is generated.

A software inspection is quite distinct from a review of the project status. An inspection is done by a few people who are peers of the developer and it is done over a limited part of the developer's work, a single module for instance. The procedure is formalized to avoid any misunderstanding about the responsibility of each participant. Inspections are uniformly applied to the work of each member in the development project. The inspection team consists of a moderator, a recorder, the author of the programming or design documents to be inspected, and perhaps one or two others. The moderator has the job of identifying a piece of work as satisfying the entrance requirements for inspection. The moderator then calls an inspection meeting and distributes the materials to all participants before the meeting. The moderator runs the meeting and is not a direct participant in the software development project to avoid any conflict of interest.

The inspection has five steps. The first is the overview where the developer describes the overall area being addressed and then the specific area under inspection. The materials distributed are design documents, code listings, and other documentation pertaining to the work being inspected. The individual participants in the inspection review these documents and try to understand the design, the coding, and so on. In the inspection itself the developer reviews the work, one line at a time in the case of coding, and explains it with a running narrative. Questions are pursued until it is clear whether an error is present or not. *The object of the inspection is to find errors and not to correct them.*

The recorder records all *defects* that are detected during the inspection of the software. Errors are called defects to direct the focus toward the software product and away from the person responsible for the product and hence the defects, the idea being that the word *defect* denotes a problem with the product whereas *error* implies a problem with the producer. Defects are recorded on standardized forms like that shown in Figure 11.26. A careful record is kept of all detected defects and their particular type and severity. Once the inspec-

INSPECTION DEFECT LIST

System: _____ Release: _____ Increment: _____ Date: _____
Unit: _____

Moderator: _____ Room: _____ Phone: _____
Inspection type:

___ Internal Requirements ___ Detail Design ___ Test Plan
___ High Level Design ___ Code ___ Test Cases

Docu-ment:	Loca-tion:	Defect Description	Defect Type:	Defect Class:

Error type IF-Interface DA-Data LO-Logic IO-Input/Output PF-Performance HF-Human Factors ST-Standards DC-Documentation Sn-Syntax OT Other

Error class M-Missing W-Wrong E-Extra

Page ____ of ____

Figure 11.26 Standardized form for recording software defects.

tion is completed, the moderator issues a written report of the inspection and determines whether the software passes the inspection, needs minor rework without additional inspection, or needs major rework with another inspection.

The developer must then resolve all questions raised at the inspection and correct all defects in the software design and/or coding. This is called the rework step.

Should there be many corrections to make, the moderator can require a follow-up step where the software is reinspected completely. This is important because a natural tendency is to assume that while the original design or code contained defects, the corrections do not. This is the opposite of experience. More defects are usually found per line of corrected coding than in the original product.

Not only does the software inspection detect defects, but it also allows the developers to gather statistics on the frequency of occurrence of defects in different stages of the development. This second aspect of the inspection process distinguishes it from *structured walk-through* methods.[5] Although the walk-through methods are similar to the inspection in the code review, the data-gathering element is not emphasized. This process of gathering information and using it dynamically as the software is developed is the control function that is analogous to the feedback and feed-forward parts of the industrial process discussed above. Frequent defects at a certain stage may indicate an underlying problem, such as inadequate problem specification or software specification. These problems are then hopefully corrected "on-line" so that future defects are minimized. Parts of the design or coding that have a significantly larger frequency of defects are flagged for observation in subsequent inspections.

Software inspections have proven to be successful in reducing development costs and they are therefore worthwhile. However, their introduction into any organization that has not previously used them is tricky. The historical picture of software development is that of "artisans" applying their individual skills to the final product, much in the way that medieval palaces and castles were constructed. While medieval kings may have been pleased at the individuality of each room in their palace, a software product with this characteristic is most definitely not satisfactory. The successful implementation of software inspections only comes with a feeling of colleageality and team work between the members of the team. Emphasis must focus on the software product and its quality, not on the human fraility of the team members who make the errors that compromise this quality. For this reason, it is imperative that the inspection process be a peer process and not be done by upper management. The purpose of the review is to benefit the software product and not to evaluate the team members.

11.6. TEAM MANAGEMENT

The organization of the software development team is built around the type of software being produced and the qualifications of the team members. Two very different team organizations are the *chief programmer team*[6] introduced by IBM in the 1970s and the *egoless team* suggested by Weinberg[7] in the same time period.

The chief programmer team is headed by a chief programmer or "ayatollah." This person is an accomplished senior software developer who holds total responsibility for the production of the software product and the management of the team. An organization chart for a chief programmer team is shown in Figure 11.27. The chief programmer has an assistant chief programmer who fills in for the chief or takes over if the chief leaves the project before completion. These two people are responsible for all important decisions and take an active part in the development of the software. In this way, the person responsible for the ultimate product plays a role in actually producing it. This is in contrast to giving the responsibility to a middle manager who supervises but does not play a role in production.

Working for the chief are a librarian and, for large projects, an administra-

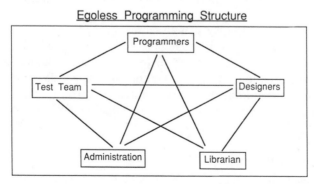

Figure 11.27 Organization structure for chief programmer and egoless approaches to programming teams.

tor. The librarian has the job of maintaining the documentation for the programmers. This is done to separate the clerical duties of programming from the intellectual aspects. By relieving programmers of the routine but essential clerical functions, their time is more effectively utilized. The librarian should be a person trained at an appropriate level to be challenged by those same tasks that are willingly relinquished by the programmers. Notice, however, that the librarian does not report to the programmers but instead reports to the chief programmer.

On very large projects an administrator may be necessary to interface with management on budgetary and other administrative matters. This person works for the chief programmer. This organization again emphasizes the central theme of the software product as most important. In most normal situations, a middle manager in charge of a project would serve as the interface to upper management.

The number of members on a chief programmer team can vary, depending on the phase of the software life cycle. At the beginning, when the problem specification and program design are done, there may be no programmers involved. But once the program generation phase is reached, the number of programmers should reach a maximum. Programmers are quickly oriented to the project because their tasks are limited in scope and are well defined by the software specification.

An alternative approach to team organization is the "egoless" team in which each member plays an equal role in the decision process. This is also shown schematically in Figure 11.27. Such a team must have true peers as members and one of them should be selected as a tie breaker in the event that there is divided opinion over a decision. The lack of a hierarchy means that all team members share in the responsibility for a successful software product.

The choice of team structure depends on the qualifications of the personnel and the characteristics of the software project. In the case of a large but straightforward software development, a hierarchical approach such as the chief programmer team is likely to be the best organization. Most decisions are over details and do not fundamentally determine the success or failure of the project. In this case, importance is placed on making a quick decision.

If the software project is reseach-oriented with little certainty in the final outcome, then a more loosely structured team may be more desirable. Here, a few experts work together, bouncing ideas off one another until a consensus is reached on the direction to proceed. In the world of engineering research, this is often the situation. The team may consist of a half dozen engineers with some additional programmer support. For a large software product, this many engineers may be required to cover the disciplines embodied in the software.

REFERENCES

1. A. A. Amsden, H.M. Ruppel, C. W. Hirt, "SALE: A Simplified ALE Computer Program for Fluid Flow at all Speeds," Los Alamos National Laboratory Report LA-8095, June 1980.

2. M. Page-Jones, *The Practical Guide to Structured Systems Design*, Yourdon Press, New York, 1980.

3. M. Fagan, "Design and Code Inspections to Reduce Errors in Program Development," *IBM Systems Journal* **15**, (182) 1976.

4. A. Ackerman, P. Fowler, and R. Ebenau, "Software Inspections and the Industrial Production of Software," *Software Validation*, Elsevier, 1984.

5. E. Yourdon, *Structured Walkthroughs*, Yourdon Press, New York, 1978.

6. F. T. Baker, "Chief Programmer Team Management of Production Programming," *IBM Systems Journal* **11** (100) 1972.

7. G. M. Weinberg, *The Psychology of Computer Programming*, Van Nostrand Reinhold, New York, 1971.

EXERCISES

1. Complete the problem specification for the SALE algorithm in Appendix A, including the data flow diagram, data dictionary, and process specification.

2. Complete the first cut software specification structure chart for the SALE algorithm, using the results of problem 1.

3. Refine the structure chart in problem 2 with attention given to module coupling and cohesion. Define the cohesion of each module using the numerical scale and types of cohesion defined in Chapter 11.

4. Make the module functional specifications using structured English, mathematical formulas, and so on, for the SALE algorithm.

5. Generate and debug code for the modules of the SALE algorithm. This should be done as a team effort with modules assigned to different teams.

■ APPENDIX A

This appendix is reproduced with permission from Los Alamos National Laboratory Report LA-8095, June 1980. Only the first 17 pages of the report are reproduced for the purpose of allowing a structured analysis and structured design exercise of the SALE numerical algorithm contained in these pages. The notation " . . . " designates that material included in the original document was omitted from this reproduction.

SALE: A SIMPLIFIED ALE COMPUTER PROGRAM FOR FLUID FLOW AT ALL SPEEDS

by

A. A. Amsden, H. M. Ruppel, and C. W. Hirt

ABSTRACT

A simplified numerical fluid-dynamics computing technique is presented for calculating two-dimensional fluid flows at all speeds. It combines an implicit treatment of the pressure equation similar to that in the Implicit Continuous-fluid Eulerian (ICE) technique with the grid rezoning philosophy of the Arbitrary Lagrangian-Eulerian (ALE) method. As a result, it can handle flow speeds from supersonic to the incompressible limit in a grid that may be moved in some arbitrary way to give a continuous rezoning capability. The report describes the combined (ICEd-ALE) technique in the framework of the SALE (Simplified ALE) computer program, for which a general flow diagram and complete FORTRAN listing are included. A set of sample problems show how to use or modify the basic code for a variety of applications. Numerical listings are provided for a sample problem run with the SALE program.

I. INTRODUCTION

Over the past decade, we have witnessed an increasing acceptance of and reliance upon numerical solutions for transient fluid flow problems. In many cases, experimental studies are prohibitively expensive, whereas high-speed computers are comparatively economical and allow a wide range of parameter variations to be examined in a short time. As a result, numerical solution techniques have become more sophisticated and the applications correspondingly more complex.

This report presents a simplified computer program to calculate two-dimensional fluid flows at all speeds, from the incompressible limit to highly supersonic. An implicit treatment of the pressure calculation similar to that in the Implicit Continuous-fluid Eulerian (ICE) technique[1] provides this flow-speed versatility. In addition, the computing mesh may move with the fluid in a typical Lagrangian fashion, be held fixed in an Eulerian manner, or move in some arbitrarily specified way to provide a continuous rezoning capability. This latitude results from the use of an Arbitrary Lagrangian-Eulerian (ALE) treatment[2] of the computing mesh. The program is named SALE, for Simplified ALE. The essential features of the ICEd-ALE combination are presented here to make this report a self-contained guide. SALE bears a strong resemblance to YAQUI, the original but more complex ICEd-ALE program.[3]

The partial differential equations solved by the SALE program are the Navier-Stokes equations,

$$\frac{\partial \rho u}{\partial t} + \frac{1}{r}\frac{\partial r\rho u^2}{\partial x} + \frac{\partial \rho uv}{\partial y}$$

$$= -\frac{\partial(p+q)}{\partial x} + \frac{1}{r}\frac{\partial r\pi_{xx}}{\partial x} + \frac{\partial \pi_{xy}}{\partial y} - \frac{\pi_\theta}{r} + \rho g_x$$

$$\frac{\partial \rho v}{\partial t} + \frac{1}{r}\frac{\partial r\rho uv}{\partial x} + \frac{\partial \rho v^2}{\partial y}$$

$$= -\frac{\partial(p+q)}{\partial y} + \frac{1}{r}\frac{\partial r\pi_{xy}}{\partial x} + \frac{\partial \pi_{yy}}{\partial y} + \rho g_y,$$

and the mass and internal energy equations,

$$\frac{\partial \rho}{\partial t} + \frac{1}{r}\frac{\partial r\rho u}{\partial x} + \frac{\partial \rho v}{\partial y} = 0,$$

and

$$\frac{\partial \rho I}{\partial t} + \frac{1}{r}\frac{\partial r\rho Iu}{\partial x} + \frac{\partial \rho Iv}{\partial y} = -(p+q)D + \pi_{xx}\frac{\partial u}{\partial x} + \pi_{xy}\frac{\partial u}{\partial y}$$

$$+ \frac{u\pi_\theta}{r} + \pi_{xy}\frac{\partial v}{\partial x} + \pi_{yy}\frac{\partial v}{\partial y},$$

where D is the velocity divergence,

$$D = \frac{1}{r}\frac{\partial ru}{\partial x} + \frac{\partial v}{\partial y}.$$

Velocity components (u,v) are in the Cartesian coordinate directions (x,y) or the cylindrical coordinate directions (r,z). When Cartesian coordinates are desired, all radii r, which appear in these equations are set to unity. The fluid pressure p is determined from an equation of state $p = p\ (\rho,I)$ and supplemented with an artificial viscous pressure q for the computation of shock waves, where

$$q = \lambda_0\ \rho \text{ Area } D \min (0,D)$$

Artificial pressures are only used in regions of compression $(D < 0)$ and are scaled proportional to the area (Area) of each computational cell, with the constant of proportionality λ_0.

The stress deviator is defined according to

$$\pi_{xx} = 2\mu\ \frac{\partial u}{\partial x} + \lambda D,$$

$$\pi_{yy} = 2\mu\ \frac{\partial v}{\partial y} + \lambda D,$$

$$\pi_\theta = \text{Cyl} \left[2\mu\ \frac{u}{r} + \lambda D \right],$$

$$\pi_{xy} = \mu \left(\frac{\partial u}{\partial y} + \frac{\partial v}{\partial x} \right),$$

in which μ is the coefficient of viscosity and λ is the coefficient of dilatation viscosity. The coefficient Cyl is zero for Cartesian coordinates and unity for cylindrical coordinates.

To facilitate its use by persons with modest experience in numerical fluid dynamics, the SALE program was written in modular form with extensive annotation and input options that provide a wide range of capabilities. In addition, SALE includes several improvements to the original YAQUI scheme that have been made since its publication. We intend that the SALE program serve not only as a useful tool for many applications, but also as a teaching aid and foundation for the development of new programs with expanded capabilities.

The basic solution algorithm for SALE appears in Sec. II of this report. Section III describes the FORTRAN program. We include a general flow diagram showing the logical partitioning of the code into a set of subroutines, each responsible for a clearly definable task. Section IV presents the results of several SALE calculations chosen to illustrate the versatility of the program. . . .

II. THE SALE SOLUTION ALGORITHM

A. The Three-Phase ICEd-ALE Approach

The basic hydrodynamic part of each cycle of SALE is divided into three phases:

1. Phase 1 is a typical, explicit Lagrangian calculation, in which the velocity field is updated by the effects of all forces.

2. Phase 2 is a Newton-Raphson iteration that provides time-advanced pressures and velocities. The purpose of Phase 2 is to allow calculations in the low-speed and

even completely incompressible regimes. The implicit, iterative scheme makes this possible with greater efficiency than a purely explicit calculation with reduced time step, as it offers a numerically stable means by which pressure signals can traverse more than one cell in a time step.

3. Phase 3 performs all the advective flux calculations. This phase is required for runs that are Eulerian or contain some other form of mesh rezoning.

A powerful feature of SALE is the ease with which different phases can be combined in various ways to suit the requirements of individual problems. For example, in high-speed applications, an explicit calculation is acceptable, allowing the Phase 2 iteration to be bypassed. For an explicit Lagrangian calculation, only Phase 1 is required. For an implicit Lagrangian calculation, only the first two phases are used. In neither of these two cases are advective flux calculations necessary, and the Phase 1 or 2 results are final results for the cycle. All these options may be selected by appropriately defining the input data.

. . .

B. The Computing Mesh

The computing mesh consists of a two-dimensional network of quadrilateral cells for either cylindrical or plane (Cartesian) coordinates. Calculations in cylindrical coordinates are scaled to unit azimuthal angle, which allows the equations to be written without any π factors. The radial coordinate is denoted by r or x, and the axial coordinate by y, with the origin located at the lower left corner of the mesh. The coordinate names in the equations are x and y. The quantity r is used to determine the geometry: r is set equal to x for cylindrical coordinates, but the expressions automatically reduce to Cartesian form if all r's are set to unity.

The vertices of the cells are labeled with the indices i and j, which increase in the radial and axial directions, respectively. Cell centers are denoted by half-integer indices $i + 1/2$ and $j + 1/2$. The mesh of cells is N_x cells wide by N_y cells high.

The mesh illustrated in Figure A.1 is in cylindrical coordinates, where the cells are sections of toroids of revolution about the cylindrical axis.

The variables in an ICEd ALE grid are of two types: those defined at vertices and those defined at cell centers. The principal variables are shown in Figure A.2, where coordinates (x and y) and corresponding velocity components (u and v) are defined at vertices. Pressures (p), specific internal energies (I), cell volumes (V), densities (ρ), and masses (M) are all assigned at cell centers.

In the equations that follow, the superscript n refers to the beginning-of-cycle values. The advancement of the solution through a time step, of duration δt, provides values at the beginning of the next ($n + 1$) cycle. Intermediate values are typically labeled with a subscript L for the results of Phases 1 or 2.

C. Initial Conditions and Preliminary Calculations

The input data supply the initial values of $x, y, u,$ and v at the vertices and ρ and I for the cells.

1. The radius r is calculated as $r = x$ in cylindrical coordinates, or $r = 1$ in plane coordinates. The coordinate system is determined by the input parameter CYL, which

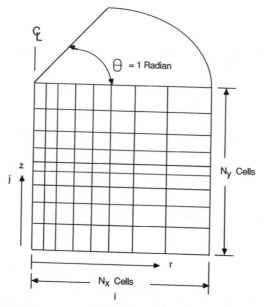

Figure A.1   A typical SALE mesh in cylindrical coordinates.

is equal to 1 for cylindrical coordinates and is equal to zero for plane coordinates. Thus, we write

$$r_i^j = (x_i^o)CYL + 1 - CYL$$

2. Cell volumes per unit azimuthal angle are given by the exact expression

$$V_{i+1/2}^{j+1/2} = \frac{1}{3} [(r_1 + r_2 + r_3) ATR + (r_3 + r_4 + r_1)ABL], \tag{1}$$

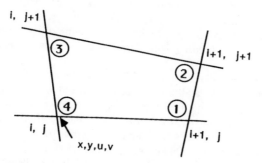

Figure A.2   The assignment of variables about cell $(i+1/2, j+1/2)$.

where

$$ATR = \frac{1}{2}[(x_3 - x_2)(y_1 - y_2) - (x_1 - x_2)(y_3 - y_2)]$$

and

$$ABL = \frac{1}{2}[(x_1 - x_4)(y_3 - y_4) - (x_3 - x_4)(y_1 - y_4)].$$

The numerical subscript notation for vertex quantities associated with a given cell is simplified to that shown in Figure A.2. It is used throughout this report and in the SALE code.

3. With the cell volumes defined, the masses at cell centers can be obtained from the product

$$M_{i+1/2}^{j+1/2} = \rho_{i+1/2}^{j+1/2} V_{i+1/2}^{j+1/2}, \tag{2}$$

but it is also necessary to assign a mass to each vertex to obtain the time advanced velocities. In SALE, we assume that the mass in each cell is shared equally between its four corner vertices, so vertex 4 in Figure A.2 for example, is given the mass

$$M_4 = \frac{1}{4}(M_{i+1/2}^{j+1/2} + M_{i-1/2}^{j+1/2} + M_{i-1/2}^{j-1/2} + M_{i+1/2}^{j-1/2}). \tag{3}$$

D. Phase 1 of the Calculation

In this phase, velocities are advanced explicitly in time in a purely Lagrangian fashion. If viscous, elastic, or other stresses are desired, they are included in this phase as well. The updating of the specific internal energies is delayed until after the optional implicit pressure calculation of Phase 2. This delay permits time-advanced pressures to be used in computing the pdV work and ensures consistency with the velocities coming out of Phase 2.

The velocities resulting from this Lagrangian calculation phase are denoted by (u_L, v_L). Pressure, viscous, and other force contributions are computed in separate subroutines, so that in each case the (u_L, v_L) values are progressively updated with each contribution. This updating is started with the beginning-of-cycle values (u, v). In the actual code, the order of updating is performed in the following sequence.

1. *Cycle Initialization.* This routine initializes the (u_L, v_L) velocities with the beginning-of-cycle values (u, v). In addition, cell densities ρ and ρ_L are calculated as the ratio of the cell mass to cell volume. Cell pressures (p) are calculated using an equation of state $p = f(\rho, I)$, although the equation of state is bypassed after the setup for implicit calculations, because the pressures resulting from the previous Phase 2 implicit solution generally prove to be a better initial guess for the next cycle iteration than the equation-of-state pressure. In the incompressible limit, we also bypass the equation of state in the setup and set zero pressures at time $t = 0$.

2. *Artificial Viscous Forces.* Here the (u_L, v_L) velocities are adjusted for contributions arising from a bulk artificial viscosity and from a coupling between alternate nodes.

a. Artificial Bulk Viscosity. For problems involving shock waves, an artificial pressure Q must be used to ensure mesh-resolvable shocks. This addition is required because mean kinetic energy is not conserved across a shock wave. Without dissipation, spurious velocity oscillations develop behind the shock to account for an excess of kinetic energy. We include the dissipation as a pressure addition, which models the fact that the pressure change across a shock is more than simple adiabatic compression.

The viscous pressure used in SALE is quadratic in the velocity divergence, and is only added to cells undergoing compression,

$$Q_i^j = \min(0, D_i^j)[\lambda_0 \rho_i^j D_i^j (\text{Area})]. \tag{4}$$

In this expression, (Area) is the area of cell (i,j), so that

$$(\text{Area}) = \frac{1}{2}[(x_2 - x_4)(y_3 - y_1)$$
$$- (x_1 - x_3)(y_4 - y_2)],$$

and D_i^j is its velocity divergence $\nabla \cdot \vec{u}$ defined as

$$D_i^j = \frac{1}{2(\text{Area})}[(u_2 - u_4)(y_3 - y_1)$$
$$- (u_1 - u_3)(y_4 - y_2) + (v_4 - v_2)(x_3 - x_1)$$
$$- (v_1 - v_3)(x_2 - x_4)] + \frac{u}{r}, \tag{5}$$

where

$$\frac{u}{r} = \text{CYL}\left(\frac{u_1 + u_2 + u_3 + u_4}{r_1 + r_2 + r_3 + r_4}\right). \tag{6}$$

The parameter λ_0 in the above expression for Q_i^j is denoted by ARTVIS in the input data list, and should be less than 0.25 to avoid excessive viscous damping. A value of ARTVIS=0.1 has been satisfactory for many applications.

With Q_i^j calculated, the appropriate contributions to the four vertices of cell (i,j) are

$$(u_L)_1 = u_1 + \frac{\delta t Q_i^j}{2M_1} r_1(y_2 - y_4),$$

$$(u_L)_2 = u_2 + \frac{\delta t Q_i^j}{2M_2} r_2(y_3 - y_1),$$

$$(u_L)_3 = u_3 - \frac{\delta t Q_i^j}{2M_3} r_3(y_2 - y_4),$$

$$(u_L)_4 = u_4 - \frac{\delta t Q_i^j}{2M_4} r_4(y_3 - y_1),$$

$$(v_L)_1 = v_1 - \frac{\delta t Q_i^j}{4M_1} (r_2 + r_4)(x_2 - x_4),$$

$$(v_L)_2 = v_2 - \frac{\delta t Q_i^j}{4M_2} (r_1 + r_3)(x_3 - x_1),$$

$$(v_L)_3 = v_3 + \frac{\delta t Q_i^j}{4M_3} (r_2 + r_4)(x_2 - x_4),$$

and

$$(v_L)_4 = v_4 + \frac{\delta t Q_i^j}{4M_4} (r_1 + r_3)(x_3 - x_1). \tag{7}$$

The asymmetry in the geometric factors in the above expressions, which also appears in other equations for pressure accelerations, arises from the difference in the effect of the boundary of the control volume on the two directions. Accelerations in the radial direction must include the forces on the ends of the one-radian section of the torus. These contributions do not enter in the axial direction.

b. Alternate Node Coupler. In a Lagrangian calculation using quadrilateral mesh cells, there are certain degenerate mesh deformations that do not result in net pressure or viscous forces. Typically, these deformations are associated with the shortest resolvable wavelengths $(2\delta x)$ in the mesh. For example, Figure A.3 illustrates two such short-wavelength deformations. Figure A.3a shows the bowtie pattern and Figure A.3b shows the herringbone pattern. In each case, the deforming cells undergo no change in volume so that no pressure variations are generated. Also, it is easily verified that no net viscous or elastic strain forces are generated at vertices embedded in the bowtie type of deformation.

Thus, to prevent such deformations from slowly degrading a solution, it is sometimes necessary to couple alternate mesh nodes with a small artificial restoring force. Ideally, this force should affect flows only at the $2\delta x$ wavelength level, but have no influence on the larger, better resolved flow variations. We introduce small accelerations at each vertex, which are based on the surrounding velocity field and tend to keep the vertex velocities from deviating too strongly from their neighbors.

A fourth order coupling scheme is effective for the bowtie mode, but a more diffusive second order scheme must be used for the herringbone pattern. The fourth order form is given by

$$u_i^j = u_i^j + \frac{a_{nc}}{4} [2(u_{i+1}^j + u_i^{j+1} + u_{i-1}^j + u_i^{j-1})$$
$$- u_{i-1}^{j+1} - u_{i-1}^{j+1} - u_{i-1}^{j-1}$$
$$- u_{i+1}^{j-1} - 4u_i^j],$$

in which a_{nc} is a coefficient that governs the amount of coupling and implies a relaxation time of a_{nc}^{-1} time steps.

The second order form is given by

$$u_i^j = u_i^j + \frac{a_{nc}}{4} [(u_{i+1}^j + u_i^{j+1} + u_{i-1}^j + u_i^{j-1}) - 4u_i^j].$$

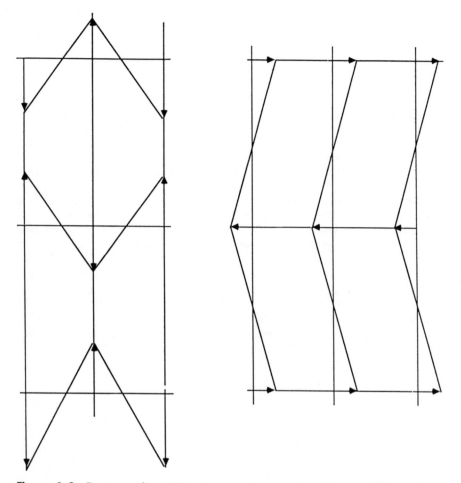

Figure A.3 Two types of instabilities between adjacent nodes: (a) bowtie, (b) herringbone.

In SALE, we combine both of these forms in the following set of expressions, in which $\xi = 1$ results in the fourth order form and $\xi = 0$ results in the second order form. Also, rather than sweeping vertices to make the contributions, we may equivalently sweep over cells and adjust the four vertices of each cell, such that

$$(u_L)_1 = (u_L)_1 + \frac{a_{nc}}{4} \left[\left(\frac{1 + \xi}{2} \right) (u_2 + u_4) - \xi u_3 - u_1 \right],$$

$$(u_L)_2 = (u_L)_2 + \frac{a_{nc}}{4} \left[\left(\frac{1 + \xi}{2} \right) (u_3 + u_1) - \xi u_4 - u_2 \right],$$

$$(u_L)_3 = (u_L)_3 + \frac{a_{nc}}{4} \left[\left(\frac{1 + \xi}{2} \right) (u_4 + u_2) - \xi u_1 - u_3 \right],$$

and

$$(u_L)_4 = (u_L)_4 + \frac{a_{nc}}{4} \left[\left(\frac{1 + \xi}{2} \right) (u_1 + u_3) - \xi u_2 - u_4 \right]. \tag{8}$$

Corresponding expressions are used for the y direction, with every u or u_L replaced by v or v_L. Note that contributions at vertices on reflective boundaries must be doubled to obtain the correct value. This is necessary here because these artificial accelerations have been defined without reference to vertex masses. In the case of all other forces, no corrections are needed for boundary vertices, because the omission of force contributions from cells on the outside of a boundary is compensated for by a corresponding omission in vertex mass.

We emphasize that node coupling is diffusive and nonphysical and should be used with discretion. In a spherical expansion, for example, the smoothing effect of too much node coupling adversely affects the sphericity. To avoid its unintentional use, we require the SALE user to supply values for ξ and a_{nc} in the input data. Rarely should a_{nc} exceed 0.05.

3. *Stress Deviator Forces.* At this point, the shear viscosity (μ) and bulk viscosity (λ) contributions are added, if either is specified, in terms of a stress deviator force. (This would also be the appropriate place to add material strength effects. These effects, however, have not been included in this version of SALE.)

For each cell, we define the divergence $D = \nabla \cdot \vec{u}$ as in step 1 above, and the four components of the viscous stress tensor as

$$\Pi_{xx} = 2\mu \frac{\partial u}{\partial x} + \lambda \nabla \cdot \vec{u},$$

$$\Pi_{yy} = 2\mu \frac{\partial v}{\partial y} + \lambda \nabla \cdot \vec{u},$$

$$\Pi_{xy} = \mu \left(\frac{\partial u}{\partial y} + \frac{\partial v}{\partial x} \right),$$

and

$$\Pi_\theta = \text{CYL} \left[2\mu \frac{u}{r} + \lambda \nabla \cdot \vec{u} \right], \tag{9}$$

where u/r is defined as in Equation (6). The finite difference expressions to compute these quantities are

$$\frac{\partial u}{\partial x} = \frac{1}{2(\text{Area})} [(u_2 - u_4)(y_3 - y_1)$$

$$- (u_3 - u_1)(y_2 - y_4)],$$

$$\frac{\partial v}{\partial x} = \frac{1}{2(\text{Area})} [(v_2 - v_4)(y_3 - y_1)$$

$$- (v_3 - v_1)(y_2 - y_4)],$$

$$\frac{\partial u}{\partial y} = \frac{1}{2(\text{Area})} [(u_3 - u_1)(x_2 - x_4)$$

$$- (u_2 - u_4)(x_3 - x_1)],$$

and

$$\frac{\partial v}{\partial y} = \frac{1}{2(\text{Area})} [(v_3 - v_1)(x_2 - x_4)$$

$$- (v_2 - v_4)(x_3 - x_1)]. \tag{10}$$

Stress deviator contributions to the vertex velocities are

$$(u_L)_1 = (u_L)_1 + \frac{\delta t}{4M_1} (r_2 + r_4) [\Pi_{xy} (x_2 - x_4)$$

$$- \Pi_{xx} (y_2 - y_4) - \frac{\text{Area}}{2} \Pi_\theta],$$

$$(u_L)_2 = (u_L)_2 + \frac{\delta t}{4M_2} (r_1 + r_3) [\Pi_{xy} (x_3 - x_1)$$

$$- \Pi_{xx} (y_3 - y_1) - \frac{\text{Area}}{2} \Pi_\theta],$$

$$(u_L)_3 = (u_L)_3 - \frac{\delta t}{4M_3} (r_2 + r_4) [\Pi_{xy} (x_2 - x_4)$$

$$- \Pi_{xx} (y_2 - y_4) + \frac{\text{Area}}{2} \Pi_\theta],$$

$$(u_L)_4 = (u_L)_4 - \frac{\delta t}{4M_4} (r_1 + r_3) [\Pi_{xy} (x_3 - x_1)$$

$$- \Pi_{xx} (y_3 - y_1) + \frac{\text{Area}}{2} \Pi_\theta],$$

$$(v_L)_1 = (v_L)_1 + \frac{\delta t}{4M_1} (r_2 + r_4) [\Pi_{yy} (x_2 - x_4)$$

$$- \Pi_{xy}(y_2 - y_4)]$$

$$(v_L)_2 = (v_L)_2 + \frac{\delta t}{4M_2} (r_1 + r_3) [\Pi_{yy} (x_3 - x_1)$$

$$- \Pi_{xy} (y_3 - y_1)],$$

$$(v_L)_3 = (v_L)_3 - \frac{\delta t}{4M_3} (r_2 + r_4) [\Pi_{yy} (x_2 - x_4)$$

$$- \Pi_{xy} (y_2 - y_4)],$$

and

$$(v_L)_4 = (v_L)_4 - \frac{\delta t}{4M_4} (r_1 + r_3) [\Pi_{yy} (x_3 - x_1)$$

$$- \Pi_{xy} (y_3 - y_1)]. \tag{11}$$

The Π terms are stored for later inclusion in the internal energy.

4. *Pressure Force Contributions.* The principal contribution to the velocities in Phase 1 comes from the pressure forces and body forces acting on the vertices.

a.   Pressure Accelerations. The difference approximations used for the pressure accelerations are

$$(u_L)_1 = (u_L)_1 + \frac{\delta t}{2M_1} p_i^j r_1 (y_2 - y_4),$$

$$(u_L)_2 = (u_L)_2 + \frac{\delta t}{2M_2} p_i^j r_2 (y_3 - y_1),$$

$$(u_L)_3 = (u_L)_3 - \frac{\delta t}{2M_3} p_i^j r_3 (y_2 - y_4),$$

$$(u_L)_4 = (u_L)_4 - \frac{\delta t}{2M_4} p_i^j r_4 (y_3 - y_1),$$

$$(v_L)_1 = (v_L)_1 - \frac{\delta t}{4M_1} p_i^j (r_2 + r_4)(x_2 - x_4),$$

$$(v_L)_2 = (v_L)_2 - \frac{\delta t}{4M_2} p_i^j (r_1 + r_3)(x_3 - x_1),$$

$$(v_L)_3 = (v_L)_3 + \frac{\delta t}{4M_3} p_i^j (r_2 + r_4)(x_2 - x_4),$$

and

$$(v_L)_4 = (v_L)_4 + \frac{\delta t}{4M_4} p_i^j (r_1 + r_3)(x_3 - x_1). \tag{12}$$

b.   Body Accelerations. Finally, any desired body accelerations, such as those arising from gravitational effects, are added to the velocities. For example,

$$(u_L)_i^j = (u_L)_i^j + \delta t g_x$$

and

$$(v_L)_i^j = (v_L)_i^j + \delta t g_y. \tag{13}$$

E. Phase 2 of the Calculation

Phase 2 provides an implicit treatment required to eliminate Courant-like time step restrictions that would otherwise be required to ensure computational stability in low speed or incompressible flows. This phase can be bypassed entirely when an explicit calculation will suffice. The purpose of the implicit treatment in Phase 2 is to obtain a velocity field that has been accelerated by time advanced pressure gradients. The time advanced pressures, in turn, depend upon the densities and energies obtained when vertices are moved with these new velocities, but because these are functions of the new pressures, the pressures are by definition implicit and are in general best determined by iteration. Our implicit approach is formulated as follows. With the subscript L again denoting time advanced values, the desired pressure p_L of cell (i,j) will be the solution of

$$(p_L)_i^j = f[(\rho_L)_i^j, (I_L)_i^j],\tag{14}$$

where the new cell density and energy are approximated in terms of their initial values as

$$(\rho_L)_i^j = \rho_i^j (V/V^*)_i^j$$

and

$$(I_L)_i^j = I_i^j + (p_L)_i^j (1 - V^*/V)/(\rho_L)_i^j.\tag{15}$$

where V is the volume of the cell at time n, and V^* is the volume the cell would have if its vertices were moved according to the current Lagrangian velocity field,

$$x_1^* = x_1 + (u_L)_1 \delta t \ , \ y_1^* = y_1 + (v_L)_1 \delta t \ , \ \ldots .\tag{16}$$

A solution for p_L is obtained by applying a Newton-Raphson iteration, for which the Phase 1 velocities (u_L, v_L) are used as initial guesses. The iteration consists of sweeping through the mesh and applying the following adjustments to each cell, once each sweep:

1. Compute V^* using the most updated values for (u_L, v_L);
2. Compute new guesses for ρ_L, I_L, and p_L from the above equations; and
3. Compute a pressure change δp, according to

$$\delta p = - \frac{p_L - f(\rho_L, I_L)}{S}\tag{17}$$

where the most updated values are used for p_L, ρ_L, and I_L, and S^{-1} is a relaxation factor to be described below.

4. Adjust the current guess for p_L by adding δp to it;
5. Adjust the velocities at the vertices of the cell to include this pressure change:

$$(u_L)_1 = (u_L)_1 + \frac{\delta t \delta p}{2M_1} r_1(y_2 - y_4),$$

$$(u_L)_2 = (u_L)_2 + \frac{\delta t \delta p}{2M_2} r_2(y_3 - y_1),$$

$$(u_L)_3 = (u_L)_3 - \frac{\delta t \delta p}{2M_3} r_3(y_2 - y_4),$$

$$(u_L)_4 = (u_L)_4 - \frac{\delta t \delta p}{2M_4} r_4(y_3 - y_1),$$

$$(v_L)_1 = (v_L)_1 - \frac{\delta t \delta p}{4M_1} (r_2 + r_4)(x_2 - x_4),$$

$$(v_L)_2 = (v_L)_2 - \frac{\delta t \delta p}{4M_2} (r_1 + r_3)(x_3 - x_1),$$

$$(v_L)_3 = (v_L)_3 + \frac{\delta t \delta p}{4M_3} (r_2 + r_4)(x_2 - x_4),$$

and

$$(v_L)_4 = (v_L)_4 + \frac{\delta t \delta p}{4M_4} (r_1 + r_3)(x_3 - x_1). \tag{18}$$

The mesh is repeatedly swept and steps (1) through (5) are performed once for each cell each sweep, until no cell exhibits a pressure change violating the inequality

$$\frac{|\delta p|}{|p_{max}|} < \epsilon, \tag{19}$$

where p_{max} is the actual or an estimated maximum pressure in the mesh and ϵ is an input number (EPS), typically of order 10^{-4}.

The quantity S used in step (3) must be chosen to keep the pressure changes bounded and progressing in the right direction. In the Newton-Raphson procedure, S is the derivative of the function whose root is sought with respect to p, the iteration variable. Here, S is the rate at which the quantity $p - f(\rho, I)$ changes as the variable p changes, and is computed numerically using the same relations outlined above. For this purpose, a small pressure change Δp is chosen, scaled to the calculation:

$$\Delta p = \frac{1}{\delta t^2} \left[\frac{p_\epsilon \rho}{2 \left(\frac{1}{\delta x^2} + \frac{1}{\delta y^2} \right)} \right]$$

Here, ρ is a typical fluid density at time $t = 0$, and p_ϵ is an input quantity (PEPS) typically 10^{-4}. The velocity changes that would be induced by Δp are used to compute the corresponding volume, energy, and density changes, and from them a new pressure. Finally, S is determined from the difference between $p - f(\rho, I)$, evaluated before and after the small change in pressure, and divided by Δp. The resulting values for S^{-1} are multiplied by an optional over-relaxation coefficient, input as OM, and stored for each cell before the iteration is begun. These quantities are not recomputed during the iteration.

The above procedure works well across a broad range of low speed flow applications, but in the incompressible limit, the procedure is modified. The reason for this is that the method is then excessively sensitive to volume changes. In this case, we replace $p = f(\rho, I)$ with

$$p = p_L + \frac{\rho_L}{\rho} - 1 \; , \tag{20}$$

which effectively holds the densities constant and results in much faster iteration convergence. Corresponding expressions are used for the evaluation of S.

It should be noted that the densities and internal energies calculated in the pressure iteration are temporary quantities used only to update the pressure. To ensure exact mass conservation, the final new densities are computed in Phase 3 after the cell masses and volumes have been calculated. The internal energy is also recalculated with time centered volume changes, which conserves internal energy, and viscous contributions are then included.

In some cases, when the pressure iteration does not converge within several hundred iterations, it is still possible to continue a calculation without serious error. Usually this only happens when the incompressible option is used. For example, a poor initial guess for velocities or pressures may require a high number of iterations to relax to an acceptable solution. In such cases, the code automatically terminates the iteration, continues the cycle, and then proceeds on to the next cycle and repeats this process up to 10 times. The code aborts if the pressure iteration still has not converged after 10 cycles.

The Phase 1 and 2 calculations as outlined above comprise an implicit Lagrangian method stable for any Courant number, and allow calculations at all values of sound speed vs fluid speed.

F. The Energy Calculation

The pressure work and viscous dissipation contributions to internal energy are calculated next. The pressures used in the work expression are those resulting from the Phase 2 iteration when the implicit option is used. In the case of explicit calculations, the pressures used are those coming from the equation of state at the beginning of each cycle.

The equation for the change in internal energy in a cycle is

$$I_j^I = I_j^I - \frac{\delta t}{2M_j} \left[(p_j^I + Q_j^I) \frac{dV}{dt} + \frac{dVIS}{dt} \right]. \tag{21}$$

Both the dV/dt and $dVIS/dt$ quantities are in time centered form, using averages of beginning of cycle and current velocities, for example

$$(u_{TC})_1 = \frac{1}{2} [u_1 + (u_L)_1]$$

and

$$(v_{TC})_1 = \frac{1}{2} [v_1 + (v_L)_1], \ldots$$

With this definition,

$$\frac{dV}{dt} = (y_2 - y_4)[r_1(u_{TC})_1 - r_3(u_{TC})_3]$$

$$+ (y_3 - y_1)[r_2(u_{TC})_2 - r_4(u_{TC})_4]$$

$$- \frac{1}{2} (r_2 + r_4)(x_2 - x_4) [(v_{TC})_1 - (v_{TC})_3]$$

$$- \frac{1}{2} (r_1 + r_3)(x_3 - x_1) [(v_{TC})_2 - (v_{TC})_4]$$

and

$$\frac{dVIS}{dt} = \frac{1}{2} \quad (r_2 + r_4)[\Pi_{xy} (x_2 - x_4)$$

$$- \Pi_{xx} (y_2 - y_4)][(u_{TC})_1 - (u_{TC})_3]$$

$$+ \frac{1}{2} (r_1 + r_3)[\Pi_{xy} (x_3 - x_1)$$

$$- \Pi_{xx} (y_3 - y_1)][(u_{TC})_2 - (u_{TC})_4]$$

$$- \frac{1}{2} (\Pi_\theta \text{ Area})[(u_{TC})_1 + (u_{TC})_2 + (u_{TC})_3 + (u_{TC})_4]$$

$$+ \frac{1}{2} (r_2 + r_4)[\Pi_{yy} (x_2 - x_4)$$

$$- \Pi_{xy} (y_2 - y_4)][(v_{TC})_1 - (v_{TC})_3]$$

$$+ \frac{1}{2} (r_1 + r_3)[\Pi_{yy} (x_3 - x_1)$$

$$- \Pi_{xy} (y_3 - y_1)][(v_{TC})_2 - (v_{TC})_4].$$

The four Π terms were evaluated in the Phase 1 stress deviator calculation using Equation (9) and stored for each cell for use here. In addition, the artificial viscous pressure Q was saved from Phase 1, Equation (4).

G. Phase 3 of the Calculation

1. *Rezone.* When large fluid distortions are not expected, a purely Lagrangian approach will suffice, allowing the computing grid to follow the fluid motion exactly. In many cases, however, large fluid motions would create devastating effects, contorting cells to extreme aspect ratios or even turning cells inside out. It is often possible to

ameliorate these effects by moving the mesh vertices with respect to the fluid so as to maintain a reasonable mesh structure. Whenever a vertex is moved relative to the fluid, however, there must be an exchange of material among the cells surrounding the vertex. SALE allows a broad spectrum of rezoning possibilities by treating this material exchange as an advective flux. The simplest case is that of a purely Eulerian flow, in which the vertices are moved back to their original positions every cycle. Between this extreme and the Lagrangian extreme lies whatever form of continuous or discrete rezoning the user wishes.

This latitude is made possible by defining a set of grid vertex velocities (u_G, v_G) over the entire mesh. For a purely Lagrangian calculation, $u_G = u_L$ and $v_G = v_L$ everywhere. For a purely Eulerian calculation, $u_G = 0$ and $v_G = 0$. For a continuous rezone that approximates a Lagrangian calculation, but minimizes excessive grid distortions, grid velocities are chosen to lie somewhere between these two extremes. In particular, the vertices are moved according to some relaxation rate to place vertices at the average position of the neighboring vertices. This usually maintains cells of reasonable size and proportion throughout a run. Once a set of grid velocities u_G and v_G have been defined, it is a simple matter to construct the new grid and perform whatever advective flux calculations that may be required.

SALE could also be modified to have a discontinuous rezone capability in this Phase of a cycle. For example, grid quantities could be interpolated onto another grid whenever distortions are excessive.

2. *Regrid.* In this step, the vertices are moved to new locations as specified by (u_G, v_G):

$$x_i^j = x_i^j + \delta t (u_G)_i^j,$$

$$y_i^j = y_i^j + \delta t \, (v_G)_i^j,$$

$$r_i^j = (x_i^j) \, \text{CYL} + 1 - \text{CYL}. \tag{22}$$

We next form a set of relative velocities (u_{REL}, v_{REL}) to simplify the later task of calculating advective fluxes. For this purpose, the vertex velocities with respect to the fluid are

$$(u_{REL})_i^j = (u_G)_i^j - (u_L)_i^j$$

and

$$(v_{REL})_i^j = (v_G)_i^j - (v_L)_i^j. \tag{23}$$

New cell volumes ^{n+1}V are calculated from the new coordinates using Equation (1), and replace the ^nV values in storage.

3. *Advective Flux of Mass, Energy, and Momentum.* This step is bypassed completely for a purely Lagrangian calculation. In all other cases the relative velocities are not zero, and we must calculate the flux of mass, energy, and momentum between cells.

The flux calculation is performed on a cell by cell basis. For every cell, we calculate the volume swept out by each of the four faces relative to their Lagrangian positions.

a. To calculate these volumes, it is necessary to first form the Lagrangian coordinates (x_p, y_p) given by

$$(x_p)_1 = x_1 - (u_{REL})_1 \, \delta t,$$

$$(y_p)_1 = y_1 - (v_{REL})_1 \, \delta t,$$

and

$$(r_p)_1 = (x_p)_1 \, \text{CYL} + 1 - \text{CYL}, \ldots \tag{24}$$

b.   Then the four volumes for the right, top, left, and bottom sides are proportional to

$$
\begin{aligned}
FR = \frac{1}{12} \Big(& [r_1 + (r_p)_1 + (r_p)_2]\{x_1[(y_p)_2 - (y_p)_1] \\
& + (x_p)_1[y_1 - (y_p)_2] \\
& + (x_p)_2 [(y_p)_1 - y_1]\} \\
& + [r_1 + r_2 + (r_p)_2]\{x_1[y_2 - (y_p)_2] \\
& + x_2[(y_p)_2 - y_1] \\
& + (x_p)_2[y_1 - y_2]\} \Big),
\end{aligned}
$$

$$
\begin{aligned}
FT = \frac{1}{12} \Big(& [(r_p)_2 + r_3 + (r_p)_3]\{(x_p)_2[y_3 - (y_p)_3] \\
& + x_3[(y_p)_3 - (y_p)_2] \\
& + (x_p)_3[(y_p)_2 - y_3]\} \\
& + [r_2 + (r_p)_2 + r_3]\{x_2[y_3 - (y_p)_2] \\
& + (x_p)_2[y_2 - y_3] \\
& + x_3[(y_p)_2 - y_2]\} \Big),
\end{aligned}
$$

$$
\begin{aligned}
FL = \frac{1}{12} \Big(& [(r_p)_3 + r_4 + (r_p)_4]\{(x_p)_3[y_4 - (y_p)_4] \\
& + x_4[(y_p)_4 - (y_p)_3] \\
& + (x_p)_4[(y_p)_3 - y_4]\} \\
& + [r_3 + (r_p)_3 + r_4]\{x_3[y_4 - (y_p)_3] \\
& + (x_p)_3[y_3 - y_4] \\
& + x_4[(y_p)_3 - y_3]\} \Big),
\end{aligned}
$$

and

$$
\begin{aligned}
FB = \frac{1}{12} \Big(& [r_1 + (r_p)_1 + (r_p)_4]\{x_1[(y_p)_1 - (y_p)_4] \\
& + (x_p)_1[(y_p)_4 - y_1]
\end{aligned}
$$

$$+ (x_p)_4[y_1 - (y_p)_1]\}$$
$$+ [r_1 + r_4 + (r_p)_4]\{x_1[(y_p)_4 - y_4]$$
$$+ x_4[y_1 - (y_p)_4]$$
$$+ (x_p)_4[y_4 - y_1]\}\Big). \tag{25}$$

These represent one half the volumes swept over by the sides moving from their Lagrangian positions to their rezoned positions, the factor of 1/2 being included for convenience. Note also the FR for cell $(i+1/2, j+1/2)$ is equal to $-FL$ for cell $(i+3/2, j+1/2)$, and FT for cell $(i+1/2, j+1/2)$ is equal to $-FB$ for cell $(i+1/2, j+3/2)$. This fact is used in the code to eliminate redundant calculations.

    c. Associated with each fluid volume crossing a cell face there are corresponding values of mass, energy, and momentum. For example, the mass crossing the right face of cell $(i+1/2, j+1/2)$ might be computed as the product of the fluxing volume $2(FR)$ times the average fluid density of the cells $(i+1/2, j+1/2)$ and $(i+3/2, j+1/2)$ located on either side of the boundary. Unfortunately, this so-called "centered differencing" leads to numerical instabilities. One way to circumvent this instability is to weight the quantity being fluxed more in favor of the upstream value. In the above example, this means the density associated with FR should be more nearly equal to the density in cell $(i+1/2, j+1/2)$ when the flux is leaving this cell ($FR<0$), or more nearly equal to the density in cell $(i+3/2, j+1/2)$ when the flux is leaving that cell ($FR>0$). In SALE, we incorporate the flux coefficients FR, FT, FL, and FB within expressions that allow various differencing forms determined from input constants a_0 and b_0:

$$a_R = a_0 \operatorname{sign} FR + 4b_0 FR/(V_{i+3/2}^{j+1/2} + V_{i+1/2}^{j+1/2}),$$

$$a_T = a_0 \operatorname{sign} FT + 4b_0 FT/(V_{i+1/2}^{j+3/2} + V_{i+1/2}^{j+1/2}),$$

$$a_L = a_0 \operatorname{sign} FL + 4b_0 FL/(V_{i-1/2}^{j+1/2} + V_{i+1/2}^{j+1/2}),$$

and

$$a_B = a_0 \operatorname{sign} FB + 4b_0 FB/(V_{i+1/2}^{j-1/2} + V_{i+1/2}^{j+1/2}), \tag{26}$$

where "sign FR," for example, equals $+1$ if $FR \geq 0$ and equals -1 if $FR<0$. Both a_0 and b_0 lie in the range 0 to 1, and the limiting cases are

$a_0 = 0$ and $b_0 = 0 \to$ centered (unstable).

$a_0 = 1$ and $b_0 = 0 \to$ full donor cell or upstream differencing (stable, but diffusive),

$a_0 = 0$ and $b_0 = 1 \to$ interpolated donor cell (linearly stable, less diffusive),

and

$a_0 = 1$ and $b_0 = 1 \to$ (stable, but more diffusive).

Note that $(a_0 + b_0)$ must be sufficiently positive for numerical stability (see Sec. III.D).

d.   In terms of these weighting fractions, the new mass and specific internal energy for a cell $(i+1/2, j+1/2)$ are then given by

$$^{n+1}M_{i+1/2}^{j+1/2} = {}^{n}M_{i+1/2}^{j+1/2} + FR\,(1\,+\,a_R)\,\rho_{Li+3/2}^{j+1/2}$$

$$+\,FT(1\,+\,a_T)\rho_{Li+1/2}^{j+3/2}$$

$$+\,FL(1\,+\,a_L)\rho_{Li-1/2}^{j+1/2} + FB(1\,+\,a_B)\rho_{Li+1/2}^{j-1/2}$$

$$+\,[FR(1\,-\,a_R)\,+\,FT(1\,-\,a_T)\,+\,FL(1\,-\,a_L)$$

$$+\,FB(1\,-\,a_B)]\rho_{Li+1/2}^{j+1/2}$$

and

$$^{n+1}I_i^j = \frac{1}{^{n+1}M_{i+1/2}^{j+1/2}}\left\{{}^{n}(MI)_{i+1/2}^{j+1/2} + FR(1\,+\,a_R)({}^{n}I\rho_L)_{i+3/2}^{j+1/2}\right.$$

$$+\,FT(1\,+\,a_T)({}^{n}I\rho_L)_{i+1/2}^{j+3/2}$$

$$+\,FL(1\,+\,a_L)({}^{n}I\rho_L)_{i-1/2}^{j+1/2} + FB(1\,+\,a_B)({}^{n}I\rho_L)_{i+1/2}^{j-1/2}$$

$$+\,[FR(1\,-\,a_R)\,+\,FT(1\,-\,a_T)\,+\,FL(1\,-\,a_L)$$

$$\left.+\,FB(1\,-\,a_B)]({}^{n}I\rho_L)_{i+1/2}^{j+1/2}\right\}.$$

e.   The advection of momentum requires an extra step, because cell momenta are not carried throughout the cycle as primary field variables. Here we use the concept of a cell centered momentum flux, which is a departure from that of a vertex centered form previously used.[3] The cell centered flux form has the advantage that momentum is fluxed consistently with mass and energy. The approach is to compute average cell centered momenta based on the vertex velocities. Changes in these cell momenta resulting from advection are computed in the same way as the other cell centered quantities. These changes are then apportioned back to the vertices. Although this scheme requires the additional calculation of cell centered averages and their average effect back on the vertex velocities, the entire process is simpler than using another set of control volumes, because it can be easily included in the advection calculation for the mass and energy. Tests with this method have shown it to be superior to all momentum advection methods based on vertex centered control volumes. In particular, it better preserves cylindrical or spherical symmetry and does not introduce diffusion across streamlines.

The first step in the momentum flux calculation is to form the cell center momenta. For every cell,

$$(UMOM_L)_{i+1/2}^{j+1/2} = \frac{(\rho_L)_i^j}{4}\,[(u_L)_1\,+\,(u_L)_2\,+\,(u_L)_3\,+\,(u_L)_4]$$

and

$$(VMOM_L)_{i+1/2}^{j+1/2} = \frac{(\rho_L)_i^j}{4}\,[(v_L)_1\,+\,(v_L)_2\,+\,(v_L)_3\,+\,(v_L)_4].$$

Then, using the flux coefficients formed in steps (b) and (c) above, the net advection changes in cell centered momentum components are given by

$$(\Delta UM)_{i+1/2}^{j+1/2} = FR(1 + a_R)(UMOM_L)_{i+3/2}^{j+1/2}$$
$$+ FT(1 + a_T)(UMOM_L)_{i+1/2}^{j+3/2}$$
$$+ FL(1 + a_L)(UMOM_L)_{i-1/2}^{j+1/2} + FB(1 + a_B)(UMOM_L)_{i+1/2}^{j-1/2}$$
$$+ [FR(1 - a_R) + FT(1 - a_T) + FL(1 - a_L)$$
$$+ FB(1 - a_B)] \, (UMOM_L)_{i+1/2}^{j+1/2}$$

and

$$(\Delta VM)_{i+1/2}^{j+1/2} = FR(1 + a_R)(VMOM_L)_{i+3/2}^{j+1/2}$$
$$+ FT(1 + a_T)(VMOM_L)_{i+1/2}^{j+3/2}$$
$$+ FL(1 + a_L)(VMOM_L)_{i-1/2}^{j+1/2} + FB(1 + a_B)(VMOM_L)_{i+1/2}^{j-1/2}$$
$$+ [FR(1 - a_R) + FT(1 - a_T) + FL(1 - a_L)$$
$$+ FB(1 - a_B)](VMOM_L)_{i+1/2}^{j+1/2}.$$

The momenta changes are finally converted to vertex velocity changes in the next step.

4. *Updating the Vertex Quantities.*

a.   We first calculate new vertex masses from averages of the new cell masses, using Equation (3).

b.   To adjust the velocities, we set initial values at all vertices, where the $(^nu,{}^nv)$ values in storage are replaced by

$$^{n+1}u_i^j = \left(\frac{^nM}{^{n+1}M} \right)_i^j (u_L)_i^j,$$

and

$$^{n+1}v_i^j = \left(\frac{^nM}{^{n+1}M} \right)_i^j (v_L)_i^j.$$

Because both the ^{n+1}M and the ^nM values are required, the replacement of ^nM values by ^{n+1}M values is deferred until after completion of this step.

c.   Finally, we distribute the cell centered momentum changes to the four vertices of the cell, in the same manner that we calculate vertex masses, that is, giving equal fractions to each vertex,

$$^{n+1}u_1 = {}^{n+1}u_1 + \left(\frac{0.25}{^{n+1}M_1} \right) \left(\Delta UM \right)_{i+1/2}^{j+1/2},$$

$$^{n+1}u_2 = {}^{n+1}u_2 + \left(\frac{0.25}{^{n+1}M_2} \right) \left(\Delta UM \right)_{i+1/2}^{j+1/2},$$

$$^{n+1}u_3 = {}^{n+1}u_3 + \left(\frac{0.25}{^{n+1}M_3}\right)\left(\Delta UM\right)^{j+1/2}_{i+1/2},$$

$$^{n+1}u_4 = {}^{n+1}u_4 + \left(\frac{0.25}{^{n+1}M_4}\right)\left(\Delta UM\right)^{j+1/2}_{i+1/2},$$

$$^{n+1}v_1 = {}^{n+1}v_1 + \left(\frac{0.25}{^{n+1}M_1}\right)\left(\Delta VM\right)^{j+1/2}_{i+1/2},$$

$$^{n+1}v_2 = {}^{n+1}v_2 + \left(\frac{0.25}{^{n+1}M_2}\right)\left(\Delta VM\right)^{j+1/2}_{i+1/2},$$

$$^{n+1}v_3 = {}^{n+1}v_3 + \left(\frac{0.25}{^{n+1}M_3}\right)\left(\Delta VM\right)^{j+1/2}_{i+1/2},$$

$$^{n+1}v_4 = {}^{n+1}v_4 + \left(\frac{0.25}{^{n+1}M_4}\right)\left(\Delta VM\right)^{j+1/2}_{i+1/2}.$$

H. Completion of the Cycle

In a purely Lagrangian calculation, the advective flux is bypassed entirely, and the end of cycle ^{n+1}u and ^{n+1}v remain to be set. In the case of an explicit Lagrangian calculation, the Phase 1 (u_L, v_L) values replace the $(^n u, {}^n v)$ values. Similarly, for an implicit Lagrangian case, the Phase 2 (u_L, v_L) values become the final values for the cycle.

$\cdots$

REFERENCES

1. F. H. Harlow and A. A Amsden, "A Numerical Fluid Dynamics Calculation Method for All Flow Speeds," *J. Comput. Phys.* **8**(197) (1971).
2. C. W. Hirt, A. A. Amsden, and J. L. Cook, "An Arbitrary Lagrangian-Eulerian Computing Method for All Flow Speeds," *J. Comput. Phys.* **14**(227) 1974.
3. A. A. Amsden and C. W. Hirt, "YAQUI: An Arbitrary Lagrangian-Eulerian Computer Program for Fluid Flow at All Speeds," Los Alamos Scientific Laboratory report LA-5100, March 1973.